ITALY
Made Easy For Seniors
An Alternative to the Escorted Tour

BOB KAUFMAN

The Gelato Press
thegelatopress.com
thegelatopress@gmail.com
USA

ITALY   Made Easy for Seniors
An Alternative to the Escorted Tour
ISBN: 9798374018103

65432

Other books by Bob Kaufman:

ITALY The Best Places to See by Rail
    An Alternative to the Escorted Tour
    ISBN: 9781985276802

ITALY Over 300 Critical Tips You Need to Know Before You Go
    ISBN: 9781677189281

ITALY Skip the Hotel and Stay at a Palace
    For the Same Price Live like Royalty
    ISBN: 9781792795626

SPAIN The Best Places to See by Rail
    An Alternative to the Escorted Tour
    ISBN: 9798684495076

Information included in this book is believed to be correct at time of publication. However, the reader should be cautioned to verify all routes and rates stated by the author with known websites on the internet. Train times stated and travel times are approximate. Hotel and attraction rates are approximate. Please consult their websites for current information. The bank exchange rate of the Euro vs. the US dollar used in this book is approximately $1.10 to purchase one Euro. As of this writing you can figure the Euro is on par with the US Dollar.

Cover photo (modified) from Tomas Marek, the Czech Republic via 123rf.com

Back cover photos and thank you for:
  The Colosseum of Rome
    Susan and John Burns, Nebraska USA

  Gondola ride in Venice
    Bob and Peggy Benson, Iowa, USA
    Mark and Wendy Stevens, Florida, USA

  The Second Temple of Hera 460BC,
    Paestum, Campania, Italy
    Lenore Brownstein and Bob Kaufman

The author can be reached at
thegelatopress@gmail.com

Acknowledgements:

Lenore Brownstein, for being sequestered with me for six months while I wrote this book, and for her assisted editing of the entire book. Evan and Mia Kaufman for their input on the title, Donald French for his numerous comments and suggestions, Jerry Bovino MD, Ashley Meli, and Paul McTigue for their chapter reviews, Mark and Wendy Stevens for their input. I would also like to thank my Francis Lewis High School history teacher, Mr. Federick Weissman for making learning history so enjoyable. And finally, Suzzette Freedlander of the DSPOT for the cover layout and:

WIKIPEDIA

Wikipedia, the free encyclopedia, has been the source of historical information, facts and figures, etc. All information is in the public domain. The writer has made a generous contribution to the Wikipedia Foundation.

Reviews on back cover

INSPIRATION
FOR MY LOVE OF ITALY
* * *

"I find other countries have this or this, but Italy is the only one that has it all for me. The culture, the cuisine, the people, the landscape, the history. Just everything to me comes together there."

FRANCES MAYES, AUTHOR
"UNDER THE TUSCAN SUN"

There is no other country in the world with more UNESCO World Heritage Sites (58) than Italy. Italy is HISTORY.

"The world is a book, and those who don't travel only read one page." – St. Augustine

---

And finally,
You will never learn from people who say
"I coulda, I woulda, I shoulda"
You only pass by here once,
So visit Italy!

MEET THE AUTHOR

Bob Kaufman has a passion for travel in Italy and Spain. He wrote his first book in 1983. He thought he would write his fifth book on Italy since few know there is an alternative for Senior travel to Italy instead of taking an expensive escorted tour. Bob is a Senior and can tell you that at 60 and over (he is now 77), travel is very different. Your body is not in the same condition as it used to be back in the "young days." Most of us have replacement parts i.e. hips, knees, etc. And yes, that Arthritis thing.

Bob has lots of experience in running tours to Italy. He has been to Italy a little over 30 times!

Bob's an Eagle Scout, and when he is not digging clams in the summer on Cape Cod, he is enjoying the beautiful American Southwest in the winter with his travelling companion partner Lenore and their little Maltese "Milo." Bob and Lenore love Italian food and of course, gelato.

TABLE OF CONTENTS

	INTRODUCTION	1
1	ORGANIZATION	11
2	WHEN TO GO AND PASSPORTS	14
3	GETTING TO ITALY	19
4	SUGGESTED ITINERARIES FOR FIRST TIME VISITORS	26
5	ROME AND THE VATICAN DAY 2,3,4	32
6	DAY TRIPS FROM ROME	82
7	FLORENCE- CITY OF THE RENAISSANCE	104
8	FLORENCE DAY TRIPS	123
9	VENICE	155
10	VENICE DAY TRIPS PADUA AND VERONA	180
11	MILAN AND THE LAKES	189
12	UMBRIA-ASSISI, PERUGIA, GUBBIO	202
13	NAPLES AREA	216
14	BARI- MATERA - ALBEROBELLO	226
15	SICILY-WEST	237
16	SICILY-EAST	258
17	BONUS CHAPTER–CORTONA TUSCANY	273
18	HOTEL SELECTION	277
19	MONEY, CREDIT CARDS, DRESS ELECTRICITY, TELEPHONES	280
20	DINING & CUSTOMS, EURAIL & SECURITY	287
UN	TABLE OF UNESCO WORLD HERITAGE SITES	292

CHAPTER 6 DAY TRIPS FROM ROME
 AMALFI DRIVE, RUINS AT POMPEII
 ISLAND OF CAPRI
 SORRENTO & POSITANO
 RAVELLO
 HERCULANEUM
 ORVIETO AND OSTIA ANTICA

CHAPTER 8 FLORENCE DAY TRIPS
 PISA & LUCCA, SAN GIMIGNANO & SIENA
 THE CINQUE TERRE

CHAPTER 11 MILAN AND THE LAKES
 LAKE COMO- VARENNA, BELLAGIO
 LAKE MAGGIORE (STRESA) LAKE GARDA
 LAKE LUGANO (SWITZERLAND)
 MILAN- WHAT TO SEE AND DO

CHAPTER 13 NAPLES AREA
 MANY DISCUSSED IN CHAPTER 6

CHAPTER 15 SICILY WEST
  PALERMO
 TRAPANI AND ERICI
 SEGESTA, SELINUNTE
 AGRIGENTO & THE VALLEY OF THE TEMPLES

CHAPTER 16 SICILY EAST
SYRACUSE, TAORMINA, CEFALU, MOUNT AETNA

MAP OF ITALY AND SICILY EXPLAINED

The map following this page is intended to give the reader a sense of the general location of cities and towns with respect to each other. It does not show distance. If you are an AAA Plus or Premier member you can obtain the AAA map of Italy, Austria & Switzerland, Florence, Milan, Naples, Rome at no cost. All you need do is contact your local AAA office. Also, feel free to make copies of my hand-drawn map and use a high-liter yellow or pink pen to layout your trip.

ITALY & SICILY
Not to any scale

INTRODUCTION

Why are so many Americans (and Canadians) flocking to Italy for a vacation? Just what is it about Italy that draws so many? Most people I know say I want to visit London or Paris, but I want to spend a week or two in Italy. Why?
Here are the reasons:

The People. On my first trip to Italy in 1972, I got lost in Rome. I opened my map, and within three minutes, I had three people trying to help me. I don't know of a more warm and gracious people than the Italians.

The Culture. I call it "La Dolce Vita" or the sweet life. Tell me do you know of any country steeped in culture the way Italy is? Italy is Western Civilization. Just think of it. The Roman Empire gave us law, architecture, art, language, and civil engineering, to name a few. The old saying "all the roads lead to Rome" still stands, and many, like the Appian Way, have been preserved along with the Colosseum and the Roman Forum. Let's not forget Italy is home to the Catholic Church with all its Renaissance art and architecture.

Speaking of the Renaissance, Italy has produced more scientists, artists and engineers, mathematicians, and doctors over the ages than any other country. Does Da Vinci, Michelangelo, Galileo, Fibonacci, Guido of Arezzo (who invented the musical staff) ring a bell (no pun intended)?

And what about that rolling landscape lined with olive trees and vineyards that stretches as far as the eye can see? Ask yourself, "Have you ever seen houses built into the hills as you will see in Positano or the Cinque Terre (the five towns)"? The landscape of Italy is just breathtaking.

An Alternative to the Escorted Tour

The Cuisine. Let's face it, who doesn't like Italian food? Each area of Italy brings a different flavor to the table. In addition, all the ingredients are always fresh. That fish you are eating in Venice was swimming in the Adriatic Sea a few hours ago. And let's not forget the wines. There are just too many to choose. My favorite is the local house wines. In Rome, it's Frascati; in Florence, it's the local Chianti from Greve. You just cannot beat the wines. And finally.

The COST. The cost of a three-star hotel is about the same price as in the USA that you would expect to pay for a "chain" hotel. The breakfasts are incredible (sorry, there are no make-your-own waffles). Rail travel is dramatically less than our AMTRAK. And, most restaurants will offer you dinner at the same prices you would expect to pay in the USA.

By now you should be convinced that you will want to come back after visiting Italy because you will enjoy it so much. And, when you throw that first coin into the Trevi Fountain, you will remember that it means "I shall return to Rome."
Turning to my travels in Italy:

In May of 2022, we decided to explore the not-so-touristy area of Italy known as Apulia-Salento. If you imagine Italy as a boot, it's the bottom half of the heel. Just draw a line between Bari on the Adriatic and Taranto on the Gulf of Taranto. Then look at the area below. That's Salento, sometimes called the Salentine Peninsular. It's certainly not the Italy I knew. No hordes of tourists. No souvenir shops selling everything from mugs (made in China, of course) to those "snow globes" and fridge magnets.

Our May trip was certainly different. I was now seventy-six, and my age was taking a toe-hold on me. I didn't enjoy that drive on the A1 Autostrada from Rome south to Naples. With all those Italians driving like maniacs, it was as dull as I-95 through the Carolinas. Instead, on arrival at Rome's DaVinci airport, we decided to skip that long drive and opted to take the train to Bari

ITALY Made Easy for Seniors

(on the Adriatic Ocean, due south-east of Rome); see Bari for four days and then rent a car and meander around Salento. No big deal, I've made many trips like this before. However, at 76, I discovered that traveling was a physical chore.

As a tour operator for almost 35 years, offering fully escorted tours (on contract to travel agents) to Italy, I found that most of our guests were usually Seniors or close to the Senior age of 60. Our fully escorted tours to Italy of eight nights would usually cost $3500-$4500 per person (including airfare) for the nine days.

Middle age folks 25-45 usually prefer an FIT (Foreign Independent Travel) visit to Italy. After reading all the tour books, they plan their entire trip, including renting a car and picking the hotels and attractions they wish to visit. Very few guests on our tours cared to do this and opted for our fully escorted tour. In other words, as Greyhound Bus Lines always stated, "leave the driving to us." I can count the total number of people in this age group (25-45) on my fingers. However, for Seniors, it was and is still the norm. But, as I stated, it's very regimented and costly.

However, there is a way for Seniors to visit Italy on practically a "shoe-string"; and I don't mean staying at a "no star" hotel with a cracked linoleum floor and sharing a toilet fifty feet down the hall. We all did this when we were kids and had no money. At least I did. And secondly, there is no regimentation with my Senior way of traveling, which you will read about in this book. So rest assured you won't read, "wake-up call at 6AM, breakfast at 7AM, and please make sure you are on the bus by 8AM, else we will leave without you."

So, if you are a Senior, don't enjoy regimentation (who does?), and don't want to part with $7,000-9,000 of your children's inheritance for an escorted tour of Italy, then you need to read this book further.

An Alternative to the Escorted Tour

WHY A BOOK SPECIFICALLY FOR SENIORS?

This book does have a "bent" or a slant. For one thing, Seniors have physical limitations, or at least the ones I know. They can't walk a mile. Most of them already have replacement parts, i.e., an artificial hip or knee. They don't want to spend $30 for a taxi ride to their hotel; they can't negotiate the Spanish Steps in Rome and on and on. So, I have targeted sites, hotels, and everything else that would make it difficult for a Senior. In other words, what I would call "how to do it if you are a Senior ." To make it easy as a Senior, I have coupled this with taking the high-speed rail system around Italy. You can bypass the rail system if you can afford a personal driver with a Mercedes or rent a car and enjoy that "white knuckle" driving!

After reading this book, you should consider purchasing my classic, *"ITALY...The Best Places to See by Rail* (available from Amazon.com or Barnes and Noble) and your trip will be delightful, stress-free, and in-expensive (as compared to the fully escorted tour).

WHAT THIS BOOK IS ABOUT AND WHAT IT IS NOT

This book is about seeing Italy for the first time (and subsequent visits) when you are in your Senior years, which I define as 60 and over. Being over 55 is also acceptable. I hear it many times when I speak to Seniors. "Oh, we are just too old to travel anymore, especially to Italy." Many have never been to Europe and don't even have passports.

Now we are 60 years older. As a New Yorker, my generation spent their summers in the Catskills in resorts like the Concord Hotel in Monticello. I don't recall too many of us going to Europe or taking cruises.

Deregulation brought about global competition in the airline industry. On the international level, TWA and PanAm now had domestic competitors flying to Europe. Suddenly, these two airlines were not the only American flagship operators with

4

ITALY Made Easy for Seniors

European destinations. The other airlines, i.e., Delta, United, American, and Continental, jumped into flying the North Atlantic. I won't get into all the rules and regulations promulgated by the European countries, but now with European Government approval, other airlines would start flying from their European hubs to major American cities. So Alitalia (now ITA) started flying from their hub in Rome to Chicago, Los Angeles, San Francisco, and so on. Competition only brings down prices.

What's most important is that airline fares came down dramatically. An air ticket from JFK to Rome in 1967 was about $700. Now that same ticket is about $450 if you go Economy Coach or get a deal. The ticket prices now, because of the inflation, are on the high side, but trust me, they will come down again. Don't consider this as an obstacle for not seeing Italy now. At most you will only save around $150 per person.

Realizing the upsurge in travel and anticipation of the future visiting hordes of people from the USA and other countries, the major countries of Europe embarked on improving their rail and highway infrastructure. As for Italy, they needed a high-speed rail system that would whisk travelers from Rome to Venice with all the comforts of a jet airliner. I remember 1970 traveling from Milan to Venice by train. I sat on a wooden seat with no air conditioning for about five hours. That was some ordeal compared to the Italian high-speed trains of today.

For us, fortunate Seniors, affordable and comfortable travel in Italy is now delightful. However, I wish someone ten years ago had told me all the stuff you will learn in this book. You will find that I have assembled it all here, so your trip will be even more pleasurable, relatively inexpensive, and nearly stress-free!

WHEELCHAIR TRAVEL

There are many tours and websites devoted to traveling with a wheelchair. I cannot possibly address this subject in my book. It is just too complex and too detailed. I can, however (and it is the objective of this book), describe what I would call "Physically Challenged." So if you have severe arthritis or any other physical ailment, and have problems walking, or climbing stairs, then this book is for you.

A WORD ABOUT THE FORMAT OF THIS BOOK
By now, you may have realized that this book uses larger-than-normal bold print. Why? That's because most Seniors have trouble reading small print. Either they wear prescription or reading glasses or have contact lenses. Hopefully, the fonts used in this book will make it far easier to read than all those other books. Since we now have the internet, I don't provide color pictures. Hopefully, you can bring back your own.

From time to time, I provide TIPS which may be outside the content of the item discussed. You may find highlighting these tips with one of those yellow or pink marker pens is a good idea. And one more thing, by now, you may have noticed I spell Seniors with a capital "S" and travelers with one "l." It's like a badge I wear. I earned it!

CHAPTER ORGANIZATION
If you are visiting Italy for the first time, it's best to pay close attention to Chapters 1-11. Try to fit in as much as possible by exploring Rome, Florence, and Venice. You can eliminate certain days by dropping suggested day trips. You should be able to do all this in 14 days. If you add Chapter 11, you can cover Milan and the lakes in 18 days with a fly-out from Milan. While there is a lot to see in Rome, Florence, and Venice, consider some of the day trips to the Italian villages of Orvieto, San Gimignano, Lucca, Pisa, or the Cinque Terre. If the laundry is drying on that clothesline from a window, you are in "real" Italy. The Italy I love so much!!

For second-time or first-time visitors who want to pick and choose more places, my recommendation is Chapter 12- Umbria-Assisi, Perugia, and Gubbio. And, if you want to experience something completely out of the ordinary, my suggestion would be Matera in Basilicata and Alberobello in Puglia. Both are about an hour apart from each other and Bari, the principal city and hub in the area.

You may consider visiting Sicily in the winter when the climate is relatively mild. And, if you can spare another 7-10 days, Sicily is the place. That's the island the toe of Italy is kicking.

STAY PUT TRAVELING

It does sound like an oxymoron. Think about it. How can you stay put and travel? Well, you can. You cut down the itinerary to 7-10 days and visit one or two cities. So, consider the day trips from Rome, Florence, Naples, and Milan (the Lakes). Consider just staying in Rome and making all those day trips. Or split the ten days to just five in Rome and five in Florence with day trips. Stay put is far less hectic than checking in and out of hotels and trying to squeeze so much into 14 days. I have written several chapters on all those day trips.

A WORD ABOUT DISTANCES- METRIC, ETC.

It is often difficult for Americans to get a feel for distance using the Metric system since we rarely use it. So I have made it simple. Remember the following facts: One meter is slightly over one yard or three feet. So when I state, "It's a little over one football field," you should figure about 100 meters. If I say "about 12 football fields," you should figure 1200 yards or a little more than 1,000 meters or almost a kilometer. After a while, you will find it easy when that Italian says, "it's just about 100 meters up the street." On purchasing food, remember that when you buy a kilo of that fresh crusty bread, it is 2.2 pounds! And most items in the supermarket, i.e., the fruit, are priced in kilograms. So, one kilogram of apples would probably be about 2.2 pounds or about three Euros ($3.30 per kilo). Don't get shocked at any of those prices. Just remember they are priced in Euros and kilos. It's best to take half the kilo price to get the price in pounds. It will be close enough.

An Alternative to the Escorted Tour

CHICAGO MANUAL OF STYLE (CMOS)
I call it Bob's manual of style! Throughout this book, you will notice I don't adhere to what is known as the Chicago Manual of Style. For example, according to CMOS, the time would be 10 a.m. In Bob's style, it is 10AM. I use BC and AD right up against the numeric. So, it would be 476AD, not 476 A.D. I spell Century with a capital "C." So expect to see the 4th Century and not the 4th century. Some words are spelled either of two accepted forms, e.g., Amphitheatre and Amphitheater. Also, some numbers are not spelled out. For example, instead of writing, "it is a little over one and a half miles to the ruins," I write it as "a little over 1.5 miles to the ruins." Just easier to read. I spell many items in Italian and English, so you get a feel for the Italian words. For example, I use Roma for Rome, etc.

THE LANGUAGE PROBLEM
There is NO problem. Most of the people speak some English.

THE TIME PROBLEM
There is NO problem if you know what you are doing. Most times are expressed using the 24-hour clock (sometimes called military time). This eliminates all problems with AM and PM. If you purchase rail tickets for 0600, this does not mean 6PM. It means 6AM. A six o'clock PM train is 1800. Just remember to add 1200. Railways, bus companies, and venues will not refund your money if you goof; however, most will accommondate you.

THE DATE PROBLEM
Europeans, especially Italians, use the format for the date as Day/Month/Year instead of our system of
Month/Day/Year. If you are booking October 8, 2023, it is written in European format as 8/10/2023. I always suggest writing it as:
Arriving Sunday, Oct 8, 2023, and not 8/10/2023
Always include the day of the week. And double-check all.
I might note Oct 8, 2023, is also World Octopus Day.

ITALY Made Easy for Seniors

MY RECOMMENDATIONS

You will notice that from time to time, I make recommendations on where to stay, where to dine, etc. All these establishments do not know me. I take absolutely no commissions, favors, or anything from them. However, all I ask is when you check into that hotel, dine at that establishment, or use the services of that private car company, you tell them that you read about them in Bob Kaufman's books on Italy.

*** MOST IMPORTANT ADVICE ***

I suggest you read this book, cover to cover, before making any plans. Many seniors will buy their air tickets, then realize about three months before their trip that friends have suggested they go to Lake Como and the Lakes District for three days instead of flying out of Rome and home from Milan. Good idea, but they are now locked into their airline schedule with a round-trip from Chicago to Rome when they now need an additional three days with a return from Milan back to Chicago. Here is something you need to know:

Air – Can only be booked 330 days before the RETURN DATE. If you book using airline points, there is usually no penalty for changing, canceling, or rebooking. If paying cash, penalties apply generally. You should check the airline's official website.

Trains in Italy can only be booked 60-90 days in advance. Schedules rarely change that much.

Hotels – book anytime without a cash deposit (learn more in the hotel chapter).

Private driver – at Rome's FCO airport two or three weeks before arrival. Same with a private driver down the Amalfi coast.

An Alternative to the Escorted Tour

And one more final word, please do not accept this book as a complete tour guide of Italy. It is not and will only give you the basics. If you want all those details (which you probably won't read anyway), purchase a five-pound book to lug around, which will give you all the details you need but won't tell *you how to visit* Italy. So here we go on to the basics.

CHAPTER 1

ORGANIZATION

INTRODUCTION

This book is very different from the other books I have written. As Sargent Joe, Friday said on the 1950's TV show *"Dragnet,"* "The facts, mam, just the facts." I don't bury all the facts I provide in paragraph form; I state them with a little comment. If you want every bit of detail on a site, best to consult one of those very detailed tour guides (2-5 pounds). I am sure you don't want to lug it around all day! And please, no complaints on this subject. Once again, "Mam, just the facts."

HISTORICAL INTERLEAVING

It is hard, or should I say impossible, to talk about Italy without involving the history of Western Civilization. I try to weave as much basic history into each city you stay in or visit. Sometimes I describe the history at the beginning of the chapter, in the middle, or at the end. Often, like the town of Matera, history is the town. I am sure you get what I mean. You should also note that I often interchange village, town, and city. I usually call very large places a "City." However, it's probably a town or a village if it's not a city.

I can't give you all the details of the history of each city. To describe the history of Rome, I would need a book of at least 700 pages. So, I am providing you with just references. For example, Pompeii was covered in ash and lava from the eruption of Mount Vesuvius in the year 79AD, about 135 years after Julius Caesar was assassinated in 44BC.

An Alternative to the Escorted Tour

THE BASIC ITINERARIES

I first provide you with a detailed itinerary for first-time visitors; however, unlike my classic book *"ITALY... The Best Places to See by Rail, An Alternative to the Escorted Tour,"* I break down daily where to stay and what to do. As for Seniors, to minimize your stress level, I lay out the day in terms of walking distances between sites, etc. Let's face it; no one wants to be stressed out or exhausted by noon unless you are an Ironman or an Ironwoman.

Concerning hotels, I will suggest three and four-star hotels where I would stay. I describe walking distances and terrain, e.g., up a long hill, etc. This hopefully will aid you. For example, you might tell the taxi driver, "could you drop us off at the top of the Piazza della Cisterna" instead of just San Gimignano? The driver would probably drop you off in the main parking lot and force you to climb about 20 steps and negotiate a six-block cobblestone street with a moderate incline. I am sure you would all agree it would be far better to be dropped off in the Piazza Cisterna and walk down the street instead of up the incline!

EXTENDED ITINERARIES

I discuss EXTRA day trips in each significant area, Rome, Florence, Venice, Naples, and Milan. So if you care not to go to Florence and only have ten days for Rome, you can make Naples and the Amalfi Coast a day trip. Likewise, you can make "Orvieto," also a day trip. So do consider my extended itineraries or day trips. Let's face it; no one wants to check into and out of hotels all day! And what's worse for Seniors is carting (schlepping) those bags back and forth to the rail station! Better to pack a day bag and head on out.

THE WRONG WAY TO SEE ITALY

I am a member of several websites on visiting Italy, or should I say "I Love Italy." I often review and critique itineraries for first-time visitors. I am amazed reading some itineraries of first-time travelers to Italy. I even get dizzy reading some of them. "We are

ITALY Made Easy for Seniors

flying into Rome, then going to Positano, then to the Cinque Terre, then to Venice, then to Lake Como, then Milan, then Taormina, and of course, flying home from Palermo. And, further, we are doing it all in two weeks." Yikes! Some people don't even know where these places are in Italy. They just heard or saw pictures of them and want to visit them.

Let's face it, Italy has more to see and do than any other country in Western Europe and perhaps the world! You cannot do it all in one fell swoop. Italy is a place, as they say, "You need to stop and smell the roses." How true. So bite off what you can chew in two weeks without feeling you need a "real" vacation when you get home. There will be plenty of time for that next trip to Perugia for the annual chocolate festival and that week-long stay in Montepulciano, where you can sample a different glass of wine every day or, better several glasses a day.

TERMINOLOGY AND DEFINITIONS

Here are the terms and definitions I regularly use in this book:
Grazie- thank you   Prego-Don't mention it (not the sauce)
Bin- The track number in the rail station
Campanile- A tower   Stazione- The rail station
Carrozza- the carriage or coach number on a train
Cena – Dinner   Pranzo-Lunch
Centro Storico- the central historic district
Colazione- Breakfast (Cola-Zee-Oh-Nee)
Crenellated Roof- It's those large notches on the top of
        the medieval castles where they shoot arrows from.
Duomo- The church, many times it's a cathedral or basilica
Ferrovia- the rail station in Venice
Firenze- The Italian word for Florence
Frecci xxxx - the high-speed trains of Trenitalia.
        Frecci is short for "Arrow ." Freccirosa would mean red
        arrow, since rosa is red.
Funicular –It's a cable car system.   Ascensore- Elevator/Lift
Scala Mobile-Escalato   Parcheggio-Parking Lot

CHAPTER 2

WHEN TO GO & PASSPORTS

WHEN TO GO

First, for Seniors, the worst time to go to Italy is June through September. There are four problems associated with this time frame. Italy is beastly hot in July and August (and equally so in the two shoulder months); second, the prices of everything are sky-high; third, there are hordes of people all over, and finally, tickets for trains and sites, i.e., The Colosseum, Vatican Museum, etc. may not be available the day you wish to visit.

I should note two issues that occur in the hot summer months. In Rome, many of the restaurants are completely closed for August. By Rome city ordinance, all A/C in many of the three and four-star hotels must be turned off at midnight and back on at 5AM. Forget about going on a Sunday to the Vatican to see the Pope. He, too, avoids the heat by staying for the summer at his summer residence in Castel Gandolfo, about 30 miles southwest of Rome. So much for the brutal heat in Rome.

You can certainly go in the months of April-May or September-October. In fact, except for the school groups, this is when most people prefer to visit Italy. However, you will encounter the same problems as in the summer months, except for the heat.

Now the best time for Seniors to visit, taking all into account, is early November, December, January, February, and late March. I have been to Italy several times during these months and can tell you that it is delightful. You should note that you must avoid travel from December 15 to January 10 because of the holiday season. Because it's winter, you can expect some rainy days.

ITALY Made Easy for Seniors

However, you can plan your days accordingly. Southern Italy i.e., Naples, Positano, Capri, Pompeii, and all the others in the Sorrentine Peninsular area, will be extremely mild, like a spring day in New York. In summary, I can personally recommend the following:

October 15- December 15
January 15- April 1

I will refer to the above time frame as Bob's "LOW SEASON."

>>>TIP<<<
If you need to watch your budget and feel that you never had the resources to travel to Europe, you will find that hotel and airfare costs will be rock bottom. A three-star hotel in low season will cost you about $100 per night with breakfast. This same hotel in high or shoulder season will cost about $200 per night. Likewise, airfares will also be at rock bottom. So, in summary, travel in the low season.
>>><<<

PASSPORTS
If you don't have a passport, you will need one. If you intend to visit Italy, you need to get one NOW. It takes about 90 days to get one. Check the government website:

https://travel.state.gov/content/travel/en/passports.html/
Make sure you are dealing with the US Government website.

And no, you do not need any "shots."

Secondly, if you have an American passport, the Italian Government (and 23 other countries) request that it be valid for six months past your return to the USA. It's called the "six-month validity rule." So if you are planning on going in November 2023, and your passport expires in January 2024, you should renew your passport NOW since you need to have at least six months forward of your expiration date.

MEDICAL INSURANCE (NOT TRIP INSURANCE)

Medical insurance is a MUST for Seniors. Do not confuse this with basic trip insurance, which usually includes cancellation (for specific reasons), loss of baggage, etc.

If you are covered under Medicare, it will not include any costs associated with hospitalization, doctors, or clinics outside the USA. Also, if you have an additional policy (a Medi-gap) to your Medicare, they usually will not cover any costs which Medicare does not cover. Suppose you don't have Medicare and instead have a substitute policy (like Medicare Advantage or a Blue Cross Blue Shield Policy). In that case, you need to check with your insurance provider on out of the country coverage. Also, many Medicare supplements will not cover any costs which Medicare will not cover. Therefore, forget Medicare and your supplement when you are out of the country.

You need Medical/Accidental Travel Insurance for your trip or a blanket policy (if you will be making lots of trips outside the USA); make sure it states:

Coverage for Accidents

-and-
Coverage for Sickness

-and-
Will it cover pre-existing conditions? What time frame?

Most of the time, they will ask you how much your trip will cost. You can do the numbers; they usually charge you about 3-4%. Yes, because we are Seniors!

ITALY Made Easy for Seniors

Consider these two scenarios: You are walking back to your hotel after visiting the Trevi Fountain in Rome. You trip on the sidewalk. You are carted into the hospital, where they inform you that you have broken your hip. Unless you have specific medical insurance for out-of-the-country coverage, you will need to pay for any hospital and doctor charges out of your pocket. If you are hospitalized in Italy, they will contact your insurance provider and bill them directly. You should take a copy of that policy or insurance card with you. Hopefully, you will not need it.

Check the internet and ensure your current provider offers accident and sickness coverages and the associated rules. I would strongly suggest that you have this type of policy in place before you board that flight to Italy, or else be prepared for parting with $25,000 for a hip replacement or whatever. Once again, do not confuse this with plain old trip insurance, which usually pays for lost baggage, overnight accommodations if your return flight is delayed or canceled, etc. What you need is OUT OF THE COUNTRY accident and sickness insurance.

A NOTE ABOUT ESCORTED TOURS
Many Seniors want to eliminate all the stress associated with all those arrangements and the actual trip. Escorted tours are the way to go. However, like cruising, some are inexpensive, and some are very pricey. Many have excellent reputations and have repeat customers for years. I ran those escorted tours for travel agent-organized groups. Thousands of people swear by them. However, there are several things you should know, and it has nothing to do with the cost of the trip.

Escorted trips or tours are highly regimented. We had a saying, and it wasn't a "Jeopardy" question. "What are 6, 7, and 8"? Answer, 6AM wake-up call, 7AM breakfast in the main dining room, and 8AM bus departure for our next city or site. Oh, did I say, "you need to be back on the coach at 4PM to head back to the hotel"? No more time for shopping? So if you want regimentation, an escorted tour is the way. No worries, that's a significant benefit. Also, with low-end tours, like cruises, be prepared for the "extras." Like the dinner plan ($495 for the week), the day trip to Pompeii ($195), the Rome by Night tour, with drinks, of course ($149), etc. Did I mention the 20% tip for the tour director and the coach driver for the week?

TRAVELING WITH OTHERS

Traveling with another couple or a buddy can also add to the experience. You may want to consider this. However, we lay down the rules every time we travel with another couple. We agree to have breakfast together and meet back at the hotel for dinner. During the day we may go to places together. However, we are free to do anything we want during the day. In this way, if we want to shop and the other couple wants to go to the Peggy Guggenheim museum in Venice, it's okay. No big deal. We can share photos in the evening or at breakfast and chat about what we did during the day. It also enhances the travel experience.

CHAPTER 3

GETTING TO ITALY

UNDERSTANDING TYPES OF AIRFARE

There are three types of airfare. Most of us are familiar with the "round-trip." However, suppose you plan on flying into one of the three major airports of Italy which offer non-stops to the USA, i.e., Rome, Milan, and Venice, and returning from a different airport either in Italy or elsewhere. In that case, you need to look at "multi-cities."

CLASSES OF FARES

Over the past five years, the airlines have restructured their categories from three classes to four: First Class, Business Class, Standard Coach, and Basic Economy. Standard Coach, called "Y" class for years, has now been broken down into standard coach and economy. Several carriers, Delta now has a class called "Comfort," which gives you about 6-8 more inches of foot room in coach. Your main concern when choosing a fare is to know the difference between the standard coach and economy fares.

In standard coach or "Y" class, you get all the amenities you always received in the past, i.e., one checked bag, seat assignment, etc. Many airlines still charge for your first and second bag, even in standard coach, unless you have a credit card or some other indicia keyed to their airline. On flights to Europe, in regular or standard coach ("Y" class), most airlines will allow you one bag (50lbs maximum) free and seat assignment. On economy or what I call "real budget," you must pay for your checked bag and seat assignment. If you don't pay online, you can pay at the airport. The first checked bag is usually $60. In addition, they will assign you a seat at the check-

An Alternative to the Escorted Tour

in counter. When checking airline fares, ensure you know what's included if it states "BASIC ECONOMY." The Basic Economy fee may not include baggage, carry-on, and seat selection. It varies by airline.

>>>TIP<<<
If you have 30 days or more before your outbound flight, try to obtain a credit card issued by a bank that is keyed to your airline. Delta is linked with American Express, American with Barclays, and Citibank. You can usually obtain bonus points, and sometimes they waive the annual fee, which will be far less than paying all those baggage fees.
>>><<<

>>>TIP<<<
If selecting seats, avoid the ones next to the toilets in the rear. Always too much noise in this area. If you can choose those "bulk-head" seats (you may have to pay a little extra (Delta Comfort Class), you will have an additional two feet of legroom. However, depending on the aircraft type, you may not have a "drop-down" tray in front of you. On newer aircraft, all the trays are now in the armrest. If you want to go to sleep, I favor the window seat. Let's face it; there is nothing outside except the ocean and darkness. If you select the left-hand window seat (the "A" seat), you will probably be facing land instead of water, as the approach to Rome (FCO-Runway 16) is in a southerly direction. The right-hand window views the Mediterranean Sea for 15 minutes until landing.
>>><<<

If you can get by with a carry-on bag for the week, you probably will save $120-150. Remember, you are going to Italy and not on a safari. There are laundromats, pharmacies, and ATMs all over the place. However, if you have the resources to fly business or first class, there will be usually no baggage fees, then go for it. Your body will thank you. You can read more on this subject in Chapter 18.

>>>TIP<<<
It would be best to compare the cost of that budget seat (basic economy) with a full coach ticket since they may be a few dollars apart. So the best would be to purchase the full coach ticket. And yes, you can sit right next to your traveling partner!
>>><<<

BEST ROUTES TO ITALY

Most Americans (and even Canadians) fly from American or Canadian domestic hubs to the three major cities: Rome, Milan, and Venice. You may want to compare the price, connections, and layover time. For example, a flight from Indianapolis to Rome may cost $750, involving a layover in Chicago or Newark and possibly another European connection. It would be better to drive (or take the bus) to Chicago (O'Hare) and fly non-stop to Rome for $450. In addition, this may get you into Rome the next day at 7AM instead of 4PM with those connections. You will also gain a day of site-seeing. The same applies to flights to Milan and Venice.

PLANNING YOUR ITINERARY

>>>TIP<<<
Before purchasing airline tickets, plan your itinerary. You can always change the itinerary, "jockey" around dates, e.g., "Should we spend four nights in Rome or three." However, you won't be able to change flights (except by paying a fee most of the time). So best to block out your outbound and inbound dates and consider extra days.
>>><<<

An Alternative to the Escorted Tour

USING FREQUENT FLYER POINTS
Most airlines allow you to change your flights if you use frequent flyer miles as long as they are for the same city pairs, e.g., Chicago-Milan. Dates and times can be changed. However, remember that additional flyer miles (points) may be required. If you need more miles, consider moving points from other credit cards to frequent flyer points. For example, if you are short, say, 5,000 miles for a Delta flight, you may be able to move 5,000 AMEX points over to Delta.

THE 330-DAY RULE
Airline tickets can usually be purchased only 330 days before the flight. If you are using frequent flyer miles, you must know that your best deals are to purchase those tickets as soon as the 330-day comes due. Note you need to take a look at the return date. If you don't get these tickets on the 330 days or within a few weeks of your dates, you may get what I call "crappy" flights.
For example, you can easily book using frequent flyer miles a JFK flight on Delta to Rome with a return from Venice 330 days prior. However, try to use your miles 90 days before your departure date, and you might have to be routed from JFK to Salt Lake City or Atlanta and even give up an additional 30,000 miles.

Remember, you can change your tickets on frequent flyer awards or put them back for a slight or no fee. Consider monitoring the points "chart" every 30 days. If you bought the ticket for 80,000 points and it goes down to 65,000, you can usually put those miles/points back into your account and book the tickets again at the lower requirement. However, if you are purchasing tickets for cash, i.e., on a credit card, the best is to wait until 3-6 months before getting the best deal.

>>>TIP<<<
Use the OTA's (Online Travel Agents, e.g., Orbitz, etc.) to locate a few flights and remember the Multi-Cities option if you are flying into Rome and returning from Venice or Milan. Then go to the

airline's website, e.g., Delta.com, and purchase (or use your frequent flyer miles) tickets there. Why? It's simple. You will have more "rights" if flights are canceled, delayed, etc. I have never bought overseas tickets on any website other than the actual carrier, i.e., Delta.com, AA.com, etc.
>>><<<

SCOTT'S (GOING.COM) CHEAP FLIGHTS

If you want to travel dirt cheap and have the liberty to be flexible on travel dates, consider a yearly subscription to GOING.COM. Scott is what I would call a "bird-dog." For as little as $39 a year, Scott will "push" ridiculously low fares, mistake or error fares. It's simple. Here is how it works. You sign up and fill out a profile, i.e., which airports you want to fly out of and where to, e.g., Europe, etc. When Scott sees a relatively low or an error fare, he notifies you immediately. So, you may get an email, JFK to Rome, basic economy on Delta for $229 round trip, valid January 10 thru March 10. Huh? Once you get this notice, you have only a day or two to get those tickets. The best is to book them immediately on the Delta.com website. You should note that Scott does not sell you the ticket. He only points you to the deal. Stated in simplicity, "It's the early bird that gets the worm," or maybe "He who hesitates is lost." You should note that you need not pay $39 for this "push" service, but you won't get all the notices.

If you want to use Scott's, it's best to make up an itinerary, and then when you are notified, "go for it." All you need do is know how many days you need, e.g., a block of 15-18 days. Also, note that many times you may have to return to your inbound airport. However, it's not a big deal to take a train back from Venice to Rome for about $50 the night before (do stay at the four-star Hotel Isola Sacre for $150 per night www.hotelisolasacra.) about two miles from FCO. There is more flexibility if you can return from the same airport you arrived.

An Alternative to the Escorted Tour

>>>SENIOR NOTE<<<
Flights to Italy usually are a minimum of 9-10 hours, most of them overnight. Several items make our Senior travel different from the others. First, consider purchasing an inexpensive pair of "compression socks" on Amazon. Compression socks will minimize the risk of a DVT or "Deep Vein Thrombosis ." In addition, consult with your doctor, but I make it a habit of taking two aspirins the day before my flight. Best that you keep your blood thin. In addition to carrying your meds in your carry-on, I bring my overnight and morning meds in one of those small sandwich bags. This way, I don't waste time rummaging around my carry-on looking for my morning pills. Also, once again, always consult with your doctor. For sleeping, I recommend Melatonin or some other natural sleep remedy, "Calm Forte" by Hyland's is one of them. Others are available.

It is also advisable to order one of those blinders from Amazon for sleeping. But remember, the flight attendants will not serve you dinner if you sleep. So best to take your sleep remedy during your dinner and put those blinders on after dinner when you are ready to snooze. Avoid having coffee. It will keep you awake.
>>><<<

Avoid having coffee or any caffeinated drink by noon on your travel date. In addition to keeping you from sleeping on your overnight flight, it will make you use the toilet more often. Best to drink water and plenty of it. If you can avoid alcohol, it's a plus unless you are in Business or First Class, then go for it and get that complimentary blanket out.

If you are flying the day flights (as opposed to the overnight flights) on American or British Airways to Heathrow, you need to check if you can make the connection down to Rome that evening. Most of the time, you will have to overnight at Heathrow airport. Also, be advised that if you are flying in and out of London on frequent flyer miles, the cost of the taxes and surcharges may be as much as $500 per person. If you want to see London for a few nights, the best would be to go directly to any European city, then fly up on a cheap fare instead of paying that out-of-sight surcharge.

My cousin thanked me for that tip and the free vacation in Paris! He flew to Paris (instead of London), spent three nights there, then took the train to London. What a brilliant idea. So instead of paying the $500 surcharge per person using his frequent flyer miles, he used it to stay in Paris and take the high-speed Eurostar train for $75. These prices do fluctuate. However, I think you get the point.

CHAPTER 4

SUGGESTED ITINERARIES FOR FIRST TIME VISITORS

ALLOW A MINIMUM OF TWO WEEKS

If this is your first time in Italy, you need to allow two weeks for what I call "The Three Capitals" tour. Jetlag will do a number on your body. Included in the two weeks are your two fly days.

For jetlag, you can figure that one day will be needed for each time zone. Italy, on Central European Time (CET), is usually six hours ahead of Eastern Standard (EST) Time. You should note that Daylight Savings Time does not coincide with these two time zones. So I figure it will take about six days to COMPLETELY recover from jetlag. I think it should be called Jet-Drag.

Reiterating, consider multi-cities where you fly into one and out of another, e.g., into Rome and out of Venice. Here is a sample itinerary for first-timers with a fly-in and out of Rome. I have included an option to fly home from Venice if you are booking "Multi-Cities" instead of a "Round Trip ."

LESS THAN TWO WEEKS

I believe Italy is best visited in two weeks for a first-time visitor. I have structured the two-week itinerary below so you can easily eliminate some days. If you are short on time, you can "scrub" several days here and there. Your most significant expense for two people traveling together will be your airfare. Keep in mind that staying that extra day in Rome to go down and see Pompeii will be that hotel room, your meals, admission, and the two-hour (each way) roundtrip on the train. So remember that you're here now, and why not spend an extra day?

On the other hand, if you are really pressed for time, you can eliminate the extra days and "whittle" down your drip to 8-10.

ROME AND THE VATICAN

Rome and The Vatican are a "must." No one I know goes to Italy without seeing Rome and, hopefully, the Vatican. You will need three calendar days here, including your arrival day, sometimes called the recovery day. I usually don't count on anything to do on your arrival day. Flights may be late especially connecting through a European hub. So by the time you get into your hotel, it may be 5PM, and all you want to do is go to sleep (only a nap) and then have dinner. If you get into the City (not the airport) by 10AM you can do the hop-on-hop-off (the hopper) bus. However, it's best not to do any hop-off (except at the end) as it will consume too much time. What you are looking for with the "hopper bus" is an orientation tour. If there are 5-6 hours before 7PM try to do a visit to the Four Monuments. Also, you will "visit" all these significant sites, e.g., the Colosseum, and Saint Peter's Basilica, in the next two days. I suggest you take a look at the extra days in Rome discussed in Chapter 6.

You may want to add one or two by eliminating days in Florence. In other words, "do" the Amalfi Drive on one of the Florence days you have eliminated. On a personal note, I have found that teenagers don't enjoy Florence and the Renaissance. However, give them the Amalfi Drive, and they will jump up and down.

SORRENTINE PENINSULAR & AMALFI COAST

Once again, if you would like to eliminate some days and stay in Sorrento, you can easily "scrub" two days from the Florence day trips, i.e., Siena and Lucca. You can take those extra days you saved from Florence, visit Venice, and then shoot down to Naples (Sorrento, Positano, etc.). You can then fly home from Naples (all are connections to the USA and Canada) or take the 90-minute train back to Rome. There are direct trains from Venice to Naples, and it's not a lot of money.

An Alternative to the Escorted Tour

MILAN AND THE LAKES

Here is another idea. After Venice, You can also use those two extra days you would have spent in Florence and head to Milan, where you can visit two of the Italian lakes, with day trips. Who doesn't want to see Lake Como and Bellagio? However, it may be desolate in December, January, and February, with many hotels and restaurants closed for the season.

VENICE

Many people have told me you only need one full day in Venice. If you take that morning train out of Florence, you will have a half day for an orientation on arrival. The next day will be a full day of site-seeing. The orientation tour consists of taking the Number One waterbus (Vaporetti) around the Grand Canal.

Many folks take an evening train (nothing to see on the way but factories) from Venice to Milan, visit Lake Como and Lake Maggiore (home of the Borromean Islands) for the next two days, and fly out of Milan. The train takes 2.5 hours and costs about $40. Please see my chapter on Milan and the Lakes. It is just something to consider.

FLORENCE

In addition to two days in Florence to see the "David" and the Uffizi Gallery, I use Florence (Firenze) as a base to see the other sites in the area. If you take my suggested day trips, you will find they are easily reachable within an hour by train or car:
The Leaning Tower of Pisa and The Medieval City of Lucca
TheMedieval cities of Siena and San Gimignano
The Cinque Terre (requires 2.5 hours each way)

RECOMMENDATION FIRST TIMERS- THE BASIC TOUR

Trust me. If you enjoy Italy the way millions of others do, you definitely will be back. So it is best to start with the basics:
ROME- The Ancient City, The Vatican and Renaissance
FLORENCE- The Renaissance and Medieval Cities
VENICE- Only one place in the world like it!

ITALY Made Easy for Seniors

MAKE IT SIMPLE- THE BASIC TOUR- NO SUNDAY BLESSING BY THE POPE:

If you want to make it simple with no stress, all you need do is follow my time-tested itinerary below. BTW, o/n = Overnight

Day 1 Fly to Rome (usually an overnight flight) o/n in the sky
Day 2 Rome- Recovery- the Four Monuments* o/n Rome
Day 3 Rome- Wedding Cake, Colosseum and Forum o/n Rome
Day 4 Rome-Vatican Museum CLOSED Sundays, see note
            below. o/n Rome
Day 5 Rome to Florence morning train o/n Florence
Day 6 Florence o/n Florence
Day 7 Florence- Day Trip Pisa & Lucca o/n Florence
Day 8 Florence- San Gimignano o/n Florence
Day 9 Florence- Day Trip Siena o/n Florence
Day 10 Morning train to Venice o/n Venice
Day 11 Venice o/n Venice
Day 12 Venice o/n Venice
Day 13 Train back to Rome- Overnight FCO airport
    Or an extra day in Venice and o/n Venice
Day 14 Fly back to the USA from Venice or Rome

Note if your Day 4 falls on a Sunday, you won't be able to see the Vatican Museum and its Sistine Chapel. So, interchange Day 4 with Day 3. You will find the Colosseum and Forum are open every day. Also, try not to arrive on Monday in Florence since the Academy and the Uffizi Gallery are closed. You can however interchange Monday for another day in Florence.

NOTE- IF YOU WANT TO ATTEND THE BLESSING BY THE POPE, FOLLOW THE ITINERARY BELOW:

THE BASIC TOUR – WITH SUNDAY BLESSING IN ST. PETERS SQUARE THE "ANGELUS":

Day 1 Friday Fly to Rome (usually an overnight flight)
Day 2 Sat Rome- Recovery- the Four Monuments* o/n Rome

An Alternative to the Escorted Tour

Day 3 Sunday - The Angelus – afternoon Colosseum and Forum
Day 4 Monday Vatican Museum (yes, it's open) o/n Rome
Day 5 Tuesday to Florence morning train or drive o/n Florence
Day 6 Wednesday Florence o/n Florence
Day 7 Thursday Florence- Day Trip Pisa & Lucca o/n Florence
Day 8 Friday- San Gimignano o/n Florence
Day 9 Saturday Florence- Day Trip Siena o/n Florence
Day 10 Sunday train to Venice o/n Venice
Day 11 Monday Venice o/n Venice
Day 12 Tuesday Venice o/n Venice
Day 13 Wednesday Train back to Rome- Overnight FCO airport
  Or an extra day in Venice and o/n Venice
Day 14 Thursday Fly back to the USA from Venice or Rome

*The Four Monuments: Piazza Navona, The Pantheon, Trevi Fountain, and the Spanish Steps. It can also be visited late in the day instead of a "hop-on-hop-bus."

In summary: If you want to be blessed by the Pope, (let's face it everyone can use a blessing) you need to figure out what day of the week you will be flying to Rome. If you will not be attending the blessing, just be mindful that you cannot visit the Vatican Museum and Sistine Chapel on Sunday, it's closed.

Feel free to use both of the above itineraries as a model. For Seniors, I have tried to minimize the walking. However, no big deal if you want to modify the two I present.

If you were lucky enough to book an "open-jaw or multi-cities," you would return from Venice. An open jaw will give you another day in Venice if you go to Milan and the Lakes.

On a final note, check to make sure you are not in Rome or Italy during one of their holidays. You don't want to purchase those air tickets only to find out you can't get a hotel room in Rome because of a holiday.

ITALY Made Easy for Seniors

When you have blocked out your itinerary, you can buy those airline tickets. Or, better use your frequent flyer miles.

A QUICK OVERVIEW OF YOUR BASIC TOUR

Instead of a bus (we call them coaches in Europe), we will use the high-speed train system of Italy to get us between the major cities. Except for driving in Rome, you will find that going to Italy is relatively easy. I will explain more later.

I have selected nice three- and four-star hotels around the train stations, except for Rome. Forgetting Rome, I provide you with hotels within a five and ten-minute walk of the train stations, which also allows you to stay right in the historic district. This does not apply to Rome, where the central train station is far from the historic district. In this case, I will try to provide you with hotels as close to the historic district as possible. Sometimes, I recommend a hotel for a taxi ride of no more than 8-10 Euros. If you are driving except Rome, I recommend parking locations close to your hotel or the historic district.

PAGE LEFT BLANK FOR YOUR ITINERARY

CHAPTER 5

ROME AND THE VATICAN DAYS 2, 3 & 4

** DAY 2- ARRIVAL, RECOVERY THE FOUR MONUMENTS

PLANNING YOUR ARRIVAL

Yes, it would be best if you plan your arrival at Rome FCO Airport, also known as Fiumicino, for the village, it is located in and also called Leonardo Da Vinci. You now need to figure out how to get to your Rome hotel. I can recommend two ways. You can drag your bags a minimum of six long blocks and negotiate three elevators or take a private car.

I don't advise the train for Seniors who have been flying all night. It will cost you about 20 Euros over the Leonard Express (28 Euros for two people) train to Rome's central rail station known as "Termini," including a taxi ride at Termini. Getting to your hotel from Termini will cost you about 15-20 Euros. When the Leonardo Express gets to Termini in about 30 minutes, you will have to fight the crowds (trust me, it is always bumper-to-bumper people) and make your way to the taxi line. So, it's best to figure with the train and the taxi, the time and the frustration you are into about 48 Euros, the total for two people, plus you get to "schlepp" your own bags.

There is a better way to do it, and it will only cost you 20-30 Euros more than the train and the taxi. You can figure that you will be bushed and all you want do is drop into bed. Oy. Now is not the time to be cheap or have your partner beat up on you! Oh, I forgot to mention you need not schlepp your bags. So, here is what is best to do:

>>>SENIOR TIP<<<
Go online and book a private car with a driver. It will cost you about 65-70 Euros. Your driver will be waiting outside those sliding doors, just past the baggage area (note they cannot come into the baggage area, however, free baggage carts are available). Your driver will be holding a sign with your name on it; very impressive and very classy! You will think you are a VIP. And you are!

Your driver will take your bags, bring you to his car (usually a high-end vehicle, e.g., Mercedes), and whiz you into Rome. Most drivers will offer you a cold bottle of water and give you a short narration of the historic sites they pass. I should note that the tip for private drivers is usually not included. Don't worry; they will accept your good old American or Canadian bucks.

I have made it a habit not to use any "portals" (sometimes called brokers) who just "job" the work to a driver they don't even know. There are numerous horror stories about "brokers" that have no control over the driver. So best is to book directly with either of these two extremely reliable firms:

Transfersrome@gmail.com
Transfersrome.com
(transfers Rome Italy tours)
Attention- Massimiliano
Phone 39 393 076 0609

An Alternative to the Escorted Tour

The other is:
Bob@romelimousines.com
Romelimosines.com
Rome Limousines Company
USA phone number- 330 942 3642
In Italy 39 342 125 0889
Bob has returned from Italy
and now lives in Ohio.

If you are starting your visit in the Sorrento/Amalfi and care not to take the train down to Naples, I would strongly suggest a private car transfer:

Sorrentocars.com a/k/a Leonardotravels.com
Info@sorrentocars.com Contact is "Ugo"
Phone 39 333 100 2426

>>><<<

Oh, by the way, avoid the "hawkers" outside the baggage control area, who will offer you a ride to Rome. You should book and pay for your private car transfer before you leave home. Book a private car and go first class for a few Euros more!

>>>SENIOR TIP<<<
It is best to advise the hotel via email a few days before your arrival. I usually inform them of my arrival time. It is best to add two hours to your flight arrival time. So, if your scheduled arrival time at FCO airport is 9AM, the best is to tell them you will arrive at about 11AM. Ask them for a quiet room away from the elevator or "lift ." There is less noise. Don't worry about noise from dropping ice cubes in the ice machine or cans of Coke dropping down into the dispensing area; there are none!

If your room is not ready, you will have time to stroll around and have a decaf cappuccino and a croissant

34

to hold you over till that room is made up.   If you are in for one of the activities and can keep your eyes open, check your bags with the front desk and head out. See my suggestions below.
>>><<<

ARRIVAL AT ROME'S FCO AIRPORT

Make sure you didn't leave anything on that airplane (meds, etc.). Getting that tablet or smartphone back long after you are far from the gate will be difficult. And trust me, Rome's new Terminal 3 requires a long walk to the baggage claim.

>>>SENIOR TIP<<<

Don't be a hero. There is a very long walk from the gate area (usually Terminal 3) to Border Control and Baggage claim. For Seniors who are mobility challenged, I recommend a wheelchair from the top of the jet-way (the gate). Advise the originating airline, i.e., Delta, American, etc., via the internet or a phone call that you need assistance (cannot walk a long way from the gate to baggage claim). By the way, there is no tipping for assistance in Italy. If you offer a tip, it will not be accepted. Also, your pusher will get you through immigration in a flash, while others will wait 5-15 minutes. Using assistance is a real plus.
>>><<<

If you are walking, follow the crowd toward the Immigration and Border control booths. Have your passports ready. The Italian Authorities will stamp your passports with your date of arrival. Do make sure you say "Grazie."

Then follow the crowd to pick up your luggage. Once you have your bags, follow the signs to the exit. Just proceed through the doors with the green lights, NOTHING TO DECLARE. If you are bringing in anything of real value, usually for resale, the guards will beckon you over for some quick questions. Hopefully, you won't have a problem, now onto Rome.

ROME OVERVIEW

Oh, Rome, the "Eternal city." History has it that this term started in the first century AD. It was the feeling that Rome would go on and on. Little did they know that in 476AD, the Roman Empire would fall apart, but certainly not the city.

Just a point in passing. Many people do not know that Rome lies in the province of Lazio. There are twenty major provinces of modern Italy. Lombardy to the north is home to Milan and the Lakes. Greater Milan is the largest in terms of population. Lazio is the second-largest province. From the center of Rome, Lazio stretches about 70 miles north to Tuscany and halfway to Naples, on the south, all along the Tyrrhenian Sea.

There is no other city in the world like Rome. I have found that people love it or hate it. I love it! I know of no other city that spans thousands of years of history. Rome is one humongous outdoor living museum. You see monuments, statues, ruins, and more everywhere you go. The problem is that you won't understand any of this unless you know some basic history of Western Civilization. It's like someone put all this stuff inside one of those old musket rifles and shot it out. There is no rhyme or reason where this stuff "landed."

Take the Spanish Steps. Yes, it was built by the Spanish. But it has nothing to do with the Roman Empire of Julius Caesar. The Spanish Steps date to about 1723, and artifacts of the Roman Empire and Ancient Rome date to about 44BC or even further back. Likewise, the famous "Wedding Cake," best known as the Monumento Nazionale of Vittorio Emanuele II (National Monument of Victor Emmanuel II), was completed in 1935. This monument to the first president of the Italian Republic is less than 100 yards from the Roman Forum of Julius Caesar's time.

ITALY Made Easy for Seniors

All this "stuff" can be found in what is commonly known as the "Centro Storico" or the historic district.

In addition, many of the monuments, particularly Hadrian's Mausoleum, also known as Castel Sant'Angelo, lie on the other side of the Tiber River, close to the Vatican.

This area known as the "Borgo Pio" which is squeezed between the Tiber River and the Vatican wall is loaded with inexpensive restaurants. It is best to have atleast a lunch or dinner here.

>>>SENIOR NOTE<<<
If you did not know by now, Rome is built on Seven Hills. That is to say, many sites of ancient Rome were built on those hills. There are some moderate hills where modern-day hotels have been built. However, as luck has it, I will recommend hotels where you do not have to negotiate some of these hills.
>>><<<

CHOOSING A HOTEL
Rome's Centro Storico is just too large to manage in this book. So I have broken it down to what I call flat districts. First, here is where I would *not* stay if I were a Senior (and why):

Off Via Sistina near the Spanish Steps. Even though there is an elevator to the top of the Spanish Steps, it would force you to always head to the bottom of the steps, known as the Piazza di Spagna to get that elevator. And take it from me, there is a long walk along the "Via del Babuino" to get to the elevator! There is a long walk up from the Palazzo Barberini, and you will be pooped when you get to the top.

Another area I don't recommend is on or directly off the Via Veneto. While it's a lovely sweeping boulevard lined with hotels, it also is on a hill. The Via Vittorio Veneto (Via Veneto) slopes down to the Palazzo Barberini, starting at the top at the Rome

37

An Alternative to the Escorted Tour

Marriott Grand Hotel Flora and passes the American Embassy just before the boulevard takes a hard right, en route to the Palazzo Barberini. In the 1950s, the Via Veneto was the place of the wealthy and the Hollywood elite. Everyone from Felline, Orson Welles, Hepburn, and more were often seen strolling on the Veneto. However, unless you are up to walking up and down this long boulevard, Seniors should avoid it.

There are areas also what I call "away from it all." It would be best if you avoided any hotel across the Tiber River. There is just too much of a walk to the historical sites. Remember, you will usually be in Rome for 3-4 days, and you don't want to take a taxi back and forth to your hotel all the time. The area of Trastevere and the area around the Vatican, Seniors, should avoid, even though Trastevere is one of my favorite neighborhoods. However, if you have lots of business with the Vatican, Trastevere is the place to stay.

>>>TIP<<<
It's best to save your hotel points (e.g., Marriott, Hilton, etc.) for use in the USA or Canada. Part of the Italian experience is staying in a European-style hotel. There is just something different about it. Yup, it's got to be the bidet. Also, many American-style hotels are not located in Centro Storico. Some of them are located a mile or two away or better, right off the GRA ring road a few miles from the FCO airport. These hotels are mainly used for conventions (congresses) and are very commercial.
>>><<<

I have chosen "Flat Areas" in and around the historical areas. If you are a Senior, this will make it easy to walk. It is like strolling in Manhattan or Chicago and certainly not San Francisco. There are more than 5000 hotels, BnB, and all other housing in greater Rome. I am sure you don't want to stay outside the City limits or at least outside the ancient walls which circle the City as it will cost you a minimum of 15 Euros plus your precious time with a taxi each way.

You should note that taxis do not "cruise," like in New York, Chicago, etc. So, don't count on "hailing" a cab on the street. You must walk to a taxi stand or go to a hotel which will usually have a taxi stand, or the hotel can call a taxi for you. There is no extra charge for this. However, please be gracious and tip the bellman or front desk clerk a Euro for calling that taxi. Also, be aware that the small streets in the area are usually one way and there is lots of traffic. You may have to resort to buses or the Metro (relatively safe). Bus tickets can be purchased at any tobacco shop; trust me, there are plenty of tabacchi shops. See my write-up at the end of this chapter.

While the Centro Storico encompasses a specific area, Rome is also made up of Ancient Rome, where the Colosseum and Roman Forum are. I have broken the touristy part, or what I call the historical part of Rome, into several non-commercial districts. Here you will find an abundance of hotels and restaurants.

These "flat" districts I favor are:
  The Pantheon and the Piazza Navona Area
  The Colosseum, Forum, Wedding Cake and Trajan's Market
  The Piazza di Spagna Area (Plaza at the base of the "Steps")
  The Trevi Fountain Area

In addition to the hotels located on hills or with a rather uphill incline, I do *not* recommend hotels in and around the Termini Train station which is very commercialized and noisy.

All the hotels in my tables are inside the ancient walls and are not on the Vatican side of the Tiber River. There are very few hotels in the Jewish Ghetto. However, you will find good BnB's and apartments.

An Alternative to the Escorted Tour

The tables consist of three or four star hotels, but not apartments, BnB's etc. Frankly, I love those Italian breakfasts in the morning which most three and four star hotels offer in their room rate. It's part of the overall Italian experience.

You will have to do your research on each one. Make sure you locate the hotels actual or "official" website and avoid using the OTA's i.e. Booking.com, Hotels.com, etc. You usually will have better bargaining power on arrival i.e. "can you upgrade us to a views of the courtyard or a better room." As Seniors, make sure

you ask about air-conditioning (if you are not going in the cool times of the year), breakfast, an elevator and do ask for a quiet room. You should forget the parking requirement as I don't recommend driving in Rome. See my tip below.

For us Seniors, I do not recommend hostels or one and two star hotels. Many of these hotels only offer a hard roll (with jam and butter of course) and a coffee or tea for breakfast. If you must stay at these hotels, always ask if they have a private bath or shower. You're a Senior, spend the extra bucks for a minimum of a three-star hotel. Your kids will do fine with their inheritance (if any). By the way, many of the four-star hotels are priced just a few Euros more than a three-star hotel. So you may want to opt for the four-star. Sometimes I cannot tell the difference between a three-star and a four-star hotel. Some four-star hotels appear to be three-star hotels, and some three-star should be four.

On another note, I cannot make any recommendation except to state that I have "stayed" at this or that hotel. So the best is to read the chapter on hotel selection and make your own decisions.

>>>TIP<<<
Do not even attempt to rent a car at the airport and drive into Rome or even around the streets of Rome. If you are not taking the train to points outside of

ITALY Made Easy for Seniors

Rome, i.e., Florence, or Naples, the best alternative is to go back to the airport and rent a car. Italy has an excellent road system (most of it toll). However, as a Senior, I would avoid driving in Rome and instead take the Leonardo Express from Termini back to the airport to pick up an auto rental. A better approach is to have your hotel call a taxi and head back to the airport to pick up your car.
>>><<<

Here are the hotels by flat areas:

AROUND THE PANTHEON AND THE PIAZZA NAVONA
This area of hotels lies between the Tiber River and the Spanish Steps. On the north side is the Piazza del Popolo, and on the south side, you will find the Trevi Fountain, about one block south of the Via del Tritone. Small one-way streets dot the area. There is easy walking to the Centro Storico and the Piazza Navona. Best to check all on the map of Rome, where you can spot the Trevi Fountain, Pantheon, and the Piazza Navona. I have segregated Trevi Fountain into a separate flat area.

Boutique Hotel Campo de' Fiore	Navona Colors Hotel	Hotel Damaso	Palazzo Lupardi Relais
M2 Hotel	Dulces in Pantheon	Hotel Carabita	Navona Essence Hotel
Kambal Luxury Suites	Navona Theatre Hotel	Hotel Barrett	Hotel Navona
Hotel Smeraldo	Lacanda Navona	Relais Teatro Argentina	Casabella Pantheon
Hotel Albergo Santa Chiara	Hotel Teatropace	Hotel Trecento	Pantheon Caesar Relais
Coronari Palace			

NEAR THE COLOSSEUM, FORUM, WEDDING CAKE, AND TRAJAN'S MARKET:
The "Monti Area" is south of the Via XX Settembre up to the Colosseum. It is an established residential area. Many hotels are off the Via Madonna d. Monti. It is just a short walk to the

An Alternative to the Escorted Tour

Colosseum and the Forum. Other historical sites will require a short bus ride or a taxi. You can walk on the major boulevards if you are up to it.

Hotel Forum	Salotto Monti	The 15 Keys Hotel	FH55 Grand Hotel Palatino
47 Botique Hotel	The Glam	The Monti Palace Hotel	The Duca
D'Aba Hotel	The Rome Times Hotel	Hotel Capo' d Africa	Hotel Bolivar
Kolbe Hotel Rome	The Dharme Boutique Hotel	Mercure Roma Centro	Relais Hotel Antigo Palazzo Rospigliosi
Sonder at Colosseum Cloisters	Hotel Griffo	Hotel Canova	Hotel Anfiteatro Flavio
Princeps Boutique Hotel	Hotel Amalfi	Hotel Borromeo	Hotel Colosseum
Hotel Valle	Hotel Verona Rome		

AROUND THE PIAZZA DI SPAGNA:
The Piazza Di Spagna is not the Spanish Steps. It is the base of the Spanish Steps, with lots of cafes and eateries. It is an area of small one ways streets. Many eateries are around the Piazza del Popolo and Via Del Corso. The Via Condotti, a small street from the Piazza di Spagna to the Tiber River, contains many high-end shops, i.e., Gucci, Louis Vuitton, etc. The Via Condotti can be very busy during the day. It would be best to avoid hotels directly abutting the Via Condotti or, better, ask for a quiet room not facing the street.

Corso Boutique Luxury	Hotel Homs	Spagna Dream Suites	Roma 55 Piazza di Spagna
Elysium Suites	The Venue Spagna	Condotti Boutique Hotel	Royal Palace Luxury Hotel
Hotel Crose di Malta	Hotel La Luminere di Piazza Di Spagna	Boutique Centrale Palace Hotel	Hotel Piazza di Spagna
Babuino 181	Hotel Locarno		

>>>TIP<<<
If you are in for a great, and I mean great Italian dinner, you must check out "Alla Rampa." Rampa, for years, has been one of my favorites, and it's easy to find. While standing in the Piazza di Spagna, looking

up the steps to the church (Trinita Dei Monti) at the top, you will note the American Express office on the right-hand side. Take a walk to the backside of the Amex office and follow the sidewalk directly under the Spanish Steps. There you will find Alla Rampa. I used to call it just "La Rampa," short for the steps. They are usually closed in August, and your front desk person should check if they are open on Sundays.
>>><<<

HOTELS AROUND THE TREVI FOUNTAIN AREA:

I don't know anyone who has visited Rome without seeing the Trevi Fountain. Next to the Colosseum and Forum, the Spanish Steps, and the Vatican, it is a must. No, this has nothing to do with the Roman Empire or Ancient Rome. It was built over thirty years, beginning in 1732. Water flows into the massive fountain from almost seven miles away. You can read more about it in all those detailed tour books.

As a tour director, I would always tell guests that this Fountain and the associated sculptures are built into the side of what seems to be an office building. It's kind of odd. The Trevi has been seen in numerous movies, including *La Dolce Vita, Roman Holiday, Sabrina Goes to Rome,* and *Three Coins in the Fountain.* Trevi always deserves a minimum of three visits. One during the day to toss those "three coins in the fountain." One to devour a gelato and enjoy the view, and finally, one to view the Trevi when it is all lit up after dinner.

A factoid, the song *"Three Coins in the Fountain"* won the Academy Award for best motion picture song in 1954. You can always listen to Frank Sinatra's rendition.

The three coins mean: One guarantees a return visit to Rome. The second represents a love affair, and the third means a forthcoming wedding.

An Alternative to the Escorted Tour

>>>TIP<<<
When you visit the fountain you must throw three coins over your left shoulder with your right hand. You do this with your back facing the fountain. Just a note. This is a major pickpocket area. There are always numerous police and many plain cloths officers mingling in the crowd. You cannot remove any coins from the fountain.
>>><<<

I will review again, all of the instructions on the coin throwing under the details of the Trevi Fountain... very important.

Mood Suites Tritone	U Visionary Roma	Hotel Barberini	Hotel Delle Nazioni
H10 Palazza Galla	The One Boutique Hotel	Concept Terrace Hotel	Palazzo Caruso
Hotel Cinquantatre	The Radical Hotel Roma	Trevi 41 Hotel	Hotel Caravita
The Cosmo Polita	The Bolivar	Collona Palace	Hotel Julia
Hotel Fellini	Hotel De Petris	Hotel Julia	Maison Trevi
Roma Resort Trevi	Al Manthia	Escape Luxury Suites	Luxury Rooms H2000 Roma
Avignonesi Suites	Piccolo Trevi Suites	Hotel Accademia	Trevi Rome Suite

FURTHER TIPS ON SELECTING A HOTEL

I have only provided a dozen or two hotels in each area. It is best to use the OTA's (Online-Travel-Agencies, Booking.com, Hotels.com, etc.) to locate hotels in the area you wish to stay. Be aware that many OTA's state "NO AVAILABILITY" *on our website*. Many hotels pull their listing off these OTA's when they have the nights you are looking for at 50% occupancy. However, when you contact the hotel directly via email, you will usually find that rooms are available. Look for their official website on the internet. Their site may appear several pages behind the first page. www.mycomfyhotel.com/central reservations is not the official website of the Comfy Hotel. You will probably find it on page 4 or 5 as www.comfyhotel.it.

ITALY Made Easy for Seniors

Please consult my chapter on "Hotel Selection" near the end of this book for details on finding the "right" place to stay.

A SHORT HISTORY OF ROME

You can't even write a short book on the history of Rome (the city). Thousands of books have been written about Rome and the Roman civilization. I will boil it down to a few paragraphs with a short timeline. The history of Rome includes the City of Rome as well as the civilization of ancient Rome.

In 753BC, Romulus founded Rome. You can read more about the myth of Remus and Romulus in all the other books on mythology if you are unfamiliar with the story.

753-509BC period when the Seven kings ruled Rome.

509BC The Roman Republic was established, kings were replaced with elected magistrates

The Gauls sacked Rome in 390BC Rome; ancient Rome gained dominance of the Western Mediterranean, displacing Carthage as the dominant regional power.

About 40BC, the establishment of the Roman Empire followed Julius Caesar's rises to power.

The Western Roman Empire begins to decline.
476AD The Empire ceases to exist, except for the Eastern Roman Empire, which is based in Constantinople

The Duchy of Rome takes over the rule of the city until the 8th Century.

The Papal States are formed and controlled by the Popes.

Medieval Rome breaks with Constantinople.

An Alternative to the Escorted Tour

The city of Rome was reduced to irrelevance, its population falling below 20,000. Rome's decline into complete irrelevance during the medieval period

Note- When you view all that "stuff" in the Roman Forum, remember all that is the remains of the Roman Empire before 476AD.

The Roman Renaissance started in the 15th Century. Rome replaces Florence as the center of artistic and cultural influence.

In 1527, the City of Rome is sacked by several warring armies from France and Spain. Famine follows, and the city's population goes from 50,000 to 10,000.

1798 Rome gets annexed by Napoleon until 1814.

During WWII, under the control of the Axis powers, several factories, etc., get bombed by the Allied forces.

Rome was finally liberated on June 5, 1944, by the Allies moving up the Italian peninsular from Sicily and the South.

In 1946 Rome was made the capital of the Italian Republic.
It is the largest city in Italy and one of the largest urban areas in the newly formed European Union.

WHAT TO SEE AND DO IN ROME
First, there is absolutely no way you can see all the sites of Rome (including the Vatican) in three or four days. You can purchase a guided tour which will have you visit 15 sites in Rome and Vatican City in one day. Forget this. You are a Senior. Unless you want to start the day at 7AM, go to 7PM, and gobble down a panini en route between the Pantheon and the Colosseum, it won't be easy. There is just too much physical stress.

ITALY Made Easy for Seniors

I have divided what to do and see in Rome and the Vatican into two categories: Those that are mandatory and those that are optional. Please note the appropriate time to visit each site. I have included the time to get to the site and, if needed, wait time in lines, etc. You should note many monuments and museums in Italy are closed on Mondays. The Colosseum and Forum are open. There are exceptions. To avoid Monday closures, you may have to juggle days around in all major cities. Also, please be aware of certain holidays where venues may be closed. Best to check their websites.

>>>TIP<<<
If you arrive early (Day 2) and your room is unavailable, there are three things you can do. One, find a café and have breakfast or lunch.   Or, two, locate a stop for the Hop-On-And-Off bus. Your hotel desk clerk or concierge will be able to help you. I always recommend the Gray Line 90 minute tour. This hop-on-hop-off (I call it a hopper) bus departs Termini Station if it is running off-season. However, I believe you can catch it at any stop. It's only 22 Euros, and you should not get off. You will find more info at www.graylinerome.it. Remember, this is an orientation tour, there are NO visits to the sites. Make sure you check the duration to make the entire loop. There are other hop-on-hop-off buses. Also, check the restroom locations.

Afterward, hopefully, you can grab a bite before your hotel room is ready. Total time should be about 3-4 hours. There are also discount coupons on the internet.

If you are ready to start site-seeing and get some exercise, you can easily do the four monuments: Piazza Navona, The Pantheon, and Trevi Fountain,

An Alternative to the Escorted Tour

and end up at 6-7PM at the Spanish Steps (Piazza di Spagna). I would suggest the cutoff time to start the four monuments walking tour would be 3PM. Note-Romans don't usually have dinner until 8PM.
>>><<<

If you are not doing a hopper bus, and your arrival at your hotel is 9-11AM, check in if available. The best approach is to take a two-hour nap, shower, and get ready to see the sites. It would be best if you avoided sleeping past two hours. If you do, you risk sleeping all day and late into the evening as your circadian rhythm fights to stay on American or Canadian time. As they say, it is best to get up and get on the street. What you want to do is get on Italian time as soon as you can. As Seniors, you can always go to sleep by 10PM after that first Italian dinner with a couple of glasses of the local "Fracatti" wine.

** DAY 2   *** MONUMENTAL ROME ***
I call this the four monuments: Piazza Navona, The Pantheon, Trevi Fountain and the Spanish Steps. There is no entrance fee to any of these sites. Tomorrow, your first real full day (Day 3), we will visit the Colosseum and the Forum.

AFTERNOON ON DAY OF ARRIVAL
WALKING – ABOUT 1.5 MILES, ALL FLAT
DAY 2- MONUMENTAL ROME- A WALKING TOUR
This day (or should I say half-day?) I reserve for the four most important major monuments of Rome: The Pantheon, Piazza Navona, Trevi Fountain, and my favorite, the Spanish Steps.

Here is how you visit all four sites with minimal walking. If you read on, I will tell you that you don't have to walk up the Spanish Steps, only down them, or better don't negotiate them. By the way, they are all flat areas.

ITALY Made Easy for Seniors

Let's face it. All day yesterday, you sat for ten hours in that uncomfortable airline seat. Now is the time to get some exercise. You can start anywhere. However, the best is to end up at the base of the Spanish Steps (Piazza di Spagna) or the Trevi Fountain since you probably will need a nourishment break.

Here is a quick recap of the routing and the walking distances between the sites:

Start-
Piazza Navona

to Pantheon (about 300 feet from Piazza Navona)

to Trevi (12 football fields from Pantheon)

to Piazza di Spagna (10 football fields from Trevi)

End – Note- All flat walking

Alternate-
Piazza Navona

to Pantheon (about 300 feet from Piazza Navona)

to For Lunch- at the Spanish Steps, about 12 football fields

to Piazza di Spagna to Trevi – (about ten football fields)
        All flat walking

To Trevi – End with a Gelato!

Start the walk at the Piazza Navona. You will need 30-45 minutes here. Perhaps enjoy a takeaway cappuccino in some of the cafes ("Two Sizes" is one of the best pastry shops in the area) on the

An Alternative to the Escorted Tour

side streets as you admire the statues and the fountains—plenty of places to sit on those stone benches.

There is no direct route. So you will have to navigate alleyways and small streets. A short walk of about four blocks will bring you to the ancient Pantheon.

The easiest way is to head for the Fontana del Moro (the forward fountain closest to the Tiber River). About 50 yards past it, there is a small street. Via di Pasquino. Here are the exact directions from Google Maps (I have printed it in a larger font, so it's easier to read).

Head south on Piazza Navona (toward the Tiber River) toward Via di Pasquino
Turn left to stay on Piazza Navona
Continue onto Via dei Canestrari
Continue onto Largo della Sapienza
Continue onto Via dei Sediari
Turn left onto Via del Teatro Valle
Via del Teatro Valle turns right and becomes Piazza di S. Eustachio
Turn left onto Via di S. Eustachio
Slight right onto Salita de Crescenzi
Turn left onto Piazza della Rotonda
The Pantheon is on your right
Note all maneuvers are about 60 feet apart
    If all else fails. follow the crowd or ask
      "Doe Vay ee ill Pantheon?" Where is the
      Pantheon?

ITALY Made Easy for Seniors

My preferred way to visit the four sites is to start at the Piazza Navona and end the day (after lunch, of course), at the Spanish Steps. If you would like to shop, you will find plenty of it on the abutting street to the Piazza Spagna, known as "Via Condotti."

After you are shopped out, walk over to the Trevi Fountain, take a lot of photos and throw those three coins in the fountain. After this is all done, enjoy a gelato in one of the many gelato stands around the Trevi Plaza. Do be very street savvy in this area, and make sure you read my chapter on security.
Here are the historical details on each site:

THE PIAZZA NAVONA- 30-45 MINUTES
The Piazza Navona is one of the most beautiful squares in Rome. The Piazza is a rectangle. It was built in 86AD by emperor Domitian. The square served as a stadium for athletic competitions. It measures two football fields in length and one football field across. At capacity, it held almost 20,000 spectators. It served its purpose as a stadium until the 17th century.

In about 1644, it was transformed by Pope Innocent X into a square of Baroque Roman art and architecture. His home, the Palazzo Pamphill, faces the plaza. Here is a brief description of those works of art:

The Obelisk in the center of the square was brought in from the Circus of Maxentius. Below it is the fountain of four rivers. The statue is the work of the Renaissance sculptor Bernini. The abutting church is the work of Rainaldi, Borromini, and others.

There are two other fountains in the Piazza. At the southern end (towards the Tiber River) is the Fontanna Del Morro. It is a basin of four tritons sculpted by Giacomo della Porta in 1575. In 1673 Bernini added a statue of a Moor wrestling with a dolphin.
At the northern end of the square is the Fountain of Neptune by Bitta. This was added in 1878 to balance the La Fontana del Morro on the other side of the square.

An Alternative to the Escorted Tour

Numerous theatrical events were held in the square for almost 300 years, starting in 1652.

The farmer's market, which also occupied part of the square, was moved in 1869 to the present Campo de Fiore (worth a visit in the morning). Please see more below.

THE PANTHEON- 30-45 MINUTES
Don't confuse this "pantheon" with the pantheon in Paris. The Pantheon in Rome is a temple and since 609AD a Catholic church. On this site, there was an earlier temple. The present temple you see, was rebuilt by Emperor Hadrian and dedicated about 126AD. The building is cylindrical. It's interesting that the height of the dome from the slab floor, is identical to the width of the building. It is one of the most famous and best preserved of all ancient Roman buildings. The earlier temple which stood here dates from Pagan times. The building is open at the top. I don't know why, but the floor gets wet when it rains.

Emanuelle II and Umberto I and Umberto's queen Margherita are buried here. In addition, the famous Renaissance painter "Raphael," is also buried there with several other famous artists.

That obelisk (about 135 feet tall including its base) and the fountain you see in the piazza (Piazza della Rotunda) just in front of the Pantheon is known as the Fontana del Pantheon. The fountain was designed and built by Giacomo della Porta in 1575. The obelisk came in 1711 at the request of Pope Clement XI. The fountain, once again, like the Trevi Fountain is fed by an ancient underground aqueduct from several miles away.

The obelisk constructed by Pharaoh Rames II for the Temple of Ra in Heliopolis was brought to Rome in ancient times (seems no one knows exactly). It was rediscovered in 1374 underneath the Basilica of Santa Maria sopra Minerva. In the mid-15th century it was then moved to the Piazza San Macuto. The obelisk stood about several hundred meters to the southeast of the Pantheon. In 1711 it was moved to its current position in what is still called the "Piazza della Rotunda".

THE SPANISH STEPS- ONE HOUR

The Spanish Steps were built with funds from the French diplomat to Rome and the Spanish Embassy. The 135 steps were built in 1723-1725. The steps go from the famous church Trinita dei Monti on Via Sistina to the base, Piazza di Spagna with its beautiful Baroque fountain, "Fontanna della Barcaccia." Of interest to note, on the right-hand side of the steps, you will find the home of poet John Keats. He died here in 1821. See my tip on visiting the Spanish Steps, where you do not have to climb the steps or the long slope on the Via Sistina. If you are going to have a coffee and a pastry, allow 90 minutes at one of the many cafes at the bottom of the steps in the Piazza. By the way, you can take great photos from the top of the Spanish Steps, and you need not climb them. Look at my tip under HOTELS AROUND THE PIAZZA DI SPAGNA for directions to the elevator, which you can use instead of climbing those stairs.

>>>CRITICAL TIP<<<

An ordinance passed in 2022 states that you are not allowed to eat or drink on the steps. In addition, you cannot sit or lie on the steps. There is now a 400 Euro fine if you are cited. I always wondered why so much bubble gum was stuck on the steps.
>>><<<

TREVI FOUNTAIN- ONE HOUR

Designed by Nicola Salvi and completed by Giuseppe Pannini (no, he did not invent the sandwich by the same name) and several others. It is Baroque in style and was built from 1732-1762. There are several statues in the Fountain. The Fountain

An Alternative to the Escorted Tour

lies at the junction of three ancient roads and aqueducts dating to 19BC. These aqueducts still supply the water to the Trevi.

Since my first visit to Trevi and subsequent visits, I have never understood why the fountain is built into the side of what appears to be an office building. This is Rome, would you not expect this gorgeous fountain to be located in a large piazza (a square)?

The Trevi Fountain you now see is the third Trevi. The first one was built in 19BC to supply water to the Romans. The name "Trevi" is derived from the fact that the Fountain lies at the junction of three ancient roads. Many modern day sculputers believe the Trevi Fountain is the most beautiful fountain in the world. It is open twenty-four hours. It is also, best to view it at night when it is illuminated.

Of most importance is the fact the Trevi Fountain is used in the backdrop of many Hollywood movies. The water comes from 14 miles away thru the ancient aqueduct, which is still in use today. The "Tritons" and horses are the main attraction in the Fountain. I describe more below on exactly how to throw the three coins into the Fountain and their significance:

It's a myth! It started with the movie 1954 called *Three Coins in the Fountain* (20th Century Fox). The song, sung by Frank Sinatra, won the Oscar for best song of the year. Here is what it means: If you throw one coin, you shall return to Rome; with two coins, you will fall in love with an attractive Italian, and if you throw three coins, you will marry the person you met. Here is what you need to do: Hold the coins in your right hand and toss them over your left shoulder with your back to the Fountain. Oh, make sure someone takes a picture of you.

After this is all done, enjoy a gelato in one of the many gelato stands around the Trevi Plaza. The fountain yields about 3,000 Euros each day, which is donated to charity. Do be very street savvy in this area, and make sure you read my chapter on security. Also, if you are caught removing any of the coins, there is a stiff fine. Many of those tourists are plain clothes police.

>>>TIP<<<
About two blocks from the Trevi Fountain on Via Marco Minghetti is an indoor shopping mall called Galleria Sciarra. Just ask any of the Italian's "Doe Vay et Galleria Sciarra"? You can usually find a taxi at the Galleria.
>>><<<

>>>TIP<<<
Since I do not know the location of your hotel, I can't give you an exact route between the sites to visit. You can figure all this out with a good map of Rome. You can get these maps online from Amazon. I recommend *"Streetwise Rome,"* by Michelin, Michael Brown, author. It's laminated and will allow you to use a water-based marker to highlight where you want to go. You can also ask the front desk or concierge for one of those free maps (they call them plans or Mappa).
>>><<<

>>>SENIOR TIP<<<
Sometimes these maps are somewhat challenging to read. I suggest you take an inexpensive plastic magnifying glass in your day bag.
>>><<<

You are now ready to walk back to your hotel or get a taxi from one of the abutting hotels on the side streets or taxi stands. Rest up; tomorrow is Colosseum day or Vatican day, your choice.

So much for what I call "Monumental Rome .

An Alternative to the Escorted Tour

** DAY 3- WEDDING CAKE, COLOSSEUM AND FORUM

HISTORIC DETAILS OF EACH MUST SEE SITE:

THE MONUMENT TO VITTORIO EMANUEL II A/N/A THE "WEDDING CAKE". 30-45 MINUTES

What is more commonly known as the "Wedding Cake" may be the last significant monument erected in Rome. Americans and Canadians see this building in many pictures of Rome but don't know what it is. But before I explain the Wedding Cake, here is some quick history. Before 1861 the land we now call Italy was made up of what they called "City-States." Even what we now call suburbs were included in the city-state. When the City States of Lazio (Rome), Firenze (Florence), Venezia (Venice) united to form what we know as modern-day Italy, they chose a king. That king was Victor Emmanuel II. He was the King of Sardinia and was brought over in March of 1861 to be the first king of the unified country known as Italy. The eternal light you see at the base of the Monument and the two soldiers guarding it is the tomb of the Italian Unknown Soldier. The Monument itself is built on Palatine Hill. It was constructed from 1895 to 1911 (finalized in 1935 with some additions) out of white marble from the area around Brescia (about one hour west of Lake Garda in the northern Lakes Region of Italy. The unknown soldier was brought over and added in 1921, right after World War I. Victor Emmanuel II, who died in 1878, is buried in the Pantheon, not at the Wedding Cake. The Monument was built to honor King Victor Emmanuel II, the Father of the Fatherland, the new Unified Italy, and the Unknown Soldier of Italy. If you have time, you can visit the museum at the base of the Monument.

TRAJAN'S MARKET AND COLUMN- 45 MINUTES

Trajan's Market was one of the first attempts to establish a "shopping mall." The ruins you will notice are built in a multi-level structure. Emperor Trajan built the Market about 100-110AD. There are numerous stalls where merchants sell their goods, i.e., baked bread, grains, beans, meats, etc. You can visit the existing ruins from an entrance on Via Quattro Novembre 94 and Piazza Madonna di Loreto. It is almost the size of a football field. The monument in front is Trajan's Column.

The column is about 125 feet tall and commemorates Trajan's victory in the Dacian Wars. A statue of Emperor Trajan disappeared in the middle ages (Medieval Era). That statue on top is a bronze figure of Saint Peter which was placed there in 1587. The column is composed of 20 round column pieces, each weighing 40 tons. Inside that long column are 185 spiral steps leading to the square platform below the statue. Even though you may be able to climb those steps (see the museum people), it is not advisable for Seniors. Suggest you send your grandchildren to the top for picture taking.

THE COLOSSEUM- 1-2 HOURS
What would a trip to Rome be without visiting the Colosseum? It's probably number one on everyone's bucket list.

The Colosseum is an oval theater in the city's center built in 80AD and still standing. It is the largest of all amphitheaters in the world. What you don't see is all the Travetine limestone facade. Over centuries it has been removed by peasants and others. It could hold about 50-80 thousand people for an event. The Colosseum was used for Gladiatorial contests, public spectacles, animal hunts, executions, and re-enactment and drama about Roman Mythology. It has a massive lower level where animals were stored and water for even depicting naval battles. Over the years, the Colosseum was sacked of all the beautiful Travertine facades, and the massive building fell into disrepair. It is listed as one of the New Seven Wonders of the World and is the iconic symbol of Rome. During the medieval period, the Colosseum was used as a hotel. The question always asked is, "what are those pockmarks or holes in the facade." From what I have been told, the holes were used to place tree branches in them and across to another hole. It was very similar to a shower curtain rod or pole. The peasants then laid over the branches animal skins to form a lean-to. Peasants would live under these lean-tos.

The cross you see in the center of the Colosseum was placed there by Pope Paul II in 2000. The cross is dedicated to Christian martyrs.

THE ROMAN FORUM- One Hour

The Roman Forum, or simply the Forum, was the heart of Rome. It lies between the Palatine and Capitoline Hills. The Forum, at one time, was the site of triumphal processions of the Roman Legions. It housed criminal trials in its courts. It was the center of government. Today, it is an area of about two football fields in length and one in width containing fragments of an ancient civilization. There are still standing columns of various buildings, including the Temple of Vesta (7th century BC). Many of the buildings were rebuilt after the rise of imperial Rome. The Senate itself was housed in the Forum. The actual area dates to the Bronze Age, about 1200BC.

Discoveries over the years have unearthed prior Roman civilizations. An interesting fact, what you see is the final layer of the Forum. It was also here in 44BC that Marcus Junius Brutus assassinated Julius Caesar.

SAN PIETRO IN VINCOLI- 30 MINUTES

The church where "Moses" is located is also known in English as "Saint Peter in Chains." It is in a church on Oppian Hill, less than three blocks from the Colosseum. The church houses Michelangelo's statue of Moses. I have seen this several times, and I can tell you that next to the "Pieta" in St. Peters, it is number two on my list of statues created by Michelangelo. It is easy to find. You need to walk up the Via Terme di Tito alongside the park on your right. You should note that there is a slight incline on "Tito ." Take a hard left at the stand-up bar at the top of the street and follow the crowd. It's free and will only add about 20 minutes to your day. The church itself dates from 439AD. The "Moses" dates from 1515 and is part of the tomb of Pope Julius II.

You are now ready to walk back to your hotel or get a taxi from one of the abutting hotels on the side streets or taxi stands. Rest up, tomorrow is Colosseum (if you did not see it today) or Vatican day, your choice. There are lots of taxi stands in the area and abutting the Metro.

** DAY 3– THE WALKING TOUR OF THE WEDDING CAKE, COLOSSEUM, FORUM AND THE MOSES.

*** The times listed in the history section above include walking to and from (the next site). Also, some items and facts I already discussed in the above History section. I reiterate them here. ***

Now that you know a little about the history of the four venues, I will do my best to describe how you visit each one in an orderly way. I recommend doing about 1.0 to 1.5 miles on the first full day in Rome. For Seniors, this will be the shortest way without doing any back-tracking. Trust me, at the end of the day; you will be pooped. With the exception of the slight incline to view "The Moses" at the Church of St. Peter in Chains, here is what you need to do:

Start your day off in the Piazza Venezia. You can either take a taxi if your hotel is too far or walk over. On arrival, note the balcony on the right-hand side of the square of that building. This balcony is where Mussolini made all his speeches to his crowd of Italian Fascists back in the days leading up to World War II.

An Alternative to the Escorted Tour

Then view the MONUMENT TO VITTORIO EMANUEL II A/N/A, THE "WEDDING CAKE ."If you wish to go to the top of the monument, it will cost you 12 Euros to use the elevator. However, you must first negotiate a flight of about 50 steps near the adjacent church and the cafe. Those 50 steps are wide and high. You will note it on the right-hand side of the monument as you face it. Then follow a passageway to the elevator. I do not recommend it for Seniors, even though there are impressive views of the City. However, if you are in excellent condition, go for it. It is easy to spot that elevator, as the café is just outside.

After taking photos of this massive white marble monument, go across the street. Then, go one block to "Via dei Forte Imperiali," and view Trajan's Market and Column. Supposedly this was the first shopping mall created. You can't buy anything here. The place has been closed for more than one thousand years. There are lots of photos to take here. For Seniors, once again, do not attempt to climb the 184 steps to the top of t Trajan's Column.

From Trajan's Market, continue walking down the Via dei Forte Imperiali. Note you will pass the Roman Forum on your right. The next stop is the Colosseum.

Continue till you reach the Colosseum and locate the ticket "holders" line.

You should purchase your timed combination ticket (Colosseum and Forum online at www.coopculture.it/en/products/ticket-colosseum-roman-forum-palatine_24h/. Several weeks before your flight to Rome. The best is to figure about 1PM entrance. They will accommodate you if you arrive early or late in the off-season. It's not a big deal. Consider purchasing the combination ticket, (instead of separate tickets) which will allow you to gain entrance to the Colosseum and the Forum.

60

>>>TIP<<<
On arrival at the Colosseum, just next to the ticket booths you will notice the bathrooms. Best to take a break before your entry. By the way, always, keep a Euro in your pocket. While it is free now, you never know when they install those turnstiles.
>>><<<

Now, after you have read up on the Colosseum, for us Seniors, you will follow the signs to the elevator (ascensore in Italian). Do not attempt to climb the stairs to the various levels of the Colosseum. If you use the stairs (not advisable), beware of tour groups that may be going down the stairs like a herd of cattle and may be pushing some people out of the way to get back to their tour bus. It is perfectly acceptable to find your way back to the ascensore and go back to the ground level. Ground floors are marked as the zero floor, not the first floor. The ground floor is called zero (0). BTW, all hotels in Italy observe the same rule.

After you finish your visit to the Colosseum, you are ready to walk across the street (follow the crowd) to the Roman Forum. I find that this is an ideal place to take great photos. Picture yourself sitting on one of those ancient Roman columns.

>>>TIP<<<
Between your visit to the Colosseum and the Roman Forum, I recommend lunch and a time to take a biological break. The only places are directly behind and to the right and left of the Metro station at the Colosseum. They are Oppio Caffe (to the right), La Biga Ristoracaffe Wine Food, and Lauras Coffe (sic) Shop (all to the left, as viewed when you are entering the Metro station).
>>><<<

An Alternative to the Escorted Tour

After you visit the Forum, it is best to walk about 3-5 blocks and view Michelangelo's "Moses." All you need do is go back to that Metro station and follow my directions from the above section on SAN PIETRO IN VINCOLI, "Saint Peter in Chains."

By now, about 4-5 PM, you should be bushed. If you are not, you probably are a Senior who is qualified to enter the Iron Man contest each year! I'm just kidding, of course. So taxi or hike back to your hotel, take a nap, shower, have a drink, and get ready for dinner. Remember, most restaurants do not open till 7:30PM or 8PM. Make sure you get lots of rest for tomorrow's VATICAN DAY. Also, it would be best to read my Chapter at the rear of the book on dining in Italy.

THE CAPITOLINE HILL (IF TIME PERMITS)
This area of Rome never gets the attention of the Colosseum, the Roman Forum, and the other vestiages of ancient Rome. This hill was the center of the Roman Empire. There is evidence that there were inhabitants on the hill dating back to 1300BC. The hill housed many of the ruins of the ancient and most important temples of the Roman Empire. You won't find them here as they are buried below the new plaza. What you now see is a square designed by Michelangelo in the 16th Century. It is known as the "Piazza del Campidoglio."

The most important item to note is that the square faces toward the Vatican and not toward the Roman Forum. This is because Michelangelo wanted to impress the populace that power and control now was with the Vatican and not the the old Roman Empire. If you go to the back of the Piazza, behind that large building you can take some great photos of the Roman Forum.

By the way, that large building at the top of the stairs houses the present day Rome City Council and a museum. There are several access points to the Campidoglio. Suggestion is just follow the crowds. Seniors should not have a problem as there are not a lot of stairs and they are gradual and wide.

ITALY Made Easy for Seniors

** DAY 4 - A VISIT TO THE VATICAN WITH LUNCH
TOTAL WALKING- ABOUT 1-2 MILES
TERRAIN – ALL FLAT

WHAT TO SEE AND DO IN THE VATICAN-
SEQUENCE OF YOUR VISIT- OVERVIEW OF DAY

The Vatican Museum requires a lot of walking. It is best visited when you have all your energy. It would be best if you arrived at the entrance to the Museum at about 10AM. Hopefully, you have purchased timed tickets between 10AM and 11AM. Then see the Museum and its Sistine Chapel. After exiting the Chapel, the facilities are next, and then the entrance to St. Peter's Basilica. If you read my tip, you will not return to the Museum's entrance area. You will go directly to the Basilica. After you visit the Basilica and take photos in St. Peter's Square, you will have lunch from about 1PM to 2PM in the Borgo Pio district abutting Vatican City. So here we go.

The Vatican City State (The Vatican) or sometimes called the Holy See, is an independent country. It is not part of Italy. The population is about 500, and it occupies almost 120 acres due west of the Tiber River. It has its police, own small army, own railroad station (not accessible), own post office, and its radio and TV stations. It was separated from Italy in February 1929 by the Lateran Treaty.

The Holy See is one of the smallest countries in the world. It is an island in the City of Rome and totally off limits to Italian Police, and other forms of security unless specifically invited. The Vatican is not a member of the UN, but is an observer.

Some quick facts about security at the Vatican. According to the Lateran Treaty of 1929, the Vatican police can call the Italian police (Polizia or the Carabinieri) to St. Peter's Square for crowd control if required. Other than that, the Vatican has its own security force. All visitors are screened before entry to the Basilica by the Vatican authorities.

An Alternative to the Escorted Tour

You won't need to show your passport to enter any Vatican City sites. However, Italian law dictates that a foreigner must always have their passport on them. That means you must carry it all the time, preferably in a secure pocket or in your day bag.

The Holy See ("See" means, in Latin, the "Chair or Office) is home to the Catholic Church and serves as its worldwide administrative headquarters or office. Of most importance, it is home to the Vatican Museums and St. Peter's Basilica.

You need to know two critical items if you will visit the Vatican. First, if visiting the Vatican Museum, you must purchase tickets online at m.museivaticani.va. If you attempt to go without tickets, you will wait in line for 1-2 hours, even off-season.

Secondly, if you want to join about 2,000 other parishioners for a Papal Audience, you need to contact your local priest or archdiocese. The papal audience, where the Pope appears on stage in the auditorium abutting St. Peters Basilica, takes place every Wednesday morning at about 10AM. Best to check with the Vatican online at http://www.papalaudience.org/schedule. Sometimes, the Pope will be away or at his summer residence at Castel Gandolfo, about 16 miles southwest of Rome, and there will be no scheduled audience.

Proper dress is required. I attended a Papal Audience in the summer of 1972, and I can tell you being in that fourth row with priests from all over the world was very moving. You usually will be escorted to your numbered seat by ushers wearing formal tails. If you are planning a Papal Audience, it will be challenging to adhere to either of my 14-day itineraries unless you allow an additional week in Rome at the beginning of your visit, or better, forget about the Angelus on Sunday morning and instead attend the Papal Audience on Wednesday morning.

Do not confuse the Papal Audience with the Sunday blessing in St. Peter's Square, known as the "Angelus." Except for the Sunday holidays, this usually takes place at 11AM and is over by 11:10AM. The Pope will bless all in attendance. I have attended three of these Angelus, and I can tell you, once again, it is very moving. Tickets are not required. It would be best if you arrived at least by 10:30. Groups are singing, and other festivities go on before the Pope's appearance from his Apartment. He appears once the Papal Flag is placed below his window.

The three main sites to see in Vatican City are The Sistine Chapel and its ceiling by Michelangelo (no, he did not paint this ceiling on his back as told in the movie *"The Agony and the Ecstasy,"* St. Peter's Square and, of course, St. Peter's Basilica with Michelangelo's statue of the "Pieta."

You should note that I only provide a short overview of Vatican City. There are loads and loads of books on the history of St. Peter's Basilica.

Here are the facts, just the facts and the details of your 3-4 hour visit to Vatican City.

THE VATICAN MUSEUM AND SISTINE CHAPEL

Most people who visit this monumental Museum are there for one reason to see the Sistine Chapel and its ceiling. As stated before, you must purchase tickets at least 8-12 weeks before you visit Italy, or else you will need to wait in a long line. This line can sometimes be a half mile long and four deep. It is NOT RECOMMENDED FOR SENIORS!

Further, there are no "porta-potties" anywhere near that massive line. In addition, the next available bathrooms are past security after you enter the Museum. If you have not purchased tickets several months before, play it safe and get on one of those half-day tours of monumental Rome and the Vatican. You should note this is not the hop-on-hop-off bus tour. Another point of

An Alternative to the Escorted Tour

information, no backpacks or rucksacks are allowed. They can be checked, but you must exit and return to the check room. ALSO, YOU WILL NOT BE PERMITTED PAST THE SECURITY CHECKPOINT IF YOU HAVE A POCKET KNIFE. So men, it is best to leave it in your hotel room.

There is too much detail to describe the actual ceiling painted by Michelangelo. It was painted "Alfresco," i.e., into wet plaster. Part of the painting is called *"The Creation."* He painted it from 1508-1512 at the request of Pope Julius II. There are other paintings on the ceiling, including *"The Life of Moses"* and the *"Life of Christ,"* all painted by Michelangelo.

Numerous tapestries adorn the Chapel, which I might note is used for several masses yearly. In addition, as we all know, the papal enclave meets here to choose a new pope when needed. This chimney is where the black smoke signals "NO Pope yet," and the white smoke tells the world, "We now have a new Pope."

Here is how you negotiate the Vatican Museum and St. Peter's:

First, with tickets in hand, you must arrive at the Vatican Museum entrance *ticket holders line* and pass through security. The entrance has those large glass doors and is flanked by Swiss Guards in their colorful red and yellow attire. You should note that the entrance to the Vatican Museum is about one-half mile away from St. Peter's Basilica. If you are taking a taxi over, tell the driver that you want the Vatican Museum (Vaticano Museum). Don't even mention the words "St. Peter's." If you read this book in your planning stage, you should have purchased your Vatican Museum tickets online, printed them, or selected your option to pick them up at will-call.

Pass through those big glass doors and then enter the security line. After passing security, it's best to use the facilities. Then you will need to make your way almost one-third of a mile down a hallway filled with the Vatican's most prized collection of sculptures, gifts, paintings, and tapestry. All you need do is follow the crowd. You cannot get lost. You need to climb several flights of stairs at the end of that hallway. Note, Seniors should avoid the stairs and take the elevators to the right.

Once at the Sistine Chapel level, you need to follow the crowd for another 2-3 blocks till you arrive at the Chapel. Once again, follow all those other tourists. They are all going to the same place.

Once entering the Chapel via the one-way entrance, you will have about five minutes to take photos. Make sure you turn off your FLASH. If it does go off, you will be approached by one of the ushers. Secondly, there is no talking allowed. Yes, you can whisper.

After viewing the ceiling of the Chapel, you will be directed to a door to your left. It's marked exit. Exiting this way will force you to view more of the Vatican Museum as you make your way back to the entrance, where you came through security about an hour ago. It is another grueling walk of about three football fields. If you have checked any bags in the cloakroom, you will have to exit this way and claim them near security.

If you want to have lunch, you have two options. You can enjoy lunch at the Vatican Museum cafeterias or exit the Museum and find one of the many places across the street from that long waiting line to purchase tickets. In addition, the street named "Borgo Pio" has over fifteen excellent inexpensive restaurants, one after another. See my tips below. After lunch, there are two options. Most folks will go over to either St. Peter's Basilica or the Castel Sant' Angelo.

It would be better to return to your hotel for a snooze and a drink before dinner if it's very late in the day.

An Alternative to the Escorted Tour

>>>SENIOR CRITICAL TIP <<<
After you visit the Vatican Museum and its Sistine Chapel and your next stop is St. Peter's Basilica, you need to follow my directions, else you will be routed back to the main entrance and the security point; a good three football fields and a lot of walking. You will then need to walk about one half mile to your right against that long waiting line for tickets, pass those stunning Swiss Guards (don't worry you can still take pictures with them later) until you make your way into Saint Peter's square. You should note that to gain access to Saint Peter's Basilica you will need to wait in line and clear security again. However, luck has it that there is a hidden secret at the Sistine Chapel for Seniors, tour groups and VIP's. Here is how you do it:

Take a look at the front of the chapel. There are two doors. One is on the left the other is on the right. There usually are ushers at both doors. If you go through the door on the left you will be forced to go back into the museum for that long walk to the main entrance where you entered, and hopefully you did not check any bags. As described in the above paragraph you will then have to take that long one half mile walk to Saint Peter's, while hugging the Vatican walls.

Here is the easiest way to eliminate that stressful walk. In addition, you will not need to go through security again. You also get to use the bathrooms immediately at Saint Peter's.

If you go through the door on the right (it is marked GRUPPO SOLO, groups only) you will go down an outside stairway. It is quite wide, but make sure you hold on to the black wrought iron railings. About four flights down you will exit directly at Saint Peters. You should make a rest stop here as the ladies and gents room is just about thirty feet to your right.   They are really nice and clean; and yes, they do have toilet seats! No need to go through security again, you are in Saint Peter's. Or better I should say the secured area.

If for some reason that usher comes over to you, just tell him "you were separated from your group and you saw them go through this door." He will open the door and say "okay, no problem"; and do thank him with a "Grazi."
>>><<<

Next stop is the Basilica itself. Best to following my directions below "**ST. PETER'S BASILICA.**" You can figure about one hour to walk about the Basilica and just marvel at its construction. You should figure another hour to participate in a Mass at one of the many alcoves. Here are the details.

ST. PETER'S BASILICA

Supposedly, St. Peter's Basilica is built over the remains of St. Peter, who was crucified in Rome. No one knows if this is true, as there was a belief that he was buried in one of the Catacombs of Rome. I don't see how St. Peter (Simon) ever traveled to Rome from Galilee (now in Israel), where he was a fisherman. Suffice it to say that in the 4th Century, on the present site, a church was constructed by Roman Emperor Constantine the Great called St. Peter's Basilica.

The Catholic church was based in Avignon, France, for almost seventy years. In January 1377, Pope Gregory moved the headquarters of the Catholic Church back to Rome. In April 1506, construction started on a new basilica. It was completed in

An Alternative to the Escorted Tour

1626 (about 120 years, a long time, about six years after the Mayflower dropped anchor in Plymouth, Massachusetts).

The architects and artists of the Renaissance designed this massive Basilica. These were Bramante, Michelangelo, Maderno, and Bernini. It is the most renowned work of the Renaissance. It is not the mother church which is a church in Rome called Saint John Lateran. St. Peter's still is regarded as the holiest of all Catholic shrines, i.e., right above Lourdes, Fatima, etc. However, it is considered the greatest of all churches in Christendom. In terms of size, it is the largest church in the world. Saint Peter's burial is directly below the high altar of the Basilica. Hundreds of Pope's and others are buried in crypts below the Basilica known as the Scavi.

You can book "Scavi" tours on certain days and times of the week. You usually need to make reservations two months in advance.

There are stringent rules for dress in St. Peter's. Once again, like the Vatican Museum, bags are not allowed in the Basilica.
If you entered directly from St. Peter's Square, you could check any bags after passing through security. There is a secured bag check to the right of the steps into the Basilica.

Also, women cannot enter wearing halter tops, short-shorts, or a "skimpy" t-shirt. There are places just outside St. Peter's on the main street (Via di Porta Angelica) where you can purchase a sizeable in-expensive scarf, which you can wrap around those exposed knees. However, if you are visiting in the colder off-season, you probably won't be wearing shorts; better to wear Capris, pants, a dress, or a skirt that falls below the knees.

Here is a quick overview of the structure.

The church is visible from all over Rome. It is massive. From the outside, those statues on top of the church, just below the dome, are the first-century apostles. You will note that there is no statue of Peter. The inside is a little more than two football fields in length and one-half in width. It is in the form of a cross with naves off on both sides near the altar. The dome and the large columns supporting it are of utmost importance. The dome is about 450 feet from the floor and about 140 feet wide at the top.

In addition to visiting the inside of the Basilica, you can visit the roof and the dome. Here is how you do it. The best is to take the elevator to the roof. It will cost you 12 Euros and eliminate a climb of about 300 steps. From the roof (I have been there twice), you can view all of Rome and into the Basilica. There is now a bathroom and a gift shop also there. If you are in good shape, consider climbing about 250 steps to the top of the dome. However, be advised that those steps are pretty narrow and winding. My advice to any Senior is NOT to go up to the top. It is just too exhausting.

>>>TIP<<<
If you wish to take a free tour of St. Peter's, you will find an information booth in St. Peter's square to the left of the Basilica, as you are facing the front. There are tours in English at about 2PM, and 3PM on weekdays and Saturdays. Best to check online as these tours do change times. Also, be advised that there is no entrance fee or tickets required to enter St. Peter's (unless you are an organized tour group). Check with the information booth about free audio tours. Also, you may find "roamers" in St. Peter's square offering you a narrated tour for 10 or 20 Euros per person. This person may take your money and place you in the security line. Many of them will never see you again! Once again best on arrival is to go to the information booth.
>>><<<

An Alternative to the Escorted Tour

If you are Catholic, you may consider attending an English Mass in one of the alcoves given several times a day. You can check on www.vatican.va/content/vatican/en.html. Be sure to stop at Michelangelo's "Pieta," which lies behind bulletproof glass. Just follow the crowd.

The Basilica is overwhelming. I have always started my groups off on the left-hand side (as you enter) and walked up and down the aisles, then finally ending at the "Pieta ." If you pass some popes under plexiglass, you guessed it, most of them have been dead for a few hundred years. They are well preserved.

After you have completed your visit to the Basilica, your next stop should be the "Square." Remember to visit the checked bags area to claim items you may have checked.

ST. PETER'S SQUARE

First, I never knew it to be a "square." If you look at it, it is supposed to be two large hands embracing visitors to St. Peter's Basilica. Once again, one of my favorites, "Bernini," designed the square in about 1686. That Egyptian obelisk you see in the square was erected in 1586. It was originally erected in Heliopolis, Egypt. Emperor Augustus brought it to the Julian Forum in Alexandria, Egypt, and in 37AD, Caligula ordered the obelisk to be moved to Rome.

Bernini designed and built those embracing hands, four columns deep. He also designed that fountain in the square in about 1675. Of importance is that Bernini had to work around the constraint of the Papal apartments (where the Pope delivers the Angelus on Sunday mornings).

Lunch follows, and I highly recommend the restaurants on the Borgo Pio. To locate the Borgo Pio, follow the Vatican wall till you reach a traffic light (at Via Sant' Anna, note the Swiss Guards). Opposite that gate to the Vatican is Borgo Pio. My favorite is the last one on the left, walking toward the Tiber River and the Castel Sant' Angelo. It's known as Borghiciana Pastificio Artigianale, and like Alla Rampa under the Spanish Steps, it is one of the best. You probably, like most Italians, will make this your main meal and have a very light dinner. You also get to steer at those incredible antipasto appetizers. There is always the inside if it's too cold for outdoor dining.

If you had a light lunch elsewhere in the "Borgo" you would hopefully have the energy to visit "Castel Sant' Angelo." I always look at this as a bonus. Or better, if you have another half or a full day in Rome. Since it is not part of the Vatican, I discuss it under optional sites to be visited. If you are up to it, it pays to see the "Castel" while you are less than a football field away. I discuss this first on the list of optional sites.

If you are now "stuffed" from that lunch (actually a dinner) at Borghiciana Pastificio Artigianale and it's about 3PM, ask the staff where you can get a taxi for your trip back to your hotel. I would suggest you don't walk it after that bountiful lunch. Arrive at your hotel for a snooze, shower, and a light dinner. The next day we are off to Florence (Firenze). Please skip down to the Firenze chapter unless you take some of the day trips I mention in the next chapter or visit additional sites I describe below. So much for our Vatican day.

>>>SENIOR TIP<<<
There is a lot of walking between visiting the Vatican Museum and St. Peters. Wear comfortable walking shoes. Make sure you take appropriate sweaters or jackets. For ladies, do not carry a heavy handbag. The Museum, Cathedral, and Square will consume at least four hours. If you couple this with lunch at the Borgo Pio and a later visit to the Castel St. Angelo, it will probably consume the entire day. So best not to plan anything else
>>><<<

An Alternative to the Escorted Tour

OPTIONAL SITES TO BE VISITED–
A THIRD FULL DAY IN ROME –OR– SKIP THE VATICAN

If you have an extra day for visiting more sites in Rome, you should consider the following by order of importance:

Castel Sant' Angelo (If you have not already)
The Baths of Caracala
The Catacombs (just one of them)
Campo di Fiore
Circus Maximus
The Villa Borghese and its Gardens

CASTEL SANT' ANGELO
If you are still in the Vatican area, and want to spend about one hour before you head back to your hotel, Castel Sant' Angelo is the place. It is also known as Mausoleum of Hadrian. This round circular structure has been around since 139AD. That's almost 1400 years before they started work up the street at Saint Peter's! Everyone that passes it on our tour buses always commented, "what is that?" Frankly, I don't know anywhere in the world, of a structure like this. Here are the facts:

Originally it was built by Emperor Hadrian to be mausoleum for him and his family. First, don't confuse this emperor with Emperor Trajan who built that massive outdoor mall and column near the Wedding Cake. Only thing in common is the last two letters of their last names.

In 139AD, Hadrian's ashes were placed in the "Treasury Room" of the mausoleum. The remains of emperors forward were also placed here. The last emperor to be interred (his ashes) here was Caracalla in 217AD. In later years the Castel was used as a prison and as late as 1900 a theatre where Puccini's third act of Tosca was performed.

There are dungeons in the Castel and a secret passageway to the Vatican. At one time this passage way, was used by Popes fleeting the Vatican to take refuge in the Castel.

That walkway over the river leading from the Castel is the "Ponte Sant' Angelo". It was also built by Hadrian. Note the Baroque statues of angels which were built at a much later point. It spans the Tiber River and connects the Castel to the Piazza Navona area. It is nice for a stroll and picture taking. However, watch out for those pickpockets. Also, the bridge is a great place to be harassed by the street vendors. Everything from fake Rolex watches to Louis Vuitton handbags, usually laid out on a blanket for a quick getaway if the "polizia" should arrive un-announced.

At many centuries the Castel was the tallest building in Rome. The building still contains many sculptures and artifacts.

Since the Castel is now a government museum, you will need to purchase timed tickets. However, if you are arriving late in the day (after 3PM) there usually is a short line. Entrance with audio tour is usually $16 per person. You can find more on the website at www.rome.info/attractions/castel-sant-angelo/. However, if you have less than one hour before heading back to your hotel, best is to just take pictures from the Ponte Sant' Angelo bridge looking back toward the Castel; great selfies.

For us Seniors, take note, there are ramps of moderate incline over the seven levels of the Castel; which will also take you to the top of the monument. There is an elevator just passed the ticket booth. You may have to ask for assistance in using it. Be aware, there is lots of walking and I do not advise this late in the day after walking all over Vatican City.

THE BATHS OF CARACALLA

Everyone asks me (this may sound funny) "in ancient Roman times did they have toilet paper." The answer is no. When you needed to take care of business, you went to a communal latrine.

75

An Alternative to the Escorted Tour

There you were given a "Tersorium." This was a stick with a small sponge on the end of it which was dipped in warm water and vinegar or salt water. After doing your business, many then went to the baths. There were baths everywhere. Of all the baths, the most famous and still well preserved are the Baths of Caracalla. They were the second largest baths in Rome.

The Baths of Caracalla were built about 212AD, (yes, by Emperor Caracalla and Emperor Severus) and were not only baths, but an entire spa complex. These baths covered over 60 acres. The Caracalla baths were about four football fields in length and a little over three football fields in width. There were 252 columns and some were as tall as 36 feet. Several million bricks were used to make the exterior and interior walls and rooms.

Water came to the baths via the Acqua Antoniniana aqueduct from the Acqua Marcia water supply. It still exists, and is located off the main road to the FCO airport, just before you get to the GRA ring road, about eight miles from the Baths of Caracalla.

The baths had hot baths, cold baths and tepid baths, in addition to a swimming pool measuring fifty by twenty-two yards. It took ten tons of wood a day just to heat the water with cauldrons or "cisterns". There were even saunas. Works of art adorned the walls of all the rooms. There even was a library. On a typical day these baths were visited by almost 8,000 bathers.

Underneath the baths there were elaborate tunnels which distributed fresh water, removed the used water and brought fresh air into the facility.

The baths were destroyed after the siege of Rome during the Gothic War, about 537AD and fell into ruin and dis-repair. The earthquake of 847AD, destroyed most of the complex remaining and left it in ruble.

There have been numerous excavations of areas under the baths including a burial area, a gravel pit and a subterranean worship area for the followers of Mithra, the Persian God.

Numerous buildings have been modeled after the Baths of Caracalla. They include the old Pennsylvania Station in New York City, and Union Station in Chicago. I might note that Pennsylvania Station was reduced to rubble in 1967 and dumped in Flushing Meadows, in the Borough of Queens.

The Baths of Caracalla are certainly worth a visit, if you have some extra time in Rome. I recommend after that nap on arrival, instead of the hop-on-hop-off orientation tour (no hop offs), that you visit the Baths of Caracalla. The entrance fee is only ten Euros. I would strongly suggest that you hire a docent at the entrance and take a one-hour tour.

You should check current hours on the internet at www.coopculture.it/en/products/ticket-for-baths-of-caracalla, where you can also purchase your tickets.

THE CATACOMBS
I was first introduced to the Catacombs in 1987 when my 16-year-old son, Scott said "Dad, can we visit one of the Catacombs." To be honest I don't recall which one. However, I can tell you we did wait in the parking lot for them to open, about 2PM.

So, after getting directions, (yes, even without a GPS), we went to one of them while en route to Florence. Remember, I don't drive in the City of Rome!

For most of you that are unfamiliar with the Catacombs, they are burial places; basically underground cemeteries. All of them are located just outside the old city walls of Rome. The two most famous are located on the old Appian Way. The San Sebastiano is located at Via Appia Antica 136 and the other known as San Callisto at Via Appia Antica 126. Each one contains several miles

An Alternative to the Escorted Tour

of tunnels with burial chambers in the walls of the tunnels. You need not worry about sleeping tonight. Most of the skeletons in the Catacombs have been removed a long time ago.

First there is a small admission fee for each site. Secondly, you can take a taxi to either one. However, getting a taxi back is a major problem. Taxi's don't usually cruise the Via Antica. So, your best bet for the afternoon is to put yourself on a tour of the Catacombs. The tours include: transportation to and from one of the above Catacombs, entrance fee, and a knowledgeable tour guide. There are several. Best to check the web.

>>>TIP<<<
If you are not fluent in Italian, best to check if they have an audio tour in English. However, see if you can book a tour with an English speaking guide. Also, the tours meet at a central point in Rome. So you need to allow time to get over to that meeting point i.e. usually a hotel.
>>><<<

CAMPO DI FIORE
First, if you are not staying at a hotel or a BnB, and have elected to stay at an apartment for three or four days while in Rome, your best bet, on arrival in Rome, in the early morning (and best by noon) is to head on down to the Campo Di Fiore, Rome's only open air market. Yes, it's open all year round. You can buy all your fruits, vegetables, cheeses, fresh pasta, hams, etc. at the Campo. Your other items like milk, wine, etc. can usually be purchased at an "alimentari" or a local supermarket (Conad, Carrefour). Alimentari's are small convenience stores who usually sell cheese, cold-cuts, canned goods and bread. They also sell beer, wine, and snacks (hint, potato chips and candy).

You should be able to locate a taxi stand nearby, however, there is one at Largo Argentina. If all else fails, simply go into a bar abutting the Campo and they will call a taxi for you. You will also find on the internet a website which lists taxi stands: www.archeoroma.org/taxi/stands/. You should also remember that there are taxi stands near every major site in Rome. However, most Italian's will know "Doe Vey un Taxi"? And one more final point, you may want to consider picking up one of those strong shopping bags for about one Euro at the Campo; just makes it easier. A better idea is to just pack one in your baggage and bring it with you.

>>>TIP<<<
If you are considering renting an apartment for perhaps four nights, your best bet is to rent one in the Jewish Ghetto abutting the Campo di Fiore. You can't beat the proximity to the Campo di Fiore; it's only a few blocks away. In addition, you will also find many BnB's around the Campo di Fiore. You will also find several mini-supermarkets in both areas. I might also note that the Jewish Ghetto, because of the Sabbath, is rather quiet all day Saturday. Restaurants however do open after sundown, which is quite early in the winter months. There are also excellent kosher restaurants in the area. Sorry, no pasta and clams and definitely no milk products for dinner. However, I am sure they will have plenty of meat dishes, and, yes artichokes!
>>><<<

CIRCUS MAXIMUS

If you have some time and want to see where that famous chariot race took place in Ben Hur, then this is it. There are actually two components of the Circo Massimo (Circus Maximus). When you visit, you will notice the large circular raceway. Yes, this is where the chariot teams raced. However, take a look behind it. Right up against the Palatine hill you will notice those red brick ruins. This is what remains of the massive stadium, which could easily hold over upwards of 150,000 people.

An Alternative to the Escorted Tour

Here are the details. The stadium and that oval shaped racetrack, in its heyday (about 500BC) was almost one half mile long and over a football field in width. What you don't see is the trackside seating. These were tiers of timber built stands. The trackside seats were reserved for senators and other distinguished guests. Under the trackside "grandstand" were shops and service buildings. This wooden structure and its bleachers were destroyed in a fire in the year 31BC. There was another fire in 36AD and another again in 64AD. Trajan was the last emperor to do extensive work on the Maximus. He added 5,000 more seats. During Emperor Diocletian's reign, a wooden grandstand section fell and killed about 13,000 people.

In addition to weekly chariot races, what we call circus's now, were also held here. Elephants, tigers and all the other beasts were displayed with various acts. Also, the Circus was a venue for what were called "ludi". They were parades, concerts and you name it. In its final years there were over 150 ludi events per year. The last known chariot race was in 549AD. That's about 73 years after the end of the Roman Empire (476AD.)

THE VILLA BORGHESE GARDENS
If you have the time, this is another one of those must see visits. It is extremely unique. This is the third largest park in Rome covering about 197 acres. In addition to the gardens it contains the Galleria Borghese. The gardens as you see them now all date from the late 18th Century. This has nothing to do with the Roman Empire or Ancient Rome.

There are several villas in the gardens. The main villa is now called the Galleria Borghese. The building itself is magnificent. Other villas on the park complex include Villa Doria Pamphili and Villa Ada. The gardens, as you see them now, were created in the late 18th century. The Villa Borghese contains priceless paintings and sculptures spread over the upper two floors. There are many free days. However, there is a two Euro timed reservation fee. More can be found at:

https://galeriaborghese.beniculturali.it. Note, the website may be fire-walled. If you have any intention on seeing the galleria, best would be to just go over to the villa or check with your concierge or desk clerk.

THE CHURCH OF QUO VADIS and THE APPIAN WAY

If you have some extra time, you might want to visit the Pyramid of Rome, the Appian way, and The Church of Quo Vadis. They are all in the same area. It is about two miles from the Pyramid. Note: you may have to take a taxi down to the Church and have it wait for you as you visit for a few minutes.

In the new testament, Peter is fleeing from the Romans down the Appian way. Peter asks Jesus, "Quo Vadis." Peter replies, "I am going to Rome to be crucified again." Peter then gains the courage to turn around and return to Rome, where he is crucified. This encounter occurred at the Church of Domine Quo Vadis on the Appian Way.

If you want to walk the Appian Way (Appia Antica, no vehicular traffic on Sundays), you will find the Church about eight football fields beyond the Porta Sebastiano gate. The Church is of medieval architecture but was rebuilt in 1600. For those of the Catholic persuasion, Mass can be said daily. More information can be found on the Church's website: For information: http://www.dominequovadis.com/en/home-2/

THE PYRAMID OF ROME

Yes, there is a Pyramid in Rome. It was built to house the body of Caius Cestius in 18BC. The interior burial chamber was opened up in 1660. Sorry to say, no one was there. The Pyramid was opened for interior visitation in 2015. Don't expect the same size as the Pyramids of Giza, Egypt. This one is only 120 feet wide with a height of about 120 feet.

CHAPTER 6

DAY TRIPS FROM ROME AMALFI DRIVE, POMPEII, CAPRI, SORRENTO, POSITANO RAVELLO, HERCULANEUM ORVIETO, OSTIA ANTICA

TRAINS AND AN OVERVIEW OF "TERMINI" STATION
The day trips in this chapter and your journey to Florence, Naples, Venice, Milan, and all those other places in Italy, will all involve travel by Italy's modern high-speed rail system. In addition, many of my places to visit, Umbria, Puglia, Sicily, and the Lakes District, are best seen by car. With respect to trains, trust me, you will spend more time and stress flying from Rome to Venice than taking the train with dramatically less hassle, not to mention more than twice the time. So, I have included a few paragraphs on Rome's Termini rail station (actually, it's a terminal), like Grand Central in New York.

Rome's central train station is known as "Termini." For all you railroad buffs like me, it does not mean terminus or terminal. It comes from the Latin word "Terme." You see, in ancient times, this was the site of underground springs used for bathing. Very much like the baths of Caracalla. When the Italians built this massive rail station in 1863, they named it "Termini" after the abutting baths. The latest major renovation took place in 1950 and is what you see now.

ITALY Made Easy for Seniors

Some quick facts: It is the second busiest rail station in Europe, second only to Paris's North Station (Nord). Termini has 33 tracks and handles 800 trains per day. Almost one-half million people visit it per day. Below the rail station is home to the Metro (subway) Lines A and B. The Metro station is marked TERMINI. Now here is what you need to know.

If you have your tickets already, you can proceed to the shopping area just behind the ticketing area and the information desks. There are three entrances for Seniors (and, of course, all others). The front is where the taxi line is, and smaller restaurants and shops flank the right and left entrances of the station.

Also, note that you need to do nothing if you have a paper ticket with a **QR** code or bar code. That piece of paper is the ticket. If you do not have a ticket, either use the red machines or wait in the ticket/information line and speak to a representative. Depending on the queues, you will need to take a number and be called. So obtain a number and watch the electronic board till your number is displayed. Many of the agents speak English, and it is so noted. Italo has their own agents with red booths. They are easy to spot.

I must admit one critical item. While waiting for your train to be called, there are just a few, and I mean a few, seats for us Seniors to sit on in that shopping gallery that abuts the ticketing area. Here is what you need to do:

Walk into the platform area where the trains are parked. Note that the tracks start at "1" on your left. About halfway down, walking toward track "25," you will see a flight of stairs. Look behind those stairs, and you will see two large elevators. These lifts will take you to what I would call the "food court." It is massive, running about four blocks in length. You should avoid those stairs; just too many people in a rush. After viewing all that really good stuff that will make your mouth water, you should decide to have a cappuccino, a pastry, or perhaps some lunch. It

An Alternative to the Escorted Tour

is important to keep your eyes on the electronic train boards located throughout the food court for your train posting.

Trains board about 20 minutes before actual departure time. Since you will have to clear security (have your ticket ready), you can figure that you must be down in the platform area about 30 minutes before departure. Security will not let you on the platform until the train is ready to board. Remember, this is Italy, and all the trains run on time (or they try to). If you arrive a minute after the posted departure time, your train will have left.

On early morning departures, about 8-10AM, you probably won't have enough time to visit the food court. However, if you need to do a grab-and-go, you will find abutting the platforms, at least six places that sell coffee, pastries, and pre-made sandwiches. Oh yes, some sell pizza (Pepperoni in the morning)?

Once your train number is posted, find your way to the platform (or bin number) have your ticket scanned, and proceed through security. Security is relatively light or what we would call "superficial." I think they are just checking for "suspicious" characters. Let's face it everyone has backpacks and roller bags.

Take a look at the posting on the electronic sign on the platform and ensure you are boarding the proper train. I find it's best to walk the platform and locate your "carozza" (carriage or car).
If you are running late, board any car and walk the train till you get to the correct carozza.

If your bags are on the heavy side (assuming you are not taking a day trip), train people or those most gracious Italians will help you with your bags. It's not a big deal for them. Also, on the "Frecci" (high-speed "Arrow") trains, there are ample places and luggage racks to stow your bags; likewise, for the Italo trains. By the way, Italo trains don't usually have cafes; instead, they have vending machines.

ITALY Made Easy for Seniors

>>>TIP<<<
It is best to always to select seats in the direction of travel. This way, you don't have to twist your neck to see what you just passed. The train has ample clean toilets (same as the airlines). There is a café mid-train. The prices are on the high side. Best that you bring your bottle of water. Once seated, you should have your ticket ready for the ticket inspector. Always have someone watch your carry-on bags, camera, etc., when leaving your seat.
>>><<<

If you do not have reserved seats in second or first class, you must validate your ticket in one of the platform's green or yellow machines. If going to Orvieto or Ostia Antica, you must do so.

HOW TO GET TO ROME TERMINI

If you are a solo traveler, have no heavy bags, and perhaps are on a budget, take the Metro. The Rome Metro lines A (RED) and B (BLUE) are pretty safe. However, for a few Euros more you can take a taxi. A single-zone ticket is all you need. Consult those auto-ticketing machines and remember to take your change or credit card. The fare for most of the inner city is only 1.50 Euros. Yes, you can buy two of them. However, note that once you use it, you only have 75 minutes to complete your journey. Make sure you hold your ticket. You may need it for the exit.

Once at Termini, either purchase a ticket from one of the red machines or Italo or head to the food court described above. Also, like the deli department at your local supermarket, you now need to take a ticket from the small machine abutting the ticket counter. Just wait for your queue ticket to be called, i.e., JL272, etc. After you have your tickets (or were fortunate to get them online before leaving for your trip), proceed to the upper-level food court, assuming you have at least 45 minutes before your scheduled departure. There are many tables and chairs here; feel free to use them even if you are not purchasing anything.

In the ticketing and information area, be aware of strangers who want to help you. They appear to work for Trenitalia or Italo but don't. If they do help, they will be wearing an official badge. If they don't wear a badge and help you, they will ask for a tip to offer you their advice. You should thank them and walk the other way or tip with a Euro if the information supplied was useful.

By the way, the toilets are modern and spotless. They all require one Euro to enter. If you don't have a Euro, all the facilities have a coin-changing machine at the entrance. After all, someone has to keep them clean, fill the soap dispensers, and all that other good stuff.

For a quick summary of Termini, I can only tell you it's a real "trip" or, better, a real experience. Secondly, allow extra time. You can always grab a bite or a café and do some people-watching. And finally, hang on to your personal belongings.

EASY, AFFORDABLE DAY TRIPS FROM ROME

If you have an extra day to spare, there are five easily affordable day trips from Rome. Three are in the Naples area. These cost about $100 per person for the day. They are:

Ruins of Pompeii
Island of Capri
The Amalfi Drive

Since they require only an hour of your time, I have excluded the ruins of Herculaneum. They are next to a section of Naples (Ercolano) with many outdoor markets and shops in a street market environment. I have included Herculaneum under the Amalfi area chapter. I might note that the ruins of Herculaneum also go by the name "Ercolano."

ITALY Made Easy for Seniors

Two other excursions worth a day are:

Orvieto- a hilltop town a little over an hour from Rome and
Ostia Antica- Near the FCO airport, about 40 minutes away
  Both of the above are easily accessible by train and will cost
  no more than $20 per person.

Thanks to the high-speed trains between Rome (Termini Station) and Naples (Napoli Centrale), you can easily do any one of the three in a single day.

Unless you want to check out of your Rome hotel and spend three days in Naples, or better, Sorrento, you can easily visit all three of the above attractions. The high-speed Trenitalia or Italo trains make the journey in under 90 minutes. If you decide to check out of your Rome hotel and take in the above three sites, here is your itinerary:

Naples Day 1 Morning train to Naples, check into your Naples hotel. Then head to visit the ruins of Pompeii.
Naples Day 2 A day visit to the Island of Capri.
Naples Day 3 A drive down the Amalfi Drive
    Either private driver or public transportation
    The early evening train from Naples back to Roma

Additional information can be found in the Naples Chapter.

If you are going to stay in the Amalfi area, I recommend that you stay in one of the hotels in Sorrento. My favorite is the Anthice Mura. My discussion on staying in Naples would take at least ten pages. However, it's beyond the scope of this book.

Staying in Sorrento allows you to do a lot of shopping, eat at great restaurants and enjoy a beautiful place perched high above the bay of Naples, with breathtaking views, especially at sunset. By the way, do have dinner one night at "Da Filipo." Have your

An Alternative to the Escorted Tour

concierge or front desk person call them, and they will pick you up and deliver you back to your hotel at no charge. What a deal! Oh yes, do remember to tip the driver both ways; a Euro or two per person is acceptable.

On arrival in Napoli Centrale, you can take the Circumvesuviana to the last stop and then take a taxi for about four Euros to your hotel. A better idea if you are a Senior would be to consult www.sorrentocars.com and arrange for a pickup at Napoli Centrale. It's best to email "Ugi" at Sorrentocars.com.
It will cost you about 100 Euros per car. However, for Seniors no schlepping bags and no hassles.

>>>TIP<<<
If you are making a day trip as one of your three days to the Island of Capri, (see below) you need only to go to Naples to catch the ferry. See my write-up below. However, if staying in Sorrento, there are ferries every two hours from the Marina Piccola in Sorrento. You need to take a taxi or else a short walk. If you are walking, there is a very steep staircase off the Corso Italia leading you down to the marina area. However, you still need to walk down a dangerous slope several blocks to the ferry terminal. For Seniors, here is a hot tip. There is a park abutting the marina area known as Villa Comunale Park. In the park, you will find the SORRENTO LIFT, which will take you down to the marina ferry terminal for only one Euro; from there, it's a two-block stroll to the ferry ticket booth over flat terrain. This is the only way to go, besides a taxi, to and from the Marina Piccolo ferry docks. For Seniors, do not attempt to negotiate the steep stairs from the Corso Italia and then that steep walk down the switchbacks. The best, once again, is the SORRENTO LIFT.

ITALY Made Easy for Seniors

It is best to ask your hotel concierge exactly where the lift is and for the ferry schedule. It's about 20 Euros each way on the high-speed ferry, which operates every two hours. More information at www.naplesbayferry.com
>>><<<

DAY TRIPS TO POMPEII, CAPRI AND AMALFI:
All visits to the Naples area start the same way.

You must work your way over to the Rome Termini rail station and take a train to Napoli Centrale. Make sure you get the train that makes the journey in less than 90 minutes. There is a train about every hour between Trenitalia, the quasi-government rail operator, and the independent rail company (NTV), better known as Italo. Their bright red trains look somewhat different from the state-run "Frecci" trains.

The Italo train at about 9:30AM makes the journey in one hour and fifteen minutes at only $23. If you spend $15 additional, you can go first class. I always suggest first class where you get a drink and a newspaper. However, I don't see the need for it. By the time you leave Rome and look out the window, you will be in Naples Centrale.

AN AFTERNOON IN POMPEII
Like the 57 other historical sites in Italy, Pompeii is also a UNESCO World Heritage Site. It is one of the top sites in Italy, attracting more than 2.5 million visitors per year.

The ancient city of Pompei (can also be spelled Pompeii) was destroyed in 79AD when the smoke, ash, lava, and pumice from Mount Vesuvius (about five miles away) covered the city to a depth of about twenty feet. Most importantly, it preserved an ancient Roman city dating to the 8th century BC when the "Oscans" built five villages there. You may see it as a "3-D" snapshot of history frozen in time for almost 2000 years.

An Alternative to the Escorted Tour

In 523BC, the Etruscans inhabited the area. The Romans came much later, taking control about 89BC. Essentially the eruption preserved the city until 1850, when it was discovered. Archeologists are still unearthing other areas of the ancient city.

In terms of making plans for the day, here are my suggestions: It would be best if you planned on a high-speed "Frecci" or Italo train leaving Termini about 9-10AM. With lunch after exiting the Ruins of Pompeii, you should be able to get a return train to Rome from Naples Centrale at about 6PM (see my tip below). You can also book a later train and hang out at the station for an hour while doing some people-watching and having a cafe. This will not rush you. It may be a rush if you short the return trip to 5PM. You are in Italy; take it easy.

So here we go to Pompeii. On arrival at Napoli Centrale, follow the signs to the Circumvesuviana Railway via the underground passageway. There are escalators and elevators. Purchase a ticket (NA3) for about three Euros for the 30-minute ride to Pompei. Note there are two outbound routes from Napoli Centrale. You need to take the train marked "Sorrento." The Circumvesuviana trains run about every 20 minutes. The exit station is marked as "Pompeii Scavi Villa Misteri or "Pompei." Loads of tourists will be getting off the train. Follow the crowd going across the street. They are all heading the same way toward the ticket booth. Seniors should note that elevators are on both sides of the rail platform. You will probably need this elevator on your way back to Naples Centrale. However, take it from the platform to the street level.

For Seniors, you should note that at the Pompeii Scavi, there is considerable walking on well-defined asphalt paths. Depending on what you want to see, you will have to walk anywhere from 10-20 blocks in different directions to take in the breath of the entire complex. I can tell you I have been there three times, and this place is awesome!

ITALY Made Easy for Seniors

There is no need to purchase tickets online or through other websites which are not the official website of the Scavi. As stated previously, ticket costs are usually marked up if you are not using the official website. In the off-season, you can buy tickets for about 16 Euros at the ticket booth. You need to check also for the entrance to the other adjoining ruins next to the main complex of Pompei. Some of the abutting sections are closed on Tuesdays.

If you want to avoid walking back to the main entrance, you can exit near the bookstore, and this will save you from doubling back to the ticket booth. I quote from the official website: pompeiisites.org/en/visiting-info/timetables-and-tickets/.

For Seniors, if you have mobility difficulties, entering from the Piazza Anfiteatro entrance, you will be able to follow the "Pompeii for all" route, with the possibility of returning from the exit to Piazza Anfiteatro or possibly from Piazza Esedra using the lift of the Antiquarium." By the way, as in most sites in Italy, all of them now take VISA and Mastercard; many also accept AMEX. Best to check at the ticket booth.

Once again, consult the website mentioned above since the Antiquarium may be closed on the day you wish to visit. Also, try not to plan a visit to Pompei on Saturday or Sunday. There are just too many crowds. Also, the last Sunday of the month is free. However, the crowd is limited to 15,000. So best to avoid any weekend day if possible.

Also, remember to download the Pompei App on your smartphone and bring your headset. You should figure about 3 hours in the Scavi. A must-visit is the two amphitheaters, the house of "ill repute," the house of the two dummies, the temple and more. The ticket booth also provides you with a map. After your visit, about 2-3PM, enjoy lunch at many of the abutting restos. You will have to exit the Scavi complex. My favorite is Ristorante pizzeria Turistico. It's at the end of that paid parking

An Alternative to the Escorted Tour

area opposite the entrance to the Scavi; easy to find. And, yes, they serve a lot more than a pizza. Do ask a local for directions if you are lost. This is the place at about 3PM you want to make your main meal for the day.

You must watch the time and allow 90 minutes to get your train back to Roma from Napoli. So here is what you need to anticipate:

Short walk to the Circumvesuviana rail station, about 10 minutes. Wait for the train for up to 20 minutes.
About a 30-minute ride to Naples Centrale then
walk the underground passage to the central station for 10 minutes. We are now at about 70 minutes.

So, a 90-minute allowance from Pompeii would be a little too tight since you need about 20 minutes to be there before the departure of your Frecci or your Italo. Best to book a return to Rome about 5-6PM. You can always hang around for an hour and have a café and a cannoli.

After you exit the Scavi or have that grande pranzo (big lunch):
1. Make your way back to the Circumvesuviana rail station.
2. Make sure you get an inbound train to Napoli, or you will wind up at the last stop in Sorrento.
3. For Seniors, note the elevator again.
You need to validate your ticket in one of those little machines on the platform.

On arrival back in Napoli, walk that underground passage (follow the signs to Napoli Centrale and make your way to the waiting room for the high-speed train (Frecci or Italo), which will deliver you to Rome Termini in about 90 minutes. Once again, note your train on the electronic boards. If it is not posted, don't worry; just have another café! They usually post times 20 minutes prior to departure. So much for your day trip to Pompeii.

ITALY Made Easy for Seniors

>>>SENIOR TIP<<<
You have complete control of your time at the Scavi. However, I have always found that you can't control the time you will spend at the restaurant. Even a request for the check and payment may take 30 minutes. Unless you are figuring a slice of pizza (instead of a sit-down lunch) on exiting the Scavi, add one hour to your planned departure on that high-speed train back to Rome. So if all the times suggest a 6PM train, take the 7PM train. A later train will eliminate all the stress.
>>><<<

DAY TRIP TO THE ISLAND OF CAPRI

First, you need to pronounce this place the way the Italians do. It is Kah-Pree, not Capri. It's an island about 19 miles off the coast of Naples. There are two towns on the island, Capri and Anacapri. The island dates to pre-historic times. Villa Jovis, one of the best preserved Roman villas, dates from 27AD. Emperor Tiberius ran the Roman Empire from here till he died in 37AD.

After the end of the Roman Empire, Naples controlled Capri. Pirates raided the island, and the French took it in 1808. Before World War One, the island was a haven for gay men. The most famous who lived and vacationed on the island were Oscar Wilde, Somerset Maugham, Alfred Krupp, and more.

The island is now a haven for the A-list and the ultra-wealthy. It's worth a visit for the beautiful views, the shopping, the food, and visiting Anacapri and the Blue Grotto. The only problem is you only have a few hours to do it. You should note cars are off-limits in the Town of Capril except for the Marina Grande and the "top-side" town of Anacapri. So all you will see are golf carts running around with luggage and supplies in Capri town.

An Alternative to the Escorted Tour

You can also follow the paparazzi, but they don't technically come out until sundown when the "well-knowns" leave their villas and yachts to go out to dinner.

On arrival (see below), it's best to take an island tour for 60-90 minutes or visit the Blue Grotto. Make sure the island tour goes to Anacapri.

If you are a Senior, I recommend an island tour without the Blue Grotto. The Blue Grotto is a cave down the island where you take a boat to the entrance, then transfer to a tiny boat that takes you into the water-filled cave for about five minutes. You can check the reviews before you go.

If you are into shopping, this is the place. One of the best souvenirs is to visit the shop which sells Capri watches for men and women. They are made in Italy and are pretty reasonable and fashionable. There are lots of restaurants off the main square (the Piazzetta). Seniors should note that most of the shopping is on well-paved walkways. Some of them do have a very slight incline. There are lots of places also to rest and take in a gelato.

Now, here is how you get to Capri:
On arrival at Napoli Centrale, you have two options. If you are a Senior solo traveler on a budget, you must take the #151 bus toward the marina. You will find it right outside the train station. Just ask the bus driver if he goes down to the marina as you want to go to Capri. If you are two or more people, it's better to take a taxi to the marina for 5-7 Euros. Just tell the driver, "Ferry to Capri," and tell him which pier (Calata di Massa or Molo Beverello), and he will take you there. It's less than five minutes away. Most of the drivers will know which pier to take you to.
There are three ferry companies offering ferry service to Capri. Just make sure you get the correct pier. For all the details on the companies and the ferry service times, best to use the portal:

www.naplesbayferry.com/en/t/napoli/capri. It is best to get the fast passenger ferry; otherwise, any ferry will do. Avoid the ferries which take cars and trucks. These ferries are slooooo.

On arrival at the Marina Grande in Capri, exit the ferry and follow the crowd to the funicular ticket booth. It will be on your right, just past that last concrete pier. All the visitors will be lining up here. For Seniors, make sure you purchase a round-trip ticket on the funicular, as the walk from the top down is quite a long way. The ticket is about three Euros round trip. Even if you are taking an island tour or a Blue Grotto tour, you will still have to purchase a funicular round trip ticket since the taxi, and the Blue Grotto boats take you back to the marina, where the island taxis hang out. After your island tour or visit the Blue Grotto, you must go up the funicular to visit Capri.

Unless you are going on a boat to the Blue Grotto or taking an island tour, after you purchase your funicular ticket, turn around and go across the roadway to the funicular, which will take you to the main square of Capri, the "Piazzetta." From this square, all roads, or should I say walkways emanate. Lots of restaurants and if you keep walking you will see the shops and fancy hotels.

>>>TIP<<<
On exiting the funicular, you will find numerous restaurants if you take a hard left down that walkway (Via Roma). My favorites are Al Capri and Villa Jovis.
>>><<<

AN ISLAND TOUR OR A VISIT TO THE BLUE GROTTO
On arrival in the marina area you will find the "Hawkers" or what you may call the "greeters." They will be offering two options. One is an island tour (best to get another couple to join you or some other singles), and the second is the tour of the Blue Grotto. As discussed above, for Seniors, I do not recommend it.

An Alternative to the Escorted Tour

You need to climb from one boat into another boat the size of a small rowboat and then wait in line (upwards of 40 minutes) to gain access to the Grotto, where you will be for about five minutes. The boat which takes you down to the Blue Grotto usually includes entrance to the Grotto. You should check, as many do not. Also, I do not believe there are any facilities on the boats which take you down to the Blue Grotto area. So best to use the facilities at the ferry terminal in the Capri marina. It is best to read Tripadvisor's reviews and make up your own mind.

After you return from the island taxi tour or your Blue Grotto experience, you will have to take the funicular to the main square in Capri Town. I then advise lunch on the Via Roma. You can then shop your heart out and stop at the Capri watch store, have gelato, and take a lot of pictures; then, you will be ready to start your journey back to Rome.

It would be best if allowed at least three hours from the time you go down that funicular before your train departure time back to Rome. The fast ferry would be two hours and the slow ferry three. Remember, you could always hang around Napoli Centrale for an hour. By the way, Italians don't like to rush. So if you arrive early, except for the local trains, it may be difficult to hop on an earlier Frecci or Italo train. Most earlier trains "close out" an hour or two before departure and there may be penalties for changing.

DAY TRIP ON THE AMALFI DRIVE
No, this is one place you do not want to rent a car in Sorrento (or any other location in Italy) and negotiate the Amalfi drive. Notice I say "negotiate" and not drive. I have driven down Amalfi drive twice over the past 30 years. Two times was enough! In California, the Pacific Coast Highway from Monterey to San Simeon is a straight line compared to the Amalfi Drive from Sorrento to Amalfi (and on into Salerno).

ITALY Made Easy for Seniors

On my last visit to the area, about three years ago, I emailed "Ugo" at Sorrentocars.com (Leonardo Travels) and asked him to send over a driver to my apartment rental in St. Agata (near Sorrento). The driver arrived promptly at 10AM and brought us back at about 5PM; no hassles. She parked the car, dropped us off for shopping in Positano, and took us to lunch (on our own) near Ravello. And, it was not a lot of money either—what a deal.

You can figure $250-$350 for the day with a private car and driver. Once again, it will be money well spent; your kids will be fine. Also, you can choose when and where to make "facility" and souvenir stops.

Now, if you do not opt for a private car and driver (way to go), there is a way to do this on a budget. "Blue" SITA little vans depart the Sorrento Circumvesuviana rail station every 45 minutes. They are marked "Amalfi." The cost for the day is about $15 per person (total round trip.) You can get on and off at each town. Check with the ticket booth inside the Sorrento train station. However, unlike a private car and driver, you won't be able to stop at souvenir places selling artisan pottery, etc. In addition, if the next van coming into Positano is full and will not be dropping off passengers, you may have to wait 45 minutes for the next van to get a seat. Also, you can't ask the bus driver to stop for a facility break or a cappuccino while admiring the waves of the blue Tyrrhenian Sea. Enough said.

Hiring a car and driver to navigate and narrate the Amalfi Drive will probably be one of the best life experiences in Italy you will have. Having your driver pick you up at Napoli Centrale if you are coming down from Rome is best. If you are visiting the Sorrentine Peninsular and staying at a hotel or apartment rental in Sorrento or Saint Agata, your driver will pick you up at Naples Centrale, drop your bags off at your hotel, and then take you down the Amalfi Drive. I am sure it will be extra, but it will be worth it. In summary, you get your transfers and the Amalfi Drive in one day. There is no need to hike over to the Circumvesuviana

An Alternative to the Escorted Tour

rail station at Naples Centrale with your baggage in tow. Let's face it; it's a drag! As they say, "no pun intended."

>>>TIP<<<
Here is another creative tip. You can see the ruins of Pompeii and "do" the Amalfi Drive all in one day. Ask Sorrentocars or other private driver firms to pick you up at Napoli Centrale, take you to Pompei for 2-3 hours, and then do the Amalfi Drive. If you arrive in Napoli Centrale by 10-11AM, you can do it all with a panini for lunch somewhere on the Amalfi Drive. You probably will not have time for a two-hour lunch. No big deal; enjoy your panini or pizza.
>>><<<

STOPS ON THE AMALFI DRIVE

When booking your private driver, you need to inform the company that you want to make several stops for souvenirs and photo ops with a visit to Positano for picture taking. You want to end the drive and turn around in Ravello after visiting the Villa Rufolo estate and gardens. Depending on the time, lunch can be in either Positano, Amalfi, or Ravello square.

Here is the sequence from Sorrento going south toward Salerno:
Positano
then
Amalfi
then
Ravello with a visit to Rufolo then turnaround and head north
Back to Napoli Centrale or drop at your Sorrento hotel.

>>>TIP<<<
You can check the ferry schedules (www.naplesbay ferries.com) as there are ferries from Amalfi and Positano back to the port of Naples. However, as stated in the off-season, they may not be running

during your time frame. You will then release your driver in Amalfi or Positano.
>>><<<

AN OVERVIEW OF POSITANO

Here are some small facts about Positano. There is what I call an upper hillside and a lower hillside. The upper hillside, for Seniors, is a challenge to visit. There are just too many steps. The lower is pretty much all ramps or slight inclines. The lower section is where most of the shopping is located. Also, walking a few blocks down to the beach is not a bad idea.

There are several excellent restaurants here for lunch. However, some may be closed in December and January.

If you are a Senior and wish to stay in Positano, make sure your hotel or BnB is flat, so you don't have to climb many stairs. You should be able to spot this on Google Earth. However, my choice is always Sorrento as a base.

RAVELLO AND VILLA RUFOLO

No visit to the Amalfi area is complete without a 45-minute visit to the Villa Rufolo and its gardens. This place is a must if the sun is shining and it is nice out. The Villa was built in the 13th Century and fell into disrepair until about 1850, when it was purchased by a Scotsman named Reid. The complex and gardens are magnificent. In addition, there are breathtaking views of the Tyrrhenian Sea. The Villa and gardens are a bargain at only seven Euros.

You return to Naples Centrale for a train back to Rome at about 7PM. Else, your driver will take you to your hotel in Sorrento.

So much for the Amalfi area. Now on to day trips around Rome.

Once again, you need to wear comfortable shoes or sneakers.

An Alternative to the Escorted Tour

A DAY TRIP TO THE TOWN OF ORVIETO

You should not confuse this with a trip to the Naples area. Orvieto is located a little over one-hour north, on the Rome-Florence rail line or the A1 Autostrada. The small city or town of Orvieto sits (it looks like a village, not my idea of a city) on a volcanic rock mesa about 200 feet above the train station.

The city lies in the southwest corner of Umbria, touching the region known as Tuscany to the North and Lazio to the South. Its actual elevation is about 1,100 feet above sea level. It is part of the metropolitan area of Terni.

Orvieto dates from the Etruscan era. In the 3rd Century BC, Orvieto was taken over by Rome. Because of its location on top of a volcanic rock mesa (or bluff), the town was impregnable to waring forces. It controlled the passage from Rome to Florence. During the middle ages (medieval times), Orvieto became a cultural center of the region. Thomas Aquinas (later to be sainted) taught theology in Orvieto before being summoned to Rome in 1265 by Pope Gregory IX. Subsequently, he became the Regent master for the newly elected Pope Clement IV. When Rome fell, Orvieto was later controlled by the Popes.

Orvieto became a papal state until it was annexed to unified Italy in 1860. If you have about thirty minutes, I suggest you also slip into the archaeological museum (Museuo Claudio Faina e Museo), where you can view ancient remnants of the Etruscan civilization which inhabited the area several thousand years ago. You will find it opposite the Duomo. There is a charge of about five Euros. So much for the history of Orvieto.

Once arriving at the rail station (stazione), you need not worry. For Seniors and everyone, a Funicular takes you from the rail station to the central plaza in Orvieto. The Funicular (or Funiculari) runs every 10 minutes. The cost is about three Euros round trip. Make sure you buy a round-trip ticket. Walking down is rather tricky, not just for Seniors but everyone.

100

ITALY Made Easy for Seniors

>>>TIP<<<
On arrival at Orvieto, look at the posted return train schedule and note the time. It would help if you figured from the time you finish your visit, you will need about 30 minutes. This allows time to get to the Funicular and get down the hill. Remember, the Funicular runs approximately every 10-15 minutes. This way, you will not have to wait long at the station for your return trip to Termini. So, if the next train to Rome is at 6PM, you must be at the upper funicular station by 5:30PM. No need to worry, the train station does have a café and toilets.
>>><<<

Very few cars are allowed in this medieval city's narrow streets, which date to about 1200AD unless you have a ZTL (Zone Traffic Limited) permit. However, a mini-bus will also take people from the rail station and the parking lot directly to the central square.

Once at the top, you will find that most streets are flat and easy to walk. The numerous streets and churches are a must to visit. My favorite is the Duomo, located in the main piazza, known as Piazza Duomo or Piazza Cahen. Have someone take a picture of you and yours on those steps of the Duomo devouring a gelato. Here's the plan for your day:

If you are planning on lunch in Orvieto, the best would be to catch a train 10-11AM. There is usually an 11AM and 1PM train, which makes the trip up to Orvieto in a little over one hour, and it's only nine Euros. Across from the Orvieto train station, you need to follow the crowd to the Funicular, purchase your round-trip ticket, and head up to the historical district on the bluff.

On arrival, plan on exploring the city and shops before lunch. The main street is the "Corso Cavour ." Suggest you walk it from the funicular station to Via Duomo. It is only a few blocks. You will find that on Via Duomo, there are also shops and eateries.

An Alternative to the Escorted Tour

If you want to take excellent photos of the entire city, you want to visit the Torre del Moro. There is an entrance fee of five Euros to climb the 250 steps of this medieval tower or use the elevator. The lift will take you up about 160 steps. I believe at this level you will be able to take great photos. At the last stop of the lift, (at the 160 step level) you still have to climb about 100 steps to the reach the top of the tower. If you are a Senior, I do not advise the climb. By the way, that clock was recently added about 1850.

As a final thought, you might want to peek into some old churches, especially the Duomo. Also, don't forget to bring back that freshly baked artisan bread.

About 5-6PM, depart the city for your trip back to Rome Termini. Even though Orvieto is on the high-speed rail line to Florence, the "Frecci" high-speed trains usually do not stop there. So, enjoy passing those little villages with your local train, and make sure you get off at Orvieto, or else you will be in Florence.

DAY TRIP TO THE RUINS AT OSTIA ANTICA
If you landed at Rome's FCO airport, you were only a "stone's throw" from the ancient city of Ostia Antica.

At one time, Ostia Antica was Rome's seaport. However, as time passed, the Tiber River silted up at its mouth, and the city of *ancient* Ostia moved closer inland. The site now lies two miles inland from the ocean. It is now only 15 miles from Rome.

The site of Ostia Antica contains ancient buildings, frescoes, and mosaics. The oldest buildings you will find here date to the 4th century BC. In 68BC, the town was sacked by pirates. The port was destroyed. Later, Rome allowed Pompey the Great to raise an army to protect Ostia. The pirates were killed a year later. The town was rebuilt with protective walls. As of 2014, only one-third of Ostia Antica has been unearthed.

102

ITALY Made Easy for Seniors

Expect to see the ancient warehouses, villas, the House of Diana, The Forum, The Temple of Venus, the baths of Neptune, the old cemeteries, and get this... the ancient synagogue.

The excavated site of Ostia Antica is open to the public. However, there is an entrance charge of 14 Euros. There is a museum with many finds. Also onsite are dining and other facilities, as well as a theatre. If you care not to do this visit yourself, best to consult your concierge or front desk clerk. You should allow five hours, including the local train to and from Ostia Antica from Termini.

If you wish to do it yourself, you can find a boatload of information and pictures, etc., at the official website:
www.ostiaantica.beniculturali.it/en/opening-hours-tickets
And do ask the information desk if the restaurant will be open for il pranzo (lunch).

>>>TIP<<<
If you arrive at the Hotel Isola Sacra near Rome FCO airport the day before you are set to fly out, you should consider a visit to the Ostia Antica Archeological park. It is two miles away and about a seven Euro taxi ride. If your are driving, drop your bags at the hotel, and then spend two hours here.
>>><<<

>>>TIP<<<
If you are checking into the Hotel Isola Sacra and it is a hot day, consider going to Rome's beach in Ostia. (Ostia Lido). Grab some towels and either drive over or taxi over. Or better ask the front desk. This is the best way to cool off. In season, there is shopping and lots of places to enjoy lunch or dinner.
>>><<<

CHAPTER 7

FLORENCE

CITY OF THE RENAISSANCE

THE CAPITAL OF TUSCANY

** DAYS 5 & 6 FLORENCE

OVERVIEW OF FLORENCE (FIRENZE)

No other city in the world has given more art, architecture, and science to Western Civilization than Florence. What Rome was to ancient times, Florence was to the end of the medieval period.

Florence is the capital of the province of Tuscany.

The Renaissance is called the rebirth period or the awakening. Remember, when Rome fell in 476AD, Europe essentially broke apart. There were no Roman legions to protect the people, and for almost 1,000 years, the countries (which did not exist) as we know them were overrun by marauding tribes.

The medieval period sometimes referred to as the "Dark Ages," was marked by the "serf" system of peasants, castles, and all that other stuff we learned about in history. I won't go into all the detail, as there are hundreds of books on the history of Western Civilization from the fall of Rome to about 1300AD.

In Italy, the City States, i.e., Florence, Venice, etc., were beginning to form. Under the city-states, normalcy was beginning, i.e., courts, defenses, laws, etc. With most of the works financed by the Catholic Church, the arts and architecture began to flourish.

You will find very few (there are some) of those Roman ruins in Florence. However, you will find numerous pieces of priceless art by the artists of the time. These works of art are housed in the "Uffizi Gallery." In addition, the Gallery of the Academy of Florence (also known as the "Galleria dell Accademia") houses Michelangelo's statue of "David." The David is a must to see. More details follow.

As for architecture, the City is bathed in it. Most of these remarkable structures are churches. They were designed and built in the 15th and 16th Centuries. However, there are other places of architecture worth noting.

No visit to Florence is complete without spending an hour or two on the Ponte Vecchio bridge. This bridge, which is the center of the gold jewelry shops in the area, goes back several hundred years. What you see now is the latest version which was built in 1345AD. The Ponte Vecchio bridge is so magnificent that the Axis powers were ordered not to bomb it in World War II.

You need not worry about walking in Florence. The historical area is compact and flat. In fact, in 1966, the Arno River, which flows through the City's heart, overflowed to all the local streets. It happened so fast that removing all the paintings in the Uffizi Gallery was difficult. Many were covered with mud which had to be painstakingly removed in subsequent years. As you walk the City, you will notice markers on the buildings indicating the high-water level of the flood of 1966.

The Accademia with David, The Uffizi Gallery, Piazza Signoria, Ponte Vecchio bridge, Mercato Nuovo, and the Duomo complex are all located within three football fields of each other.

An Alternative to the Escorted Tour

There are so many shopping places; my favorite is the Mercato Nuovo. I will describe more later. In addition, numerous squares and restaurants dot the area. If you have additional days, there are many places to visit on the other side of the Arno river, known as "Oltrarno." The Pitti Palace and the Boboli Gardens are the most famous and most visited.

GETTING TO FLORENCE (FIRENZE)

The best way to travel from Rome to Florence is via the "Frecci" high-speed or the Italo trains. There is a train about every 30 minutes. The trains make the run in as little as 90 minutes. Seniors should consider going First Class for about $25-$30. The second class runs around $20. First Class has more comfortable seats, and you get a newspaper, snacks (cookies or crackers), and a drink on all the Trenitalia Frecci trains. For all first-class passengers, the same holds. All trains allow you to bring your food and beverage. Wine with meals is served in first class on Italo trains for more than 70 minutes of all journeys. Best to check their current website.

When making your reservations, you must take the train from Rome Termini to Firenze Santa Maria Novella (SMN). However, if you are close to Rome's other train station, "Tiburtina," you can certainly originate there.

>>>TIP<<<
Certain "Frecci" and Italo trains fill up fast. Many trains around 8AM on weekdays are usually sold out in first-class as they accommodate one-day travel of business folks. Also, many second-class seats are sold out on Friday afternoons and Sunday evenings as weekenders buy tickets to see relatives and get out of Rome for an escape weekend. The best is to plan your rail to Florence and Florence to Venice or Milan as soon as you can "fix" those dates. Also, you should note that some tickets only go on sale 60 or 90 days before the travel dates. On inter-city travel,

the best is to use Raileurope, Trenitalia, or Italotreno.it to purchase your tickets. Note the competitor, Italo, has non-peak coach fares throughout the day for as low as ten Euros. Best to check their website: italotreno.it.
>>><<<

>>>TIP<<<
Did you know you can fly into Florence or even Pisa an hour away? If you have been to Rome and want to start your two-week holiday in Florence, you can find many flights. However, they are all connections from the European hubs. So consider flying to Amsterdam, Paris, Lisbon, etc., and connecting to a flight to either Florence or Pisa. Buses and trains are every hour between Pisa (PSA) and Florence.

For some reason, there are always much better fares in and out of Florence. If driving from the Pisa airport, it's a little over an hour on the A11 Autostrada. There are tolls that accept all credit cards. The toll gate machines are easy to operate.
>>><<<

TWO DAYS IN FLORENCE WHAT TO SEE AND DO

Two weeks in Florence would do it. However, we don't have two weeks. So here are my suggestions for the two days. These two days can be interchanged. However, I recommend visiting the Accademia on your first day in Florence. For Seniors, this will allow less walking for the entire day. Here is your suggested itinerary for the two-day visit:

First day-
Train about 9-10AM from Rome Termini to Florence
Arrive in Florence and drop bags at the hotel.
At about 12:30PM head on over to the Accademia to see David.
Visit the Piazza Della Signoria for lunch at about 2PM.

An Alternative to the Escorted Tour

Shopping after lunch at the Nuovo Marcato, about three blocks away. This outdoor market is one place to purchase affordable items, especially for Christmas.

By the way, it's okay to haggle over price.
You are in a real bargaining position if you buy two or more of the same, e.g., scarves, etc.

About 4-5PM, head on back to your hotel for a snooze, a drink, and dinner about 8PM

Second Day-
Timed visit to the Uffizi Gallery at about 11AM.
About 1PM visit to the Duomo (also view the Scavi, it's free).
About 2-3PM lunch again at Piazza della Signoria.

Then 3-5PM shopping on the Ponte Vecchio bridge.
Notice I did not say buying. You may find it too pricey. However, you do need to bring back some souvenirs! At the far end of the bridge, you will find plenty of places to have gelato or a panini to hold you over till dinner, about 8PM.

THE ACCADEMIA AND THE UFFIZI

You should also make reservations to see "David" at about noon: https://www.galleriaaccademiafirenze.it/en/tickets.
It would be best to book your timed reservation for two hours past your arrival time into Florence, either by train or car. You can figure about 30 minutes to view David. However, the ticket holders line, security, etc., will bring you to a full hour.

The next day, it is best to visit The Uffizzi Gallery around 11AM. You will also need timed tickets. You can figure one to two hours at the Uffizzi. These reservations will allow you to have lunch at about 2PM. Seniors, remember that dinner (Cena) is about 7:30 or, better 8PM, Oy! Even though it can be done, it is difficult and stressful (especially for Seniors) to do both David and the Uffizzi in one day, especially if you are coming up from Rome by car or train. Both of these museums are booked several months in advance. So when you make those train reservations, you need to get your tickets for the Accademia (Academy) on the day of arrival into Florence and the next day for the Uffizi.

You won't have to do a lot of walking to view the "David." You pass through security, and "walla," there's David in front of you. "David," because of its sheer weight, stands a few feet off the entrance on the ground floor. It is 17 feet in height and was chiseled out of one massive block of marble by Michelangelo in 1504. On the other hand, the Uffizi requires lots of walking. So much for preparation for Florence.

After you have checked into your hotel or checked your bags with the bellman, you are off to see the town. The first stop is the Galleria dell Accademia to visit "David." The best is to pick up one of those free maps from the front desk or the concierge. It's only a few blocks to the Accademia. And because Florence is on the border of being called a "maze," I would suggest you keep asking "Doe Vay et Accademia Gallery," or follow the crowd.

MICHANGELO'S DAVID
Michelangelo's David is the symbol of Florence and the Renaissance. You cannot visit Florence without seeing David. David "is" Florence.

Here are the facts: It stands almost 17 feet tall and weighs six tons. It was chiseled by a 26 old Italian artist, Michelangelo 1501-1504. It's the David we all know, from the Old Testament, complete with that slingshot on his left shoulder, which he used to take down Goliath. His right arm appears larger than his left. He also seems to be cross-eyed.

David also symbolizes Florence's defense of civil liberties embodied in the Republic of Florence, an independent city-state.

An Alternative to the Escorted Tour

The independent republic was threatened on all sides by more powerful states. Florence, like David, would not be bullied.

There were two attempts to chisel David for placement on the roof of the Cathedral of Florence (The Duomo). The two chosen artists gave up (one quit after ten years of work), and the unfinished work lay in a yard in Florence for 26 years before Michelangelo started the work effort. The final work was erected in the Palazzo Signoria (Palazzo Vecchio), where a copy of it stands. In 1873 it was moved to the Galleria dell' Accademia, where it stands today. If you go to lunch in the Palazzo della Signoria, you can't miss that copy of David.

The David was originally intended to be placed on top of the Duomo. However, weighing six tons, it was too heavy to lift onto the roof of the Duomo. In addition, the roof probably would not support this weight.

The original marble block came from Carrara, which is near Massa. If you are taking a day trip to the Cinque Terre, you will pass Massa on the right-hand side of the road. You can't miss it with all those white blocks of marble in the yards.

In 1527 when David debuted, anti-Medici protesters pelted David's left arm with stones, breaking it into three pieces.

Of significant interest is the fact that David is not circumcised. Since David was Jewish, he would have been circumcised. However, this is consistent with Renaissance art, as most biblical males are shown not circumcised.

Security is tight at the Gallery of the Academy of Florence. There have been several attempts on David. The most recent occurred in 1991 when a deranged person snuck a hammer into the hall and started destroying David's left toe.

The only thing now which can harm David is an earthquake. In addition, archeologists are worried about the vibrations of viewers' footsteps harming the statue.

THE DUOMO
The Duomo is right up there with the David as a symbol of Florence as a must-see. The appearance of the Cathedral and the other buildings in the complex are striking. It was originally called the Cathedral of Saint Mary of the Flower (Fiore in Italian). The massive basilica is officially the Cathedral of Florence, now called in Italian "The Duomo of Firenze" It appears in practically every photo of the City. You can't miss those red bricks which cover the dome.

The Duomo was begun in 1296 in a Gothic style of a design by Arnolfo di Cambio and was structurally completed by 1326. The dome was engineered by Filippo Brunelleschi, the famous architect, engineer, and sculptor of the Renaissance. It is the largest brick dome ever constructed. The exterior is made up of two colors of green and pink marble, which has a white border. It is a 19th Century Gothic Revival façade designed by Emilio De Fabris. In round numbers, the Cathedral is 500 feet long and has a height of 380 feet. It is one of the world's largest and the largest medieval building in Europe.

You can visit the inside of the Duomo. Of most importance are the Roman ruins below the floor of the church. They can be viewed via the stairs next to the bookshop.

Also, the painting in the dome itself represents the Last Judgement. There is no charge to enter the Cathedral.

>>>SENIOR TIP<<<
While you can visit the top of the dome of the Duomo for Seniors -DON'T, there is no elevator, and you need to walk up 463 steps. Several other places on

the other side of the river afford a beautiful view of the City. For pictures and photo ops of the City, after you cross the Ponte Vecchio bridge, consider a six-block flat walk to the Pitti Palace or the Boboli Gardens, which abuts the Palace.
>>><<<

>>>TIP<<<
You can purchase a three-day combination ticket to the Uffizi Gallery, the Pitti Palace, and Boboli Gardens for 50% off the price of single tickets. More information can be found at www.visitflorence.com.
>>><<<

DETAILS OF THE DUOMO COMPLEX
There are two other buildings in the Piazza del Duomo. They are the Baptistery and Giotto's Campanile. The Campanile is that tall tower. Including the Cathedral, the three buildings are part of the UNESCO World Heritage Site. Those two other buildings are decorated in the same style as the Cathedral.

The tower is known as Giotto's Bell Tower. You guessed it, designed by "Giotto ." It was started in 1334 and completed in 1359. The Campanile stands 400 feet and is about 45 feet on each side. If you are fit enough, you can climb the 414 steps. There is no elevator. It is not recommended for Seniors. In addition to Giotto's design, Pisano and Talenti also worked on the tower. Those many hexagon pieces of inlaid artwork depict scenes from the Old and New Testaments.

There are now seven bells in the tower. The first was installed in 1705, and the last five in 1956.

The Baptistery (or Baptistry) building was built 1059-1128. It is of Florentine Romanesque design. There is also one more building you may want to visit on a separate ticket or one of the combination tickets. It is called the Museum dell' Opera del Duomo. It's right in front of the Cathedral and is committed to conserving the Duomo and other artworks. Here you will see the works of Michelangelo, Donatello, and more.

It should be time for lunch when you have completed your visit to the Duomo complex. So head to the Piazza d Signoria. It's only a few blocks away.

LUNCH ON THE PIAZZA DELLA SIGNORIA
The Piazza della Signoria is sometimes called the Palazzo Vecchio. It is the equivalent of a city hall plaza in most major American cities. It is the meeting place of the Florentines. And is located just a few blocks from the Piazza del Duomo and one block from the Uffizi Gallery.

That big building you see is the town hall. You can't miss it with that crenellated fortress-type roof. The tower, or campanile with its crenellated top, is a part of the main building. It overlooks the copy of Michangelo's David. Remember, when the original was moved to the Academy, they needed another to replace it. So what you are looking at is the replacement.

The name "Signoria" comes from the name of the ruling body of the Republic of Florence.

The square had several names. It wasn't until the Medici duke's residence was relocated across the Arno River to the Pitti Palace that they renamed the square "Signoria."

That building to the right of the Palazzo Vecchio (as you face the city hall) is known as the Loggia dei Lanzi. It backs the Uffizi Gallery. It is basically an open-air sculpture museum.

Around the Piazza, you will find numerous restaurants, stand-up bars, and pastry and gelato shops. Oh, I forgot to mention the excellent sandwiches at several shops.

An Alternative to the Escorted Tour

THE UFFIZI GALLERY

In terms of Renaissance art, the Uffizi Gallery is second only to the Academy and its David. The name "Uffizi" comes from the building which houses all these priceless paintings that used to be the offices of the official Florentine magistrates or judges. Hence the name Uffizi means official. The building was started in 1560 and completed in 1581. The Uffizi is right up there with the Louver and the Prado. It was built for Cosimo I de' Medici. The top floor was made into a gallery for the Medici family to house their collection of Roman sculptures.

You can purchase your Uffizi tickets online at https://www.uffizi.it/en/tickets

Unless you are into sculpture, I recommend you start your visit at the Uffizi on the floor right below the last sculpture floor. You will need two hours to work your way down from floor to floor, viewing all the great paintings of the Renaissance. These paintings are priceless and include Michelangelo, Botticelli, and others. If you are a Senior, feel free to take the elevators.

THE NUOVO MERCATO

After you visit the Uffizi, your next stop should be the Nuovo Mercato, originally called the Mercato del Porcellino. This mercato is where you want to do your inexpensive shopping, and I don't mean bottle openers or snowglobes that say Florence, which are made in China. They have everything from silk ties to leather jackets and beautiful handmade ladies' handbags and wallets. Also, if you purchase a boatload of items, expect to haggle on the price. Also, they take most credit cards and will give you a better price if you pay with good old Euros. I might note that there are also numerous stand-up bars around the Mercato. In this area be very street savvy, and watch your wallet and handbags. Here is how to get to the Mercato:

ITALY Made Easy for Seniors

The Nuovo Mercato is easy to find:
1. Exit the Piazza della Signoria by locating the "Il Bargello" restaurant ask any of the locals or one of the Polizia or Carabinieri.
2. Go past the Bargello about one block.
3. Take a hard right on Via Calimala, and you will see the market about one block up.

Suppose you are finished at the Nuovo Mercato and still have some energy. In that case, you can turn around and walk about four blocks to the Ponte Vecchio bridge for some high-end shopping and a gelato (on the other side of the bridge) before you head back to your hotel for a snooze and dinner.

Hopefully, I will have whet your appetite and get you "psyched" on your visit to Florence. So here we go.
.

ARRIVAL IN FLORENCE AND HOTELS
When your train arrives at the end of the line at Florence's Santa Maria Novella (SMN) station, you will find three exits after clearing the platform area. The main entrance is in front of you.

As you exit the station, if you look directly in front, you will notice the Santa Maria Novella church. Just a few words on the church: The Dominican Order built a new church in 1221 to replace the older 9th Century church. Construction started about 1276 and lasted 80 years. The Romanesque-Gothic bell tower and sacristy were finally completed. In 1360, Gothic arcades were added to the façade. The church was consecrated in 1420.

The basilica, the cloister, and the chapter house contain art treasures and funerary monuments. There are frescoes by masters of Gothic and early Renaissance. Unlike many other treasures in Florence, which the church financed, these were funded by the most important and wealthy Florentine families. By doing so, they ensured themselves a burial place on consecrated ground. This church is worth a minimum of a one-hour visit to admire these magnificent frescoes. Now back to your arrival at the Santa Maria Novella Stazione.

You should spot your hotel in relation to the train station. It is best if you exit the station on the right-hand side since there are several hotels I have selected in this area. It is best to spot your hotel on Google Maps. If it is on the left-hand side of the station as you look at the map, then exit on the right-hand side as you leave the train. The boulevard is clearly marked Via Luigi Alamanni. For Seniors, exiting onto Via Luigi Alamanni, will save you a few blocks of walking. If your hotel is not on the left-hand side, proceed through the main or front entrance, where most of the hotels are located. They involve walking 1-4 blocks. Just watch the traffic. If you are going to Venice or Milan, the hotels I have chosen allow you to walk back to the station instead of taking a taxi. If you want to stay at several upscale four and five-star hotels, you will find them abutting the Arno River. The walk over to the Arno River is too far. So follow the signs at SMN to the taxi line.

>>>TIP<<<
If you want an authentic experience staying at a 16th Century palace, this opulent, all-suite hotel is a 13-minute walk from the Duomo di Firenze. It is called Palazzo Magnani Feroni. The palace sits one block back from the other side (Oltrarno) of the Arno River. You will need to take a taxi, as it is located about one kilometer from the SMN station. As of this writing, in late 2022, it is temporarily closed for renovations. I have stayed at the "Palazzo" and can personally tell you it's a "10" and a real experience. It should be open for the 2023 season. If you are driving, they have parking in an old carriage house.
>>><<<

ITALY Made Easy for Seniors

As Seniors, it's best to stay at any hotel within that four-block radius of the SMN rail station. However, you should note that you will have to walk over to the historic district, where you will find the Uffizi Gallery, the Piazza Signoria, Ponte Vecchio Bridge, and the Duomo complex, in addition to all the other interesting sites. I should note that for some reason, as you get closer to the Arno River, the hotel prices seem to go up.

For Seniors, if you book a hotel on the other side of the Arno River (Oltrarno area), you will have to take a taxi or drag your bags over one of the bridges. You should avoid, if possible, the crowds at the Ponte Vecchio bridge. Once again, it is best to stay at the hotels mentioned below, which are within four blocks of the SMN rail station.

HOTELS AROUND THE SMN RAIL STATION

C-Hotel Ambsciatori	Hotel delle Nazioni	The Adler Cavalieri Hotel	The Holel Boccaccio
The Hotel Montreal	Hotel Alba Palace	The Rivoli Boutique	Hotel Palazzo del Borgo
Hotel l' Orologio	The Domus Florentiae Hotel	The Hotel Lombardia	Grand Hotel Baglioni
The Hotel Universo	The Hotel Croce di Malta	NH Florence Hotel and Spa	Hotel Golf
Hotel Arcadia	Hotel Embassy	C-Hotel Joy	Hotel Argentina
Florence Center Train Station (hotel)			

>>>TIP<<<
Just a note on my favorite restaurant... Do check out the Osteria Cinghiale Bianco. It's a short walk on the other side of the Arno from the Ponte Vecchio bridge. In case you don't know your Italian "Cinghiale" is wild boar, which is excellent in wide noodle Pappadelli. The Osteria Cinghiale is easy to find. Take a hard right at the far side of the Arno River after crossing the Ponte Vecchio bridge. Then go up about 2 blocks and you will see the Cinghiale on the left hand side. It's about a fifteen-minute walk from

117

the train station and you can gauge it from your hotel. If you are too bushed, take a taxi for about seven Euros. On the return, if you are too tired to walk back, they will call a taxi for you. Also, not a lot of Euros here.
>>><<<

Once you check in or at least drop your bags you are ready to explore the City of the Renaissance: The David, the Uffizi, the Duomo, the Piazza Signoria, Rialto Bridge, and of course the Nuovo Mercato

MONTECATINI- STAYING WITH THE LOCALS

The Village of Montecatini Terme (note you need the Terme) is about 50 minutes from Firenze. It's also 40 minutes from Pisa and Lucca and a little over two hours from the Cinque Terre. Montecatini makes an ideal base for exploring the area. In addition, hotels are almost half what you would expect to pay in the historic district of Florence. There is also an abundance of restaurants. Known for its natural underground thermal springs, Montecatini is one of eleven UNESCO World Heritage Spa sites in Western Europe.

There are two other points you ought to know about this beautiful town. First, as I stated above, it is an excellent base for exploring the area. Secondly, it has a lovely main street loaded with bakeries, shops, pastry shops, clothing stores, and you name it; public parks abut the central area. These, including a supermarket are within walking distance of most hotels. Talk about the hotels. Secondly, would you believe there are over 400 hotels and BnBs in Montecatini Terme?

And thirdly, the reason for all these shops and hotels is that folks from all over Europe flock here to "do" the baths. The baths give the town natural mineral baths. Like Baden-Baden in Germany and many of the natural baths in Hungary, Montecatini Terme is right up there. The baths are located (just like Saratoga Springs, NY) in those parks. I might note that the baths are works of art with Roman columns and statues. Even if you don't go in, they make great pictures. The baths are public, however there is an entrance fee.

There are many furnished apartment rentals within a few blocks of the two rail stations and the main street (Corso Roma). If you have a family or want to do "self-catering" without a maid knocking at your door at 9AM to tidy it up, this is the place.

No stay at Montecatini Terme is complete without an afternoon visit to Montecatini Alto. The Alto is a small town atop a hill in Montecatini. It was built in medieval times. There is a church and the remnants of a medieval wall around the old town. There are about six restaurants and a very old church. You'll find lots of shops selling hand-made items of the area.

Half the enjoyment of visiting Montecatini Alto is the funicular. It dates from 1898. The fee is about $8 round-trip. It runs approximately every 30 minutes. If you arrive early, there is a café abutting the base station. Note I do not believe the funicular accepts credit cards. Also, check with your concierge, hotel desk person, or that information stand in Montecatini for the funicular's operation days and hours. In the off-season, I believe it runs only on the weekends (Friday usually included). For Seniors, do not attempt to walk up to Montecatini Alto. A walk down is fine but watch those cars. It is best to take a taxi to the top if the funicular is not operational. You can also drive; however, it's scary, and there are not a lot of parking spaces at the top. I always advise having lunch on the Alto or a gelato late in the day. There are great views up here. Also, you can walk around to the old hospital at the edge of the hill. You can easily figure 3-4 hours for your visit to the Alto with lunch.

An Alternative to the Escorted Tour

Five four-star hotels located on or right off the Corso Roma are:
Hotel Puccini – one of the best, book direct with "Pasquale"
Hotel Columbia
Hotel Minerva Palace
Albergo Terme
Ercolini & Savi (best location, one block off the Corso Roma)
   It's an American style hotel with large rooms.

You can also locate other hotels on the parks, just a few more blocks from the Corso Roma. In addition, there is a beautiful residential area lining the street known as Viale IV Novembre. Here you will find many elegant four-star hotels, of which my favorite is the Croce di Malta, at the end of the street on the right-hand side, opposite one of the parks or, should I say, mansions. You may want to also consider the Hotel Biondi. If staying at the Biondi best is to stay in the main building and not the annex.

If you have a large party (a family), consider renting an apartment instead of several hotel rooms. There are plenty of cafes to have breakfast if you care not to enjoy it in your rental.

>>>TIP<<<
I can only recommend you go to Tripadvisor and look at "Montecatini Terme Restaurants with a View." if you stay in Montecatini, consider one of your nights dining at one of the fabulous restaurants located on the hills backing the town. You will find at least six of them if you do not have a car, best to take a taxi. Also, Seniors, be aware that if you have issues driving at night, you must take a cab as most of these restaurants are on hilly, dark roads that are difficult to negotiate. It would be better to have lunch during daylight hours, if they are open. And, do make sure you request a table with a view. My favorite is the Montaccolle. For Seniors, best to split the pasta and the main dish, and order an appetizer.
>>><<<

120

There are two rail stations on the "Firenze-Viareggio" line in Montecatini. The Corso Roma is about one mile long, and they placed the bus terminal at the beginning of the Corso Roma. So unless you are connecting with a bus to go somewhere else, most folks get off the train at the second stop, which is known as "Montecatini Centro." Fares usually run $3-7 each way for all your day trips (Florence, Pisa, and Lucca). These day trips exclude the Cinque Terre towns. Trains run about every 30 minutes during the day. I cannot say enough about Montecatini Terme. I have stayed here about six times and every time I go back I enjoy it more.

DAY TRIP TO FLORENCE FROM MONTECATINI

One more point. Suppose you are interested in making a day trip to Florence from Montecatini. In that case, I suggest the Academy when it opens, then the Duomo, then lunch, and finish at the Uffizi Gallery before heading back around 7PM from Firenze SMN station. You can even have dinner and do shopping at the Nuovo Mercato, along with a stroll over the Ponte Vecchio Bridge. A full-day trip to Firenze will bring you to about a 9 PM train back to Montecatini Centro. Other than that, consider two days in Florence to do all the sites or better, pack your toothbrush and a change of clothing and stay overnight in Florence.

If you are not staying in Florence but in Montecatini, when that train pulls into the SMN station, you still have to exit the train, go to the front main lobby and purchase a one-way ticket for that 50-minute ride to Montecatini Centro. You can do this through those red machines. During most of the day, the trains run about twice an hour. So, don't worry about missing the train. And do remember to validate your ticket in those yellow or green machines at least one hour before you board that train, else you will have to do a lot of explaining to the ticket examiner.

An Alternative to the Escorted Tour

ANOTHER IDEA- ONE DAY IN FLORENCE

If you are pressed for time on your Italy visit (definitely not recommended), consider leaving Rome or Venice on a train at about 6-7PM for Florence. You can easily visit the David, The Duomo, and Uffizi Gallery the next day. There is no time to take a nap here or smell those roses. You probably will have to scrub the shopping or swap it for the Uffizi. If, as they say, "push comes to shove," skip the Uffizi and do all else. No big deal. But it can be done. There is just enough time to pick up your bags at the hotel and head out for your next stop in the evening. The best hotel closest to the rail station is the "Florence Center Train Station Hotel." You cannot find a more convenient hotel. It is best if you booked direct.

OTHER SITES IN FLORENCE

Leonardo Da Vinci made his mark on the world (he also invented the helicopter) and he made his mark on Florence. There is one notable museum worth visiting. The Leonardo *Interactive* Museum is only 50 yards from the Academy. There are about fifty interactive machines which Leonardo invented. This place is great for kids. The adult admission is about $10.

If you have about 2-3 hours, do consider the Firenze Hop-On-Hop-Off bus. Consider this bus a good tour on the day of arrival in Florence and reserve the Academia, Duomo and Uffizi visits for later days in the week.

If you are into red wine, you will find many tours to the Chianti wine country located only 10 miles south of Florence. The most popular towns are Greve (pronounce Gra Vay) in Chiani and Montepulciano famous for its Montepulciano d'Abruzzo. If you are renting a car, it is best to leave it in the hotel garage in Firenze and take a half-day escorted tour. These tours will include all wine tastings, and you can rest assured you will not be pulled over by the Carabinieri for a DUI citation. Best to check online for Florence wine tours.

CHAPTER 8

FLORENCE DAY TRIPS

PISA & LUCCA

SAN GIMIGNANO
&
SIENA

THE CINQUE TERRE

OVERVIEW- THE THREE FLORENCE DAY TRIPS

If you have two or three extra days in Florence, a/k/a, the capital of Tuscany, you should plan on enough time to fit in all these four locations. Some of them can be done on the same day. Pisa and Lucca are easy to do in one day. For Seniors, Siena and San Gimignano are a little more complex. If you are a Senior, I have made it relatively easy to visit San Gimignano at the end of the day after leaving Siena at about 2PM. If you can spare a whole day, you can also pay a visit to the Cinque Terre or, should I say, one of the five towns. You pick it. But my favorite is Manarola. Not too much history in the five towns, just beautiful villages with gorgeous houses painted with those pastel colors strung against the mountainside, often confused with a picture of Positano on the Amalfi Coast.

An Alternative to the Escorted Tour

Siena and San Gimignano are easily reachable by train or car in one hour from Florence; about two hours from Montecatini. Both towns have ample parking.

There is ample public parking at both Lucca and Pisa. You should note that in Pisa, all cars must park in the large municipal lot about one-half mile away from the Tower complex. However, a courtesy tram every 10 minutes will take you to and from the Tower. The best way, without any hassles, is to take the train. Trains run about two per hour between SMN and Pisa Centrale. The trip takes about one hour. You can drive it also in one hour. There are tolls. Your credit card will work without any problems.

First, here is a quick overview of Pisa and Lucca:

Both Lucca and Pisa lie due west of Florence toward the Tyrrhenian Sea. They are only 27 minutes away by a connecting train. So you can take the train to either and hop that "shuttle" train to the other. You can return to Florence from either Lucca or Pisa. If you are staying in Montecatini, you can only return from Lucca since Montecatini is on the Viareggio line.

PISA
If you don't know the name or what's in Pisa, you should probably be planning a visit to New York City, not Italy. Yes, everyone knows the Leaning Tower of Pisa. It's a must to visit. For Seniors, it's all easy—flat walking to and from the Tower complex. You will need 2-3 hours here. Timed tickets are available if you want to climb the 300 steps to the top of the Tower. Sorry, there is no elevator. The cost is about $20 per adult. For Seniors, NOT RECOMMENDED. Too much waiting in line and too many stairs to climb with everyone pushing you up those stairs. Other than that, there is no charge for admission to the complex known as the Square of Miracles. Here is a short history of City of Pisa.

124

HISTORY OF PISA

The name "Pisa" means in Etruscan "mouth." the town of Pisa dates to about 200BC. In ancient times, about the 5th Century BC, it was inhabited by the Etruscans. It lies at the mouth of the Arno River. It's the same Arno River you see in Florence. At one time, the actual city of Pisa was closer to the Ligurian Sea. However, over time it has receded from 2.5 miles to about six miles from the coast. This river recession made Pisa an excellent port on the Mediterranean (actually the part of the "Med" known as the Ligurian Sea), the next port being Genova to the north and Ostia (Rome's old port) to the south. If you are driving up the coast road, you can see that marshy area where the sea was about 2,000 years ago. Before the river receded, ships could navigate up the Arno into the city.

In the 1980s and 1990s, archaeological remains were discovered dating to the 5th Century BC. Of considerable importance was the discovery of a tomb of an Etruscan prince.

At about 180BC, Pisa became a Roman colony. The Romans used the port as a base for warring against the Gauls and Ligurians.

During the final days of the Roman Empire (about 476AD), Pisa became a leading trading partner of destinations that could easily be reached from its strategic port. These were the islands of Sardinia and Corsica and the port cities of France and Spain.

Over the years, the Pisans were naval warriors and fought against dozens of invading navies. Most of the time, they were successful. In about 1290, the Pisans lost a major sea battle with the Genoese fleet (from Genoa). From here, it was all downhill for the Pisans. The maritime strength of Pisa would never be again. Pisa continued to be just a trading port.

An Alternative to the Escorted Tour

THE LEANING TOWER OF PISA

First, few travelers realize that the Leaning Tower is actually in a complex called the Piazza dei Miracoli or the Plaza of Miracles. The complex is also a UNESCO World Heritage Site. It contains the Pisa Cathedral, the Pisa Baptistry, and the Tower, also known as the Campanile. The complex is about two blocks wide and five blocks long and is enclosed by a wall. There is also a small cemetery, but it is known as a "Camposanto" or the holyfields, which dates from 1464. It's that large, long building on the far left, which abuts the perimeter wall as you enter the complex. You will notice if you look on the other side of the Baptistery and the Basilica. The Camposanto is home to 84 Roman sarcophagi and numerous works of art.

There is no charge for entering the Plaza of Miracles. However, there is a charge for climbing the Tower.

To climb the Tower, you must purchase a timed admission ticket and then wait in a long line. There is no elevator, and you must negotiate 296 steps against opposing tourists coming down. For Seniors, very important; I do not recommend climbing the Tower for the view or standing outside the top of the Tower for a photo op. You will see many tourists taking that picture of their partner or a friend pushing up the Tower.

The website is https://www.towerofpisa.org/tickets/.

Here are the technical facts about the Tower:
It is 183 feet from the ground to the top; you can figure out about ten stories. After a "heave-ho," with lead weights and a pushup of the Tower with a new concrete base, the corrected lean is slightly less than 4%. Taking into account the foundation, the Tower is almost 200 feet tall. The outer diameter is about 50 feet, and the inner diameter is 25 feet. Before the correction, the lean was 6%, and it appeared that it would fall eventually. The weight of the Tower is 16,200 tons; there are seven bells in the belfry.

Here is a quick recap of the construction:

It took a little over 200 years to build the Tower ultimately. The foundation was a gift of Donna Berta di Bernardo in 1172AD. In 1173, the primary stones which still form the foundation were laid. In 1178 the Tower began to sink during the second-floor construction. This sinking occurred because of the extremely weak subsoil. Construction was halted for almost 100 years as Pisa went to war with Genova, Florence, and Lucca. In about 1264, it was observed that the soil under the Tower was becoming unstable since the existing structure was compressing the underlying soil. In that year, they noticed that the Tower was beginning to tilt. So, in 1272, work restarted with cut marble from mountain pits near Pisa. Construction proceeded by making one side of the Tower floors taller than the other. They felt that this would correct the leaning.

Work stopped again in 1284 when Genova defeated the Pisans at the Battle of Meloria. Work continued several years later until the 7th floor was completed in 1319. The belfry was added in 1372. There are seven bells, each representing a note from the major scale. The completion of the belfry was achieved in 1655. The Tower continued to lean.

In 1990, the Tower was at a tilt of almost 6%. If nothing were done, the Tower would ultimately fall. Over the years before 1990, numerous efforts were made to restore the Tower to an upright position. However, some even worsened the tilt. The Tower was closed in 1990 and re-opened in 2001 after a significant stabilization effort. The effort involved pushing the Tower back with lead weights, removing the bells in the belfry, removing soil, and replacing the foundation under the base of the Tower.

Here is how they did it:

Finally, in 1993, the Italian Government devised a plan to tilt the Tower back to at least 3-4%. It was decided not to eliminate the lean since the "Leaning" Tower was a key tourism draw. Let's face it, who would come to see the Tower of Pisa if it were not

An Alternative to the Escorted Tour

leaning? The British proposed, and the Italian Government took them up on the offer. The plan worked with the lead weights used to bring it back temporarily as it fell back in a 3-4% tilt into a hole created by 43 screw augers removing the earth. The lead weights were then removed, and the Tower re-opened. It should last now for almost 300 years. The Tower tilt, since 2001, has been measured. In 2008, the Tower was completely stabilized, and there was no more progression in the tilt.

There have been four earthquakes over the course of the life of the Tower. For some reason, it is believed that the soft earth below cushioned the quake's shock, thus allowing no damage to the Tower. So much for the history of the Tower.

If you have the time, I suggest you visit the Basilica and the Baptistery near the Tower.

Of interest, aside from the lean of the Tower, is that Galileo (the astronomer) who lived in Pisa is said to have dropped two cannonballs of different masses to demonstrate that their speed of descent was independent of their mass, thus reinforcing the law of free fall. Regarding Galileo, Fibonacci, the famous mathematician (The Fibonacci sequence), was also from Pisa and lived about 400 years before Galileo.

Abutting and entering the complex are fast food, gelato stands, and souvenir shops. There are lots of shopping at those stalls. You can negotiate the price. Depending on the day of the week, you will also find those "Senegal or Dakar Merchants" selling everything on blankets, from fake Rolex watches to copies of Gucci handbags on the walkway leading up to the Tower. Best to buy them before the local police raid them, which usually takes place every 3-4 hours. And yes, you can negotiate the price.

No visit to the Tower complex is complete without a visit to the Cathedral of Pisa. The Cathedral is the large church in the Plaza of Miracles. Here are the basic facts: Its style is medieval

128

Roman, also known as Romanesque architecture. It is dedicated to the Assumption of the Virgin Mary. It is the oldest of the three structures, consecrated in 1118.

Construction began in 1063 and was completed in 1092. Enlargements were made in the 12th century, and a new façade was also built.

There was a fire in 1595, and the roof had to be replaced. The inside of the Cathedral is definitely worth a visit. Of interest to note are the coffered matrix ceiling and the Renaissance paintings. The dome of the Cathedral underwent restoration from 2015-2018.

That smaller round building which I might add is also tilting, is the Baptistery which replaced an older baptistery. It is officially called the Pisa Baptistery of St. John. Construction started in 1152 and was completed in 1363. Yes, 1363! It was the second building to be built on the Plaza of Miracles. It was a "slow build," taking 211 years. Because of the soft soil below, it, like the Tower of Pisa, also began to tilt. It now tilts .6 degrees (a little more than one-half of a degree).

Leaving the Plaza of Miracles is quite simple. It will cost you about three Euros more than two people taking a bus back to the central rail station. Note Pisa has two rail stations. You want Pisa Centrale. You can easily walk it. The distance is about one mile, and it's flat. However, after doing all that walking, on the return, Seniors should consider spending the six Euros and taking a taxi, else take that 15 minute walk.

On exiting the complex, go straight past those food stalls to that main boulevard (Via Bananno Pisano), and you will see several cab stands there. If you are parked in that massive parking lot, the best is to spot that tram for your return trip. I believe it departs from the same place as the drop-off point.

An Alternative to the Escorted Tour

LUCCA

Lucca is one of the walled cities of the medieval ages, which is not on the top of a hill. However, most of the wall and the old gates remain. Lucca is all flat and home to Giacomo Puccini (1858-1924), the famous operatic composer (Madam Bufferfly, La Boheme). Lots of restaurants and just a delightful place to stroll and visit all the churches and squares. You will also need three hours here; if you figure lunch, anticipate four hours. There is no charge to enter the town. Also, along with the easy walking, the city's main gate is directly across from the rail station. If you are taking the train, it is best to note the return times to Florence and Montecatini. Driving is easy as the A11 affords two exits for Lucca (east and west). Either one will bring you into town. On the A11 there are tolls which accept all credit cards. Parking is plentiful in Lucca. However, make sure you feed those meters.

There are several ways to plan your visit to Lucca.
1. The classic half day from Pisa in the morning.
2. A full day in Lucca
3. A half day in the morning and then onto the Cinque Terre for an overnighter, you are only an hour away.

Like many towns in this area, the Town of Lucca was inhabited by the ancient Etruscans. The City's name appears to come from the Ligurians (Ligurian Sea), who settled this area after the Etruscans. It means "marsh" and dates from about the 3rd century. In about 180BC the Romans took over and created a town hall in 89BC. The wall around the town is actually from the medieval era and not from Rome or ancient Rome times.

The Romans did create the rectangular street plan. The outline of the original Roman amphitheater can still be seen in the Piazza dell' Anfiteatro. What is left of the amphitheater sits about nine feet below the center of the large oval piazza. It was built during the 2nd century and could hold 10,000 spectators.

130

ITALY Made Easy for Seniors

Lucca was an important city and medieval fortress in the 6th century. In 553AD the city was taken over by Narses. From 576 to 797 the Lombards came down from Lombardy, took it over, and made it the capital of the duchy, which also included a large part of Tuscany and the province of Viterbo (part of the same province of Rome "Lazio"). Lucca minted their coins.

There was a significant presence of Jews in 859, led by the Kalonymos family. The City was one of the leading destinations of the Via Francigena, which was one of the major pilgrimage routes to Rome from the north.

The main products of Lucca during the 11th century were silk fabric woven with gold or silver threads. Production of silk and woven silk products continued for the next 200 years. In 1160, after Matilda of Tuscany passed away, the City became an independent commune with a charter. For almost 500 years, Lucca remained an independent republic.

About 1273 and again in 1277, and as far into 1789, the French Revolution, Lucca was controlled by numerous foreign entities. From then on, Lucca would be the second largest Italian city-state after Venice, with a republican constitution.

Lucca lost its independence in 1860 when it became part of the Kingdom of Sardinia under the control of the Grand Duchy of Tuscany. It became part of the Italian state in 1861.

Okay, so much for a short history. Now, what do we do in Lucca? Here is a list:
If you have a full two hours, consider walking on top of the wall around the city. It is about 2.5 miles. For Seniors, don't feel you must walk the entire wall length. You can stop for a café and a gelato at the halfway point or when you are pooped. There are numerous places where ramps have been installed that you may exit onto the local streets of the town.

An Alternative to the Escorted Tour

Look around for the Guinigi Tower. It is built between two mansions that date from the 14th and 15th centuries. You can climb the tower. However, there are an awful lot of stairs in this 135-foot-tall tower. Note it's the one where trees are growing on the top. There is a taller tower (campanile) next to the Cathedral of Lucca. This one has a crenel top and is about 210 feet tall. Work on that church started in 1063 and was redone in the Gothic style in the 14th century. It is worth a visit.

If you want to have lunch, stop at one of the many eateries at the Piazza dell Anfiteatro (Plaza of the Amphitheater).

There are numerous churches and squares to visit in Lucca. Shopping is also excellent as there are many souvenirs of the operas by Puccini.

I saved the best place to visit as the last in line. However, you might want to make it your first stop. It's the Puccini Museum. If you are an opera fan, this is the place! You would need an hour or two here. It is located at Corte San Lorenzo, Number 8.

Next up is Siena and San Gimignano if you can plan another day.

SIENA AND SAN GIMIGNANO- A DAY TRIP

OVERVIEW

As stated before, these medieval Tuscan cities can be visited on the same day. Just a little planning is needed. First, you must visit Siena in the morning and have lunch there. Once you are on top of the hill, there is flat walking throughout the historic center. If you depart the "Campo," the main square, at about 1-2PM you will have enough time to visit San Gimignano, the Medieval town of towers. If you see the town the way I suggest, San "Gimi" becomes all downhill. Using my suggestions allows a stroll and final shopping before you leave the area. To visit both cities on the same day, you must depart a local train from Florence's Santa Maria Novella 9-10AM. At this time, don't purchase any additional rail tickets. You may be too bushed to visit San Gimignano or wish to stay in Siena all day.

>>>TIP<<<
If you are planning on visiting San Gimignano in the afternoon, I usually don't suggest purchasing any "heavy," e.g., salami, a bottle of wine, souvenirs in Siena. You will be forced to carry them around San Gimignano. You can buy most of the stuff that you see in Siena also in San Gimignano. The best souvenirs in San Gimignano are the area's products, wine, salumi, olives, etc.
>>><<<

SIENA
Siena is a hilltop town built in the medieval ages. Like many historical sites in Italy, it is also a UNESCO World Heritage Site. In addition to the historical significance, Siena is best known for the twice-annual horse race and exhibition known as the "Palio di Siena" held in the "Campo ." The term "burnt sienna" comes from the fact that the buildings in the Palazzo are all that burnt red/yellow color known now as "burnt sienna." Note it's not a mistake. The color has two "n" s.

The City of Siena has made it easy for us Seniors to visit the historical center. In the past 20 years, the City has built escalators and people movers. There are now three escalator complexes. I think the one from the rail station may be the longest escalator in the world outside of the ones you see at airports. It stretches almost three football fields. That's about 1000 feet. It will lift you to the top of the historic district in about 10 minutes.

>>>TIP<<<
Before you leave the rail station, find out when the trains depart for San Gimignano (going north). The fare is less than $4, and the journey is less than 45 minutes. The best is to check with the ticket agent. Make a note for trains around 2-4PM which will

133

An Alternative to the Escorted Tour

allow you about two hours to visit San Gimignano. You don't want to arrive at the Siena rail station only to wait 40 minutes or so for the next train to "San Gimi." Note, the stop is called Poggibonsi-San Gimignano.

If you are driving, you can figure about 40 minutes. The main road to San Gimignano is a national road. You can't miss it. All you need do is follow the signs to Firenze and exit at Poggibonsi-San Gimignano. There are no tolls.
>>><<<

If you are arriving by train, follow the signs to the escalator, which will take you to Porto Camollia. There are plenty of public parking lots if you are arriving by car.

I usually recommend parking directly against the City walls. Just follow the road around the walls, and you will see lots of parking "Parcheccios." Remember to purchase a ticket from the machine, or else you will have a costly souvenir on your windshield when you return.

On arrival at the top of the hill, you must make a strategic decision. Do you head for the Piazza del Campo first or see some of those gorgeous churches? The problem with Siena, it is just one giant maze, and I mean an absolute labyrinth! My suggestion is to make your way to the Piazza del Campo and locate a place for lunch. Then after lunch, you can explore some of the churches. My first choice is, without a doubt, the Basilica Cateriniana San Domenico followed by the Duomo di Siena. A first runner-up is the Basilica of San Francisco. All of them contain exquisite Renaissance works of art.

Once you make your way into the "Campo," you may be tempted to climb the Torre del Mangia, which is that big tower (about the same height as a football field) in front of you. For Seniors, this is a no-no attempt to climb (especially after lunch), as there are 200 steps and no elevator. If your kids or grandchildren want to climb the tower, there is an admission charge of ten Euros per person. You can figure a half-hour for the up and down. That building to the right is known as the Palazzo Pubblico or, better, the city hall. It is now a museum.

If you are of the Jewish faith, you may want to spend a few minutes after lunch visiting the Synagogue of Siena (at least the medieval one). It's easy to find because it lies on the street directly behind that large tower (the campanile)—the one you don't want to climb. Just follow the signs to the "sinagoga," or ask any one of the locals.

A SHORT HISTORY OF SIENA- JUST THE FACTS
From what we know, Siena was founded at the beginning of the 4th Century BC as a Roman Colony during the reign of the Roman Emperor Augustus. However, it is believed that about 900 BC, it was inhabited by a small group of Etruscans who called it Saina. The Roman colony was called Saena Lulia. It did not flourish under Roman rule because it was "off the beaten path," i.e., no significant roads and ports existed.

For about 600 years, control of Siena bounced around between various archdioceses, namely Arezzo. It was not until the beginning of the 10th Century AD that Siena became an important trade route between Rome and Florence. In the 12th Century, Siena went to war against Florence.

Siena was a major Italian banking center until the 14th Century. The oldest bank in the world still in existence is the Monte dei Paschi bank of Italy. The bank has been operating since 1472.

During the Renaissance, the arts made their mark on the churches of Siena.

An Alternative to the Escorted Tour

The Campo was a marketplace just before the 13th Century. It was built on a sloping site and paved over in red bricks with a herringbone design.

Here are some questions you probably want to ponder as you eat that great pizza in the Piazza del Campo, or better, wait for it to be delivered to your table:

Q: Why is the Piazza divided into nine pie-shaped sections? Does this represent a pizza?
A: No, each wedge represents one of the nine politicians (the committee of 9) who laid out the Piazza of Siena a/k/a "The Campo" during the 12th Century.

Q: What's with all those flags?
A: Each one represents one of the neighborhoods of Siena.

Q: And finally, what's with that fountain in the middle of the square? Or shall I say, at the top of the square?
A: That fountain is known as the "Fonte Gaia" or Joyous Fountain. It was built in 1419 by that committee of nine. The fountain serves as the watering hole for the area as it was the end point of several conduits. It is still in use today. However, the water out of this fountain is not potable any more. So, don't drink the water!

If you are ready to leave Siena and go to San Gimignano, you need to walk back to the Porto Camollia or take a taxi to the train station. If you care not to walk back to the train station, there is a major taxi stand at the Piazza Independenza. The taxi stand is no more than one block from the Piazza del Campo. In terms of proximity, it is about one block behind that gorgeous fountain known as Fonte Gaia. If you are lost, ask one of the locals, "Doe Vay et Piazza Independenaz- Taxi." The fare back to the stazione usually runs about ten Euros. If you know where you parked your car, the taxi will also take you back there. You can figure about twelve Euros.

136

Now onto San Gimignano. If you have driven, follow the signs to Firenze. If going by rail, board the train bound for Firenze and make sure you exit at that Poggibonsi-San Gimignano station.

SAN GIMIGNANO- THE TOWN OF TOWERS

No other town or city in the world compares to this place. This is not New York or Chicago. These towers go back 800 years, not eighty. I love it!

About ten years ago, I walked into a real estate office and asked about buying a home here. That's how much I love this town, not to mention it has the best gelato shop in all Italy, or maybe in the world! Let's face it how many times have you downed a gelato of cream with saffron and pine nuts?

>>>TIP<<<

If you are arriving by train from Florence or Siena at the Poggibonsi-San Gimignano rail station, you need to note the times for the return trains to Florence. If you are staying in Montecatini Terme, you still need to change trains in Florence (SMN).

If you are going on to Montecatini Terme, one ticket will do it all. On arrival at Firenze SMN, you won't have to buy another ticket from SMN to Montecatini. However, it would help if you still gauged your time back to the station. My suggestion would be to allow 30 minutes in total. The taxi ride back to the station is only 10 minutes. However, you must find a taxi (in the main parking lot next to the "Coop" market) and buy that return ticket at the station. You may consider a bus back to the station, however it takes about twenty minutes and it may not be worth it even if you are on a tight budget, as a taxi will cost you 12-15 Euros. The bus departs from the main

An Alternative to the Escorted Tour

parking lot and will cost you no more than two Euros. Now on to the history of San Gimignano
>>><<<

Here is a quick history of San Gimignano:

It is a walled hilltop medieval town in the province of Siena, Tuscany. And, yes, it is also a UNESCO World Heritage Site. It is best known for its medieval architecture and a dozen towers remaining. Those towers you see are houses. The town dates from about the 3rd century BC when it was an Etruscan village. Two brothers, Muzio and Silvio, fled the Roman Republic for a hilltop village called Valdelsa. The brothers built two castles atop that hill and called it Silvia. The name was changed in 450AD by Bishop Geminianus. The Bishop was able to spare the destruction of the two castles from Atilla the Hun.

In the 6th and 7th Centuries, the wall was built around the town. From about 900AD forward, the village was controlled by Volterra's bishops, another medieval hilltop town a few miles away. The small town was called the "Castle of San Gimignano."

During the middle ages and the Renaissance, San Gimignano was a stop-over on the Via Francigena road, stretching from England across Europe and through the Apennine Peninsula, now known as Italy. This stop-over point hosted pilgrimages en route to Rome and further to the Holy Land through ports on the Apennine Peninsula.

In 1199AD, the fledging town became independent of Volterra. Public buildings and churches were built. However, this peace did not last long. For the next 200 years, there were conflicts between the Guelphs and the Ghibellines, and to further add more conflict, the wealthy families of San Gimignano began to fight each other; enter the towers.

138

The competing families of San Gimignano started to build tower houses to house their families. At the end of the medieval period, there were 72 tower houses. Today 14 remain standing. As each tower was erected, the next tower to be built had to be taller. This competition was like "keeping up with the Jones."

This competition continued until the town council said no tower could be taller than the campanile tower abutting the Palazzo Comunale, which is 230 feet tall. The city continued to grow until the Black Plague hit most of Europe in 1348, when about half of the population of San Gimignano died. Florence later governed the town. You will note throughout the Town Gothic houses built in the Florentine style. Many of the towers had to be leveled to the height of the abutting buildings. This lasted until the 19th Century when San Gimignano became a tourist attraction. The present-day towers can be seen for miles.

Oh, one more item. People always ask, "What happened to all the other towers"? Simple, they were lost to wars, neglect, and finally, urban renewal.

Here is a little geography of the town. First, only three sides of the old wall still exist. The fourth wall was torn down during the 16th Century. There are now only eight entrances from the road which encircles the town. If you have a car, it's a nice "drive-around," and will take you no more than ten minutes to circumnavigate the town.

I have visited San Gimignano about a dozen times. There are two main piazzas. The first is the Piazza della Cisterna. It looks like a triangle. You can't miss it. It is the one with the water well in the middle. The well dates from 1346AD. Across from one end is the Hotel Cisterna, and on the other side is the Hotel Leon Bianco. On the other side of this triangle, you will find the famous Gelateria Dondoli, supposedly the best gelato in Italy.

An Alternative to the Escorted Tour

The second piazza is the Piazza Duomo. It's just off the Piazza della Cisterna next to the Dondoli Gelato shop. With your back to the well, go toward the right passing the side of the Hotel Leon Bianco. In about 200 feet, you will come to the Piazza Duomo. The first building on the left is the Palazzo Comunale. It is essentially the town hall. You can't miss it as it has a campanile (Torre Grossa) on the right side of it. Continuing to your right is the Collegiate Church. If you continue past the Collegiate Church several blocks, you will come upon a small square with a street to the right and one to the left. The Piazza Agostino is named for the Church of Sant' Agostino on that square. All three churches are worth a short visit to view the beautiful artwork on the walls and ceilings.

NAVIGATING AROUND SAN GIMIGNANO

San Gimignano is one town that is not a maze and one town where you want to do some serious shopping. There are two main streets, and they are wide. The first one (Via San Giovanni) starts from that small park, "Piazzale Montemaggio" at Viale Roma and works its way uphill at about a 5-7% incline. It starts at the beginning, where you come up from the parking lot and pass the "Coop" supermarket. It would help if you watched those stairs or take the ramp.

San Giovanni is lined with all types of shops and eateries. In about six blocks, it takes a bend to the right and goes under a house (yes, a house) before coming out at the Piazza Cisterna; note the line on the left in front of the Dondoli Gelato shop (Gelateria Dondoli). As you pass the city hall with that big tower and the Collegiate Church, bear to your right down the Via San Matteo until you get to Via Cellolese, then go right for about two blocks. Here you will find the Piazza St. Agostino with the church by the same name located on it. If you don't make the right-hand turn on Via Celloese, you will wind up going out the Porta Matteo gate onto the ring road. You must turn around, walk back a block, and take a hard left.

There are ample public facilities in the town, or better, swing into a stand-up bar or a sandwich shop and ask to use the toilet. I find it best to order an Americano Coffee and THEN head for the toilet (WC). It's not a requirement but a nice gesture.

140

ITALY Made Easy for Seniors

HOW TO VISIT SAN GIMIGNANO

If you have decided to drive here, you will find a municipal parking lot about three blocks from the Piazzalle Montemaggio park at the beginning of the Viale Roma and San Giovanni. A medium-sized supermarket (The Coop) and café abutting the parking lot. You cannot miss it. Follow the ramp and steps to the right, bringing you up to the Viale Roma at the park's far end. If you are driving, you can follow that ring road until you get a parking spot. Remember do feed that meter, or else a ticket. Because San Gimignano is a hilltop town, what goes up must come down. So either way, you will huff and puff. For Seniors, there is an easier way. Just follow my tip below.

>>>TIP<<<

For Seniors, the best approach is to take the train from Siena or Florence to Poggibonsi-San Gimignano. Then instead of taking that bus, which will go to the parking area at the bottom of the hill next to the Coop, take a taxi to the top of San Gimignano. When you get into the taxi, inform the driver that you want to go to the PIAZZA DELLE CISTERNA, the Hotel Cisterna. It will cost you about 15-18 Euros (remember, we don't tip the driver in Italy; however, it is okay to let them keep the change, i.e., the coins).

Once you are in the Piazza, all you need do is walk the flat area to St. Agostino, turn around, walk back to Piazza delle Cisterna, have that gelato at Dondoli's, and then walk down the hill toward the Coop supermarket to the main parking area. This is the checkpoint where all the tour buses park.

All you need to do now is spot the municipal bus that will take you to the stazione. If you want to splurge (and go in class), find another couple and take one of those taxis to the stazione. You probably will be

An Alternative to the Escorted Tour

packed with souvenirs, cheese, salami, bottles of wine, and all that other good stuff. Remember, you are going to the Poggibonsi-San Gimignano stazione, where you will get a train to Florence, or if you are going to Siena for the afternoon.
>>><<<

>>>TIP<<<
You may want to view the movie "Tea with Mussolini" (MGM and Medusa films 1999). It was filmed in the Hotel Cisterna on the square of the same name. When you are in the square and have finished your gelato, drop into the hotel to view the main lobby where they filmed the movie.
>>><<<

Return by train or your rental car to Florence or Montecatini. You should be at your hotel about 6-7PM, just in time for a snooze, a shower, and dinner at 8PM.

ITALY Made Easy for Seniors

THE CINQUE TERRE

First of all, let's get it right. The Cinque Terre pronounced, "CHINK-QUAY-TER-RAY ." The Five Lands (five towns) is a coastal area against the Ligurian Sea (part of the Mediterranean) about 75 miles south of Genova and 60 miles north of Pisa. It is part of the province known as Liguria. The five towns which are UNESCO World Heritage sites are (starting from the north) Monterosso al Mare, Vernazza, Corniglia, Manarola, and Riomaggiore. They are one of the National Parks of Italy. Due to the beauty of the colorful houses perched on the cliffs, the five towns have been one of the most photographed areas of Italy.

Several towns, namely Manarola, are often confused with Positano in the Amalfi area south of Naples. The Cinque Terre has become Italy's "hot" tourist spot in the past thirty years. In peak season, the towns are flooded with day trippers from all over Italy. Rail, small roads, and boats connect the five villages. Footpaths and hiking trails also connect the towns.

The towns were accessed only by boat until 1874, when the Italian State Railway (FS) decided to connect La Spezia in the south with Genoa in the north. Tunnels were bored in the rock mountains abutting the sea until all the towns were connected. For most of the journey via rail, the trains will pass through 51 tunnels connecting the five villages. It was a significant engineering feat considering it was done in 1874 when the tools (tunnel boring machines) used today were unavailable. Some tunnels are so short that the trains need to stop in them to access the stations. In addition, the train tracks are laid about four feet from the ocean and are perched on the rocky incline.

You can visit one of the five towns if you have a whole extra day. I have found that it is doable to see two of the towns but difficult. So here are my recommendations:

First, you need to read this paragraph two or three times. Do NOT attempt to visit any of the five towns by car. Second, if you have rented a standard transmission car, you will probably burn out the clutch, the brakes, or both. Secondly, you risk an accident if you are backing up (especially in a downhill location) in any parking areas, which may also be difficult to find. If driving, you will probably only make it to the first town, Riomaggiore.

>>>TIP<<<
If you insist on driving, your best bet is to drive to La Spezia Centrale rail station and find a parking space. You may have to walk about eight blocks—no big deal. For Seniors, it's all flat. At La Spezia Centrale, you will join the herds of people and those tour buses full of tourists waiting for the train (about every 20 minutes) to go up to the five towns. It's about twelve minutes to the first town Riomaggiore and another five minutes to Manarola. So once again, don't drive!
>>><<<

QUICK HISTORY HERE OF THE FIVE TOWNS
Like the other 57 other UNESCO World Heritage Sites, the Cinque Terre is also one. The Cinque Terre is also the smallest National Park of Italy. As far as I know, there are no historic Roman sites to visit. As far as we know, the Cinque Terre towns go back to the 11th Century. At that time, the inhabitants began to terrace the hills and grow olives and grapes. Farming continued until the 19th Century and into the 20th Century when the houses you see began to flourish. It wasn't until the 1900's that the Cinque Terre towns became a tourist attraction.

The environment continues to do a number on the five towns. Over the last twenty years, torrential storms have caused many landslides. In addition, the Cinque Terre is in a low Earthquake zone. In January 2023, there were several tremors of 1.0, and in 2022 the area was hit with five quakes of more than 4.0. So if you are there and the ground rumbles, don't worry.

ITALY Made Easy for Seniors

HOW TO VISIT THE CINQUE TERRE

I describe a day trip to Manarola either from Florence or Montecatini Terme. It is best to depart between 8 and 9AM.

It would be best if you took a train to Manarola. There is no other way around it unless you take a day trip on tour (best to check with your hotel). That bus tour is a good idea. They still will take you to La Spezia rail station for that 12-minute ride to Rio Maggiore. There may even be enough time at the end of the day to visit Pisa. However, be advised that it will probably be a long day with a departure at about 8AM from Florence. If it's a mini-van tour, expect it to be about $150 or more per person. Best to do it on your own: It is simple and cheap.

You will note I advise a ticket to Manarola. It is the second village. As I write this book, the "Via della More" (walk of the Lovers) connecting Riomaggiore with Manarola is still "knocked" out due to two significant landslides. Even if it were repaired, I would not recommend it for Seniors. While the walk is flat and only about three-quarter miles between the towns, there are two steep flights of stairs on each end of the path. Also, except for some nice restaurants, I have never seen the need to visit Riomaggiore except to gain entrance to the "Via della More." Which means in English, "The walk of the lovers."

If you are a Senior and in great shape, there is another alternative to the Walk of the Lovers. The "Beccara" is a trail over the hills between the two towns. The route is almost one mile long. The only problem is that you need to climb up a hill of about 800 feet and then down that hill on the other side. There are approximately 620 steps on each side of the trail. You need to start your visit in Riomaggiore and not Manarola. Also, don't be shocked when that train stops in a tunnel in Riomaggiore. You must exit the train in the tunnel and walk up to the station. Best to follow the crowd.

An Alternative to the Escorted Tour

If you are planning an overnighter to the Cinque Terre to see the other towns, you will find later in this chapter a description and what to see in Corniglia, Vernazza, and Monterosso al Mare.

If you are visiting several towns, staying overnight in one of the inns or BnBs is best. My first choice for an overnighter is Vernazza, followed by Manarola. It would help if you packed a carry-on with your toothbrush and a change of clothing. Also, don't expect to find any major hotels in the Cinque Terre. Seniors, you need to consult Google Earth to check the location of your BnB. Most of them will require a steep walk uphill from the rail stations.

If you want to visit several towns, staying in La Spezia for the evening is best. Here you will find many inexpensive, friendly hotels; all you need to do is walk to the La Spezia Centrale rail station. Note, make sure you go to Centrale, as La Spezia has two stations. Trenitalia runs more trains from March through November, stopping at all the Cinque Terre towns. The train is known as the Cinque Terre Express and starts in La Spezia on the south and the resort town of Sestri Levante on the north.

If you want to stay at some upscale hotels in the area, I recommend the four-star hotels in Sestri Levante. It's only a 40-minute fast run to the Cinque Terre towns. In season you can expect the Cinque Terre Express trains to make the journey in about 25 minutes as they do not stop at many of the local stations before they get to Monterosso al Mar.

If you plan to spend a minimum of five days at the Cinque Terre, consider the most northern town, Monterosso de Mar. Unlike the other four villages, the town is a resort town with lovely beaches. However, this will not help you in the off-season, when most of the "luxury" hotels are closed for the winter season.

Also, if you want to see all five towns or several, there is a Cinque Terre unlimited day ticket, allowing you to shuttle to and from any of the towns via rail. It is best to check with the ticket agent.

If you are into hiking and are physically fit, consider hiking the "Blue Trail" which connects all five towns. There is a charge of about $8, and there are checkpoints along the way. It would be best if you started early, as the entire hike is about 11km (about 7 miles) and takes nearly six hours without any nourishment stops. Water and proper dress are required. If you decide it's too much and you are pooping out, you can always swing into the closest town and take the train back to your base town hotel for only one Euro. Note for Seniors; it is not an easy trail as you need to go up and down those steep hills.

>>>TIP<<<
If you are in excellent shape and wish to hike any parts of the Blue Trail, be aware that a law was passed in 2019 prohibiting wearing flip-flops, sandals, and pumps. The government was tired of air-lifting tourists out of the area with broken hips, ankles, and legs. There is now a fine of 2500 Euros, and rest assured that ticket punchers on top of the hills we catch you.
>>><<<

HERE WE GO TO
Most trains from Florence or Monticatini will get you to the southern entrance of the Cinque Terre, La Spezia. Usually, all trains stop here en route to Genoa. It is a major connection point. Because of the price difference I favor the local express trains to La Spezia, also there is lovely countryside to view. Using the local train to La Spezia will add about 20 minutes and save you about $10. Some regional trains do not require any change, even in La Spezia, and run straight through to Manarola. I do not believe at this time that there are any fast "Frecci" trains operating to La Spezia or the Cinque Terre.

An Alternative to the Escorted Tour

>>>TIP<<<
Out of the La Spezia station, make sure you are sitting on the left-hand side of the train (in the direction of travel). Keep your eyes on the windows. About six minutes into that first tunnel, you will see the Ligurian sea through those windows cut into the tunnel walls. The sea comes and goes in a few seconds. Also, ensure your train out of La Spezia will stop in Manarola, as many do not, as many make the first stop in Sestri Levante and go on to Genoa.
>>><<<

The first stop is Riomaggiore. Don't get off the train! The second stop will be Manarola, your stop. If you are sitting in the back of the train, don't be shocked as the back of the train stops in the tunnel at some of the stations. Yes, the tunnel. It's freaky. When the train begins to move out of the Riomaggiore station, make your way to one of the exit doors and make sure you have all your personal stuff, or else they may wind up in Genova. When the train makes the next stop (Manarola), exit the train and follow the crowd. For Seniors, you do not have to climb those two flights of stairs or even negotiate that long ramp. You will find the elevator opposite the toilets; behind the souvenir shop and ticket booth. Once at the upper level, follow that long tunnel about three blocks into the center of the town.

When you exit the pedestrian tunnel with all that Italian graffiti, go to your left to that small plaza, where you will notice a ramp to your right. That small plaza above the train line is excellent for photographing Manarola's main street (Via Renato Birolli). That ramp of about 100 feet will take you down to Via Renator Birolli, for shopping and the eateries. It's about a 10-minute flat walk to the "marina." Don't expect a large marina with lots of boats and yachts. There isn't one. Here you will find one of my favorite restaurants, "Ristorante Marina Piccola ." Absolutely great seafood with pasta dishes. Do request one of the outdoor tables if it's nice out.

148

ITALY Made Easy for Seniors

If you are tight for time and are not going to have an Italian lunch, you will find lots of places selling fried calamari to go in a paper cone. Also, I don't know why, but most of the pizza I have seen here seems to be Sicilian style. In other words, it's that spongy pizza or what I would call pizza made with Focaccia bread. Probably, the pizza makers here, came from Sicily.

After lunch (Pranzo), exit the restaurant and go to your right, toward the steps to the beach; turn around and snap some photos of the gorgeous painted houses on the cliff.

One more item I should note, there is an excursion boat out of La Spezia if you don't want to take the train. However, this boat does not operate out of season.

Also, for Seniors, the area past the entrance to that passageway (tunnel) to the station is all uphill. However, there are a few souvenir shops past the ATM unit on your right. The ATM is easy to spot since there is only one in town.

CORNIGLIA

Corniglia is the middle village of the Cinque Terre towns. At last, checked the population was around 200. It sits like Manarola, on a bluff about a football field back from the Ligurian sea. Very few tourists visit Corniglia.

First, while it has a rail station (after Manarola and just before Vernazza), it has no streets. So access by automobile is impossible. It has what I would call "sought of access" to Manarola. It defines the saying, "You can't get there from here;" if you are driving, best to plan on bypassing Corniglia. Since there is no direct road to Manarola from Corniglia, you need to go to the outskirts of Vernazza on Via Stazione, where you pick up the SP51 road going south toward Manarola.

An Alternative to the Escorted Tour

Here is the real scoop on Corniglia: To get to the heart of the town from the rail station, you need to climb the "Lardarina." The Lardarina comprises 33 flights of stairs and about 380 steps. Get this; all of them are switchbacks. Oy! There are lots of rest stops. From the top of the Lardarina, there are sweeping views to the left and right of the other four towns.

For Seniors, this walk up the Lardarina is not recommended. Once at the top of the Lardarina, you will find a short main drag known as Via Fieschi. Here you will find little streets with BnBs and small restaurants. However, you won't find any authentic multi-room hotels. If you are the type of person who works out at the gym every day and is in great shape with no cardiac issues, you will find the beginning of the Lardarina at the northern end of the train station just as it goes into the tunnel. Better to go down the Lardarina instead of climbing it.

>>>TIP<<<
There is a mini-bus that meets the arriving trains. This mini-bus will take you to the top of the hill and drop you right in the heart of Corniglia. There is a charge of about one Euro. You may need to purchase a ticket at the rail station. As usual, you should note the train return times.
>>><<<

VERNAZZA

Vernazza, better known as town number four, lies just below Monterosso al Mare. I love this town. If you are overnighting from Florence or Montecatini, this is one of the best places in addition to Manarola to stay. First, it's the only one of the Five Lands with a harbor. It's got a lovely sandy beach. It has plenty of BnBs and excellent restaurants and is predominantly flat walking. However, be advised that many of the BnBs require access via a staircase or ramp. You should check with your innkeeper, and remember the ground floor is the "zero floor," not the first floor. So best to ask, "Is the room on the ground floor or the first floor" (piano terra, or primo piano)?

Also, if the room is on the first floor, you probably will have to negotiate some stairs since most of these places do not have lifts or elevators. If walking up stairs creates a problem, better to check in at Monterosso al Mare or Riomaggiore for accommodations with elevators.

Vernazza is off-limits to all cars. There is, however, a small parking lot located about a quarter mile from the town. Once again, because of the walk and the difficulty driving in the Cinque Terre, a car is not recommended, especially for Seniors.

The town is home to "Pesto" (actually, it was invented in Genoa). If you don't know what it is, it's pretty simple. You crush together pine nuts, olive oil, basil leaves, garlic, grated parmesan cheese, and presto; that's Pesto. It may come from the words "Mortar and Pestle," which are used for crushing the ingredients. You can purchase it already made, and it's a great gift to bring home from Vernazza. You will find many dishes made with it, e.g., Pesto Pizza.

Vernazza also has one of those unique rail stations. The train station itself is quite short. So, most trains stop in a tunnel. Don't get shocked if people open the doors and start walking in the tunnel. On another subject, since they didn't have room for the tunnel, it was placed under about 3-4 blocks of the houses in town. So if you are staying overnight, don't be surprised if you hear a very slight rumble as the train passes a hundred feet underneath your bed.

Hopefully, you will be taking the train. So, after exiting the train onto the platform, you will find stairs and an elevator, which will take you down to the Via Roma. The Via Roma is the main drag of Vernazza. In several blocks, it becomes Via Visconti as it works its way down to the harbor, the beach, and the castle.

An Alternative to the Escorted Tour

The Doria Castle dates from around the 11th Century and was used as a lookout for invading pirates. In 1284, the fortress was taken over by invaders from Pisa during the Battle of Meloria. Ultimately, Genova won. During WWII, the Germans used it as an anti-aircraft position.

If you stand on the jetty at the end of Via Visconti, you can take some awesome pictures of those fishing boats moored together (there are no piers). You can then turn around and take more breathtaking photos of the painted houses, much like Manarola.

If you are physically fit, you can take the ninety-minute hike to Monterosso al Mare. For Seniors, if you are not in great shape, I do not recommend this hike.

You will find many restaurants mainly serving seafood on the side streets of Via Visconti. If you want to dine outside (weather permitting) and enjoy a gorgeous sunset, visit Gambero Rosso Restaurant. It's that restaurant with all the umbrellas at the beginning of the concrete walkway to the boats at the end of Via Visconti. But show up early (at the opening time) as the place fills up quickly. Make sure you check the sunset time. Best to visit here in October, April, or May. On now to the resort town of Monterosso al Mare, Monterosso of the Sea.

MONTEROSSO AL MARE
This is one place you would not expect to be part of the Cinque Terre. It is not like the other towns—first, not enough pretty houses with lots of colors on the hillside. Secondly, it is a beach resort. You should note that this is Monterosso al Mare, not Monterosso! Monterosso is about 230 miles away near Padua. On the Ligurian Sea, Monterosso is the largest of the five towns and has a population of about 1500.

The town is divided into two areas: the old town and the new town. A pedestrian tunnel of about three blocks connects them.

152

Vehicles can also pass through this tunnel, so best to be cautious. The northern or most western town, the oldest town of the two areas, is known as "Fegina." It has the longest beach in the Cinque Terre and a lovely beach compared to the other "postage stamp" beaches. Fegina is also home to the Monterosso Al Mar train station.

If you are driving, you should enter from the Genova (northern or western side) and not through the four towns to the south because of the very steep and curvy road, SP38 (Via Roma).

There is ample beach parking for the day in a large muni lot at Fegina beach. If you are staying overnight at a hotel or a BnB, you need to check with your hotel and obtain a pass; else, you will be ticketed for a ZTL (Zone Traffic Limited) violation. That ticket is pretty pricey; trust me, they have a habit of catching you in a few months. I know from experience!

If you are not too concerned about all those pretty houses perched on the hillsides of the other four towns and want to enjoy a place that is also a reasonable resort, then Monterosso is the place. If you wish, you can pay three times the price a few miles up the road in Portofino, but you would need to get back to the main line to the Cinque Terre for all your day trips. So the best is to camp yourself at one of the many resort-style hotels in Monterosso. You will find most of the hotels in Monterosso lie in the flat area abutting the beach for about six blocks in length.

If you are going out of season but in September or early June, you probably will find the beach warm and swimmable. There still will be crowds. Of the other four towns, this one is the liveliest. They do not roll up the sidewalks when the tourists go home for the day.

An Alternative to the Escorted Tour

Here is a little history about Monterosso al Mare:
First, that church on the hill is the church of San Francesco (same as St. Francis of Assisi). It divides Fegina with the new section of Monterosso al Mare. There is an attached Capuchin convent. The church was built in 1619-1622 and was consecrated in 1623. In 1819, Napoleon took it from the friars and converted it into a fort of the Ligurian Republic under the first French Empire. After Napoleon's fall in 1816, it was given back to the Capuchin Monks.

In 2013, a significant landslide destroyed several pieces of the convent, historic wall, etc. Most of the rubble spilled down the hill onto the driveway connecting the two towns. Inside the monastery are beautiful paintings. However, to view the church, the town, and the cemetery, you need to climb about forty steps and negotiate a path with several switchbacks. For Seniors, not advisable unless you are in excellent shape.

Monterosso dates to about the 11th Century. There are remnants of medieval fortresses and watchtowers. These were used to spot invading marauders and pirates. Other than that, not too much history as Monterosso is a "new" town.

CHAPTER 9

VENICE

OVERVIEW

Venice is very much like Rome; this is one city that is undoubtedly unique. Yes, I can say this. I have been to Amsterdam, Bruges, and other places where canals are all over. However, none of these and others can compare to Venice. There is only one Venice in the world. Many say it is the most romantic city in the world.

Venice is massive. It sits in a lagoon about 2.5 miles from the mainland. Back in time, it was used to protect the inhabitants against marauding tribes. To conquer Venice one would have to mount an invasion by sea, which would be nearly impossible in medieval times.

Today, a roadway and a rail link connect the central lagoon island with the mainland, known as Venice Mestre. The rail system ends about 300 feet before the "Grand Canal" at the Santa Lucia rail terminal.

With the exception of the end of the motorway at the Piazzale Roma, there are absolutely no automobiles in the Venice Lagoon islands since there are no roads, only canals. All transportation is via water boats comprised of government (ACTV) operated vaporettos, water taxis and charter boats. Note gondola rides are not allowed on the Grand Canal. So don't expect one of those gondoliers to take you for those forty minutes down the Grand Canal. Also, they do not sing "Oh Solo Mio," that's strictly in Napoli. However, residents can use the Grand Canal for a few "blocks," and gondoliers making deliveries.

An Alternative to the Escorted Tour

There are over 118 islands in the Venice Lagoon, connected by 400 bridges. Several other islands in the Lagoon are not connected to the main lagoon complex. They are the islands of Burano, Murano, and Torcello; all three are worth a visit. There are several other islands worth mentioning.

The "Lido" is a long barrier island at the end of the Lagoon. It is a resort area with a beautiful beach facing the Adriatic. The Lido is absolutely dead in the off-season. From October through May, even the birds head down to Sicily. If you spend extra days in either May or September, a day at the Lido is undoubtedly in order. Here you will find lots of BnBs and smaller hotels. You will find many restaurants and shops on the wide boulevard called "Gran Viale Santa Maria Elisabetta." On exiting the Vaporetto, you need to take a hard right, then walk about one block to the Gran Viale. This boulevard is lined with shops, gelato stands, cafes, and restaurants.

Two other islands border the Grand Canal which are not considered in the six Sestieris (or districts). They are Giudecca and San Giorgio. If you can spare an extra day, these two islands are worth a visit. Vaporetti also reaches these two islands.

A SHORT HISTORY OF VENICE

There is minimal early history about Venice. Roman sources believe there were fishermen living in the marshy Lagoon about 421AD. That year, the first church was established by these "lagoon dwellers" as San Giacomo. Warring tribes, mainly in Lombardia (Northern Italy), made their mark on the people until they finally got fed up and fled for safety to the marshes of the Lagoon. In 568AD, the first central government was formed.

More and more Veneti fleeing from the Lombardy region of the north started to inhabit the marshy areas. For several hundred years, the people in the Lagoon were governed by the Byzantine Empire (Eastern Roman Empire, which survived after 476 AD). In 726AD, the people in the Lagoon broke away from

Constantinople, formed their government, and elected their first Doge (duke). In 810AD, the Franks tried to conquer the Venetians living in the marshes but failed.

In 828, the Venetians smuggled from Egypt the body of Saint Mark. The Venetians declared Saint Mark, the patron saint of Venice. Venice became a world trading center as its population swelled. About 1200AD entered into several wars with Constantinople and Genoa.

In about 1348, the Black Plague destroyed a good portion of the inhabitants of Venice. Ships arriving in Venice had to wait 40 days before they could enter for fear of infected sailors. This 40-day waiting period is where we get the term (Quarantine, from 40). The plague struck again in 1630. Napoleon conquered Venice and dissolved its government in 1797. Austria took control over Venice in 1815.

In 1866, the Austrians were defeated by the Prussians. The Venice City state became part of the new Kingdom of Italy with other city-states, i.e., Florence, Milan, etc., under the leadership of the key Italian unifier Giuseppe Garibaldi.

CONSTRUCTION OF THE CITY
Now that you know a little about the city, you are probably thinking about how these little islands were connected. First, you need to realize that they did not bring in lots of dirt or what we call "material" from the mainland and fill the marshy areas. Instead, they did something very novel. Sticks of Oak and other durable trees were cut and brought in from the mainland on boats. These Oak sticks were then pounded into the marsh until they reached a solid footing. In addition, they were positioned very close to each other and lashed together to make what we would now call a pylon (piling). Flat boards were placed on these pylons to spread the weight needed to carry the load. Bricks were laid on top of these boards until a foundation was created. The

An Alternative to the Escorted Tour

Venetians then bridged together each little island they created to form canals between them.

Now mind you, like Rome, Venice was not built in a day, a month, or even a year. It took several hundred years to make it into what it is now.

WHAT TO DO IN VENICE

You will need a minimum of two full days in Venice, better would be three full days or a week. There is much to do here, even in the off-season.

Days 10, 11, and 12
Here are the must-dos:
  Vaporetto trip down the Grand Canal
  Shopping at Rialto Mercato
  At San Marco Piazza:
    Visit the Basilica of San Marco
    Visit the Doges Palace/Bridge of Sighs
    Visit the Campanile
    A café in the Piazza San Marco
    A gondola ride for 45 minutes
       not allowed on the Grand Canal
  If you have an extra half day- The Peggy Guggenheim
   Extra day trips:
      Morano, Burano, and Torcello
      The Lido- No visit during November-March

HOW TO GET TO VENICE

If you are traveling from Florence, there are high-speed, Frecci and Italo trains every hour or two. The journey takes about two hours and thirty minutes from Florence, and costs $35-40. If you are starting your Italy visit and flying into VCE- Marco Polo Airport, you need to take the shuttle bus to the Piazzale Roma as there is no rail service from the airport to the central rail station known as Santa Lucia (Venice SL). If you are not staying in the

Lagoon but in "Mestre" (rhymes with pastry), on the mainland, the bus will let you off opposite the Venice Mestre rail station. From here, you should be able to walk to your hotel in Mestre, as many of them are only 1-4 blocks from the rail station.

If you are flying into Venice, booking hotels in or around San Marco Piazza is best. All the buses and taxis stop at the Piazzale Roma as they can go no further. If you have booked a hotel around the train station in the Cannaregio district, all you need do is go to your left after you exit the train station. There are just a few small bridges of 4-8 steps up and 4-8 steps down. These few steps should not present a problem.

NAVIGATING YOUR WAY AROUND VENICE

The Lagoon is almost like one of those corn mazes during the Fall in the USA. It is one mind-boggling maze. However, the Venetians of today are smart. So you will notice at all street corners (or alley corners) a sign pained in black indicating which way to the Ferrovia (rail station), San Marco, and to the Rialto Bridge. Try not to get confused. There are several ways around this maze to your destination. Just follow the signs. When in doubt, follow any sign. Trust me; it will get you to either of the three major locations.

>>>TIP<<<
Note, Seniors have no reason to go down all those steps in front of the rail station and take an unexpected fall. On exiting the train tracks, immediately go to your left on the way to the toilets, and you will see an exit. Exit the track area, and you will be on a ramp that will bring you down to the Grand Canal. You are now in Venice,-- and you need to get to your hotel. Here's how. By the way, best to grab that Euro now and use the facilities before leaving the station.
>>><<<

159

An Alternative to the Escorted Tour

SELECTING A HOTEL IN VENICE OR MESTRE

While you can apply all my selection criteria to anyone visiting Venice, I have tailored it to Seniors. First, some geography about Venice. If you look at a map of Venice, it looks like a coupler they use in railroading to connect two cars. You can also look at it as an open wrench. In summary, best to describe it as two interlocked hands. The main lagoon complex is composed of six districts or Sestieris.

These six districts have their mayors. Cannaregio is where the Santa Lucia train station is (also known on all the signs as the Ferrovia (way of the iron). If you want to stay close to the locals and don't want to do a lot of walking over big bridges (20 steps up and 20 steps down), Cannaregio is the place. It is also home to the Jewish Quarter.

The district, known as San Marco, is home to St. Mark's Basilica, the Doge's Palace, The Campanile (that big red brick tower), The Rialto Bridge, and of course, St. Marks Piazza. St. Marks is also home to the gondola fleet. And yes, if you want to take a gondola ride, you will have to get one in front of the Hotel Danieli (actually on the border of San Marco and Castello), where most of the Gondoliers hang out. More later on this.

San Polo is the smallest of the districts. It shares its fame with the western side of the Rialto bridge.

The Dorsoduro district is home to several well-known art galleries, of which the Peggy Guggenheim is the most visited. I will bet you didn't know there was a Guggenheim in Venice.

Castello is on the far eastern side of the historic district. It is a mix of one side of tourists and hotels and the other side of the locals. It is worth a stroll if you have an extra hour or two.

The sixth Sestieri is the transportation hub (non-rail) of the historic district. This is the home to the Piazzale (another word for plaza) Roma, where the causeway terminates. It is also home to the terminus of the local buses which go to Mestre and other places on the mainland, including the airport bus. Also of importance is the original car park. However, a monster garage was recently built on one of the abutting piers (at Tronchetto). Hopefully, you will not need any of this information since you will be arriving by train or flying into Venice Marco Polo Airport. If you are driving it is best to compare parking prices at Tronchetto or one of the parking lots in Mestre.

By the way, don't look for those big modern American-style hotels in Venice. You will find only a few, if any, in the Lagoon area. However, because hotels can have elevators and be built on solid ground instead of marsh, you will find them in Venice Mestre. We are now ready to find our hotel.

First, here are some quickies on selecting any hotel in the Lagoon. It is best that you follow my recommendations below. However, for Seniors, this is your best bet if you are not staying in the Cannaregio district abutting the train station. Here is the alternative: Instead, on coming down that long ramp from the train station, look to your right; and spot those porters in the sky blue outfits with those hand trucks. They are here, if you wish, to take you to your hotel if you care not to port your bags or don't know where your hotel is located in the big maze.

>>>TIP<<<
You must discuss the fixed price (including the Vaporetto fees for you and the porter). You can purchase the Vaporetto tickets at the Grand Canal's yellow and black booths (ACTV) just in front of the rail station. Remember, you still may have to walk across that humongous bridge known as the Ponte Degli Scalvi bridge. If you are going to hotels in and around San Marco (see my table below), you will need to take the Vaporetto anyway and will not have

161

An Alternative to the Escorted Tour

to cross the Degli Scalvi bridge. By the way, those Vaporetti (Waterbuses) tickets are not cheap. You can take any combination of Vaporetti for 75 minutes (except the Lido) after you validate it for 7.5 Euros on the boat. So you can figure without the porter fee (which is tariffed, so you really can't haggle), it will cost you about $25. The porter will take you to the Black and Yellow booth and instruct you to purchase the tickets for him and others in your party. The porter fee will run another $40-50. You will have to pay in Euros as no credit cards are accepted. Guys, take it from me; this is not the time to show your other half you are a "hero." Let the porter do the schlepping! You will be glad you did.

A private water taxi from the rail station is not cheap. If you are fortunate, you can arrange a private water taxi to pick you up in front of the train station. However, ensure they will port your bags into your selected hotel. You can figure about $100-$200 for this service.
>>><<<

>>>TIP<<<
If you are flying in or out of Venice, you should also check out the water taxis, which will come directly to the airport (there are several slips) and take you to your hotel. However, bear in mind that this is pricey but the least stressful. Also, some water-taxi transfers are "shared," so be advised that the taxi may make several stops before yours. Best to ask if it will be private or shared. It is also the fastest from the airport to your hotel. One such firm is www.motoscafivenezia.it. I believe they are all tariffed, so there is no price negotiation.
>>><<<

162

ITALY Made Easy for Seniors

For all Seniors who have mobility challenges, i.e., walking up twenty-five steps and down another twenty-five steps, I recommend staying in the Cannaregio district, which is directly to your left as you exit that ramp on your left from the station. This way, you do not have to cross the Grand Canal (over the Ponte Degli Scalvi bridge) or cart your bags on a Vaporetto down the Grand Canal. There will be plenty of times to take the Vaporetto completely down the Grand Canal for many photo ops.

Here are the closest hotels to the rail station. Note they are all on the left-hand side of the station (as you walk toward the Grand Canal), about 2-5 blocks. Several are also in the Jewish Quarter, which is excellent if you are a Sabbath observer or enjoy Kosher food. And further, don't worry about hearing those trains. They don't make any noises when they are parked at the station.

CANNAREGIO HOTELS –NEAR THE TRAIN STATION, NO NEED TO CROSS THE PONTE DEGLI SCALVI

NH Venezia Lucia	Hotel Abbazia	Hotel Belle Epoque	Hotel Nazionale
Hotel il Mercante di Venezia	Hotel Amadeus	Hotel Marte	Hotel Universo e Norde
Hotel Bellini	Hotel Antica Casa Carettoni	Hotel Agli Artisti	Hotel Santa Chiara at Piazzale Roma

The Cannaregio district is quaint, with many small hotels and lots of restaurants, etc. For Seniors, there are; however, small bridges. Most of them are 4-6 steps over smaller canals.

If you want to go to San Marco, you can easily hop a Vaporetto at the Santa Marcuola stop and exit at one of the two San Marco stops (both start with the words San Marco).   Likewise, if you are going to the Rialto area, you can exit the Vaporetto at "Rialto" (not Rialto Mercato) and avoid climbing the Rialto bridge. This is another huff and puffer. If you are just going to the Rialto Market exit the waterbus (Vaporetto) at the Rialto Mercato. It's an easy flat walk to San Marco from the Rialto stop. Please see my write-up on the details of the Vaporetto system.

An Alternative to the Escorted Tour

The Vaporetto down the Grand Canal zig-zags back and forth between stops on each side.

If you are staying at one of the hotels around San Marco and if you have luggage, you have three options. First, hire a porter, as I described above.   Second, do it yourself, i.e., buy a ticket for 75 minutes and get that Number 1 Vaporetto and exit at either the San Marco Valarresso or the San Marco Giardinetti, or skip the Vaporetto, lug those bags over that monster bridge (the Ponte Degli Scalvi) then cut across to your hotel. I don't recommend this final option for Seniors unless you have only carry-on bags.

In addition to the monster bridge, you will have to negotiate about a dozen smaller bridges, not to mention that most of the walkways are only eight feet wide. I would strongly suggest you use my second option or, better, go for it with option one and that porter. If you want to schlep your bags (option 2), it's best to email your hotel and ask them, "what is the closest Vaporetto stop on the #1 Line"?

HOTELS AROUND SAN MARCO PIAZZA

Hotel Saturnia & International	Hotel Al Ponte Sospiri	Hotel Concordia	Hotel Casa Nova
Hotel Firene	Hotel do Pozzi	Hotel Flora	Hotel San Moise
Hotel Torino	Hotel dell Opera	Hotel bell Sito e Berlino	Palazzo del Giglio
Royal San Marco Hotel	Ambassador Trerose	San Marco Palace	Antico Panada

>>>TIP<<<

The Vaporetto lines are complex. For example, #2 is an express and bypasses every other stop on the Grand Canal except the popular ones, i.e., Rialto, Ferrovia, San Marco, and Piazzale Roma. The best when you have some time is to load your smartphone with a three or four-day pass. It may still work out if you are in Venice for two or three days. All you need do is hold it up to that funny meter when you enter the boat, and you will get 75 minutes without the

164

need for validation of a paper ticket. Just purchase your electronic ticket online.
>>><<<

You can see more comments below on using the Vaporetti.

STAYING IN VENICE MESTRE

Here is a discussion on staying in the mainland section of Venice, known as Venice Mestre. Mestre is not in the lagoon area. There are many reasons people stay here. For one thing, you are out of all those crowds and day-trippers visiting Venice. Did you know the population of Venice is 50,000 at night and 250,000 during the day? You can go into Venice any time you want since there are trains every 20 minutes from Venice Mestre to Venice Santa Lucia station, and it's only one Euro.

Mestre has over twenty hotels, all within a five-minute walk of the station. All buses from the airport make a stop in front of the Mestre rail station. You don't have to cart your bags up and down all those bridges. In addition, if there is an "Acqua Alta" (see below), you won't have to worry about slogging through all that water and living with wet shoes for the balance of your trip.

>>>TIP<<<
In 2015, the new T1 Tram Line opened between Mestre and the Piazzale Roma. The T1/T2 Tramline has two branches in the Mestre section of Venice. It now opens the possibility of staying at an additional twenty accommodations, many with free parking. Note- It does not stop at the Mestre Rail Station. More information can be found at:
https://actv.avmspa.it/en/content/tram
>>><<<

An Alternative to the Escorted Tour

VENICE MESTRE HOTELS ON LAND SIDE OF THE LAGOON, NEAR VENICE "MESTRE" RAIL STATION

Hotel Plaza	Campanile Venice Mestre	Hotel Regil	Hotel Trieste
Quality Hotel del Fino	Hotel Aaron	Ecohotel Villa Costanza	Hotel Mundial
Hotel Villa Serena	Alla Bianca	NH Venezia Laguna Palace	Hotel Ville Adele
Hotel Adria	Best Western Tritone	Hotel Roberta	Best Western Bologna

In the past, we have found the Plaza Hotel to be the best hotel opposite the Mestre rail station. It is a four-star American-style, very reasonable hotel with an excellent breakfast. However, in the Mestre section there are other four-star hotels which require a short bus ride to the Piazzale Roma as they are not close to the Mestre rail station. There is paid parking in most of them.

On the negative side, I have always found that there are not a lot of restaurants around the Mestre rail station or even a 5-6 block walk. There are many coffee shops and light "eateries" in the hotels. So best if you are up to it, after that nap, go back into the Lagoon for dinner and view all of Venice at night, especially San Marco's square. If you want to take it easy, you have one of the best seafood and fish restaurants 10 minutes away; see my tip.

>>>TIP<<<

There is one restaurant that rates a "10" across the board. It is so good and reasonable that our tours used it for two dinners when we were in Venice. "Ristorante Bepi Venesian" is located directly behind the Plaza Hotel off that small park in Venice Mestre (not in the lagoon). It's a 10-minute walk from the Plaza Hotel or the rail station. "Bepi Venesian" is run by three brothers. You cannot beat the fresh fish dishes. In addition, all dinners are served with crusty bread and, oh, those olives. To find it, all you need do is walk up Via Piave and take a right at the first

166

ain street (Via Sernaglia) until you come to the end of that park. You will find the "Bepi" one block up. >>><<<

** DAY 10 TRAIN OR AUTO TO VENICE

ARRIVAL VENICE HALF DAY- ORIENTATION
DOWN THE GRAND CANAL, RIALTO MERCATO, RIALTO BRIDGE AND THE PIAZZA SAN MARCO

The best approach is to take a train from Florence at about 10AM or earlier, without sacrificing that wonderful Italian buffet breakfast. You can figure out your train arrival time in Venice, or Venice Mestre will take another hour to find your hotel, check-in, and grab a light bite. Let's face it, as usual, when you arrive at your hotel at about noon, your room probably will not be ready. So best to check your bags with the desk clerk and head on out.

If you are staying around the Mestre rail station, you must walk to the train station (about 1-3 blocks) and buy a ticket to Venice from one of those red machines. They will take your credit cards. You cannot board a Frecci, Italo, or the Orient Express, only local trains. You need not worry, as the conductor will not let you board anyway. Make sure you validate your ticket at one of the machines on the platform. Once boarding the train; in about twelve minutes, you will arrive at Venice Santa Lucia station. Make sure you hold on to that ticket, as the ticket collector will inspect it for validation.

DOWN THE GRAND CANAL-VENICE ORIENTATION

On the first day in Venice, it's best to get a "feel" for the City. So after arrival at Venice Santa Lucia station or the Piazzale Roma it is best to head down to the closest Vaporetto stop and buy a ticket. All the single-ride tickets are the same price, except for the multi-day passes. For 75 minutes of travel, it will cost you 7.50 Euros. And yes, that black and yellow ticket booth at the Vaporetto stop will take your credit cards. If possible, I suggest returning to the Santa Lucia (Ferrovia) train station Vaporetto

An Alternative to the Escorted Tour

stop unless you are closer to another stop. The Piazzale Roma also has a Vaporetto stop. Get your 75-minute ticket and catch a Number 1 Vaporetto. Make sure it is heading toward Rialto Mercato. It will probably zig-zag back and cross the Grand Canal. Take photos as you go down the canal, and be prepared to exit at Rialto "Mercato." Note, for Seniors, I said Mercato. There are two stops. You want the Mercato stop. You do not want to get off at the Rialto stop. This will force you to go over the Rialto Bridge. You will have a chance to cross this bridge on your way to San Marco.

You can shop to your heart's content if you get off at Rialto Mercato. Also, you should note that there are public facilities here; however, ensure you have that one Euro coin with you.

>>> VERY IMPORTANT TIP <<<
There are two items to note on your first Vaporetto trip. You need to validate your ticket in that little green or yellow machine on the boat or the pier, and secondly, you need to be real street savvy. Watch out for strangers who may bump against you and force you to part with your wallet.
Be extra cautious of who you stand next to.
>>><<<

It should be about 3-4PM before you are ready to take a short walk, about three football fields over to Piazza San Marco. You won't have too much time here. There are several ways through the Venice maze to get to San Marco. You can follow the crowd. If you think you are lost, look at those black-painted signs on the corners of the buildings.

First, you must cross the Grand Canal by going over the Rialto Bridge with your back toward the Mercato. Halfway over the bridge, there are great photo ops. Just don't drop your camera or smartphone in the Canal. Also, if you want a nice photo op, ask another tourist to take a picture. Don't ask a stranger. Now, continue over the bridge, and as you exit, take the pathway to the right (Pescaria S. Bartolomio), passing the Rialto Vaporetto stop. You should note that if you go over the Rialto bridge and go toward your left, it will dead-end and you will be forced to turn around and backtrack. Sort of like one of those corn mazes. Continue following the crowd, and if you don't make any shopping, pastry, or gelato stops, you should arrive in San Marco in about fifteen minutes. There are several small bridges to negotiate, no big deal.

After arriving in Piazza San Marco, you will understand why I say Venice is one giant maze. Just follow those painted black signs on the corners of the buildings.

On arrival in Piazza San Marco, you will only have time to acquaint yourself with the area. On your left, as you enter the Piazza (assume you are walking in from the Rialto area), you will notice the Basilica San Marco and the Doge's Palace to the right. The Doges were the kings who ruled the Venetian City state.

Directly in front of you at the foot of the lagoon (the Piazzetta San Marco area), you will note two large columns with statues on top (part of the Colonna di San Todaro). Moving to your right, you will note the Campanile, that very tall red brick tower. And, finally, as you move further to the right, you can take in the full Piazza of San Marco. Note that this is where you came into the Piazza; through that arch is the famous clock tower. Those two little "knockers" come out every hour and hit that big bell. So do not confuse this with the massive clock on the top of the red brick tower in the square known as the San Marco Campanile.

>>>TIP<<<
There are public toilets in the Rialto Marcato. You should find them relatively clean from my last trip over there. Be advised that each person will need a Euro for entry. There is usually a coin changer next to the turn styles. Those Euros pay for the matron or

169

the attendant to keep the place clean, the toilet paper, and the paper towels. Great idea. To locate them, spin your head around, and you should see some signs. When in doubt, "Doe Vay et Toilet?"
>>><<<

>>>TIP<<<
Italy is a little advanced regarding cleanliness at the supermarket, or the fruit stands. You cannot pick up fruit or vegetables with your hands or even feel them with your fingers! Either the vendor will select them and place the product on the scale, or you must put on a plastic glove. Makes sense!
>>><<<

There will probably not be enough time to visit any of the sites. However, if there is a very small line you might want to visit for a few minutes the ornate Basilica of San Marco. Best approach is to take a lot of photos and shop the square. By the way, it is now illegal to feed those pigeons and seagulls in Saint Mark's square. If you are caught doing it, there is a hefty fine.

>>>TIP<<<
If one of those pigeons or gulls does a number on you, do not attempt to wipe it off. You need to let it dry, and dry hard. Then with a credit card (I'm assuming the one you rarely use), brush it off. You may want to consider this a sign of good luck and purchase one of those lottery (lotto) tickets from a tobacco stand or one of those folks selling them on the street. Good luck.
>>><<<

After a snack or a gelato, it is best to make your way back to your hotel. If you are in the San Marco area, it should be a short walk back to your hotel. If you are staying in Mestre or near the rail station you need to take the Vaporetto back. Since it's late in the

170

day, the best approach is to get the #1 Vaporetto going in the opposite direction and exit at the Ferrovia (rail station). Also, note that it may go the opposite way, i.e., toward the Piazzale Roma (where the buses and taxis arrive). Try not to panic. The next stop will be Ferrovia. If you are inclined to get, some last-minute exercise go back through that arch with the clock on top and make your way to the Rialto bridge. Cross the bridge and follow the signs to the Ferrovia. You will also need to cross that big bridge near the rail station (the Ponte Degli Scalvi bridge). Note for Seniors with severe mobility issues; you might find this far too stressful. From either stop at Saint Mark's, it would be best to take the Vaporetto #1 back to Ferrovia. Then, you won't have to climb up and down the Ponte Degli Scalvi bridge.

If you are into walking and do not care to cross those two bridges, you can take a leisurely walk through the Cannaregio district. The best is to make your way over to the base of the Rialto Bridge (not the Mercado side). Don't climb those steps. Instead, locate about two blocks before the base a wide alley and go directly toward the Burger King (don't laugh). The BK is after that first small canal bridge. Then find through the maze the Strada Nova. Trust me; you probably will get lost several times. Not a problem; a lot to see. Just keep asking those locals, "Doe Vay et Ferrovia" and hope they point you in the correct direction. Also, if you are seeing the sun setting you are going toward the rail station. The Strada Nova will bring you to the Jewish Quarter and then the rail station.

** DAY 11

DAY TWO IN VENICE

This day should be a full one. I assume you made that Vaporetto trip down the Grand Canal, shopped at the Rialto Market, crossed the Rialto Bridge, and did the San Marco orientation. So here we go with Day 2 in Venice.

171

An Alternative to the Escorted Tour

Best to take a gondola ride before lunch. Make your way over to San Marco Piazza. It would be best if you arrived 10-11AM. Head directly to the Gondola parking area in front of the Danieli Hotel. It's on the Riva Degli Schiavoni Strada, which parallels the Grand Canal. Take a 40-minute gondola ride. See below for just how to do it.

>>>TIP<<<
Those gondolier rides are tariffed. They all charge the same rates, which the City of Venice approves. For a 40-minute ride, the charge, say, is 150 Euros. So if there are two in the gondola, you will be charged 150 Euros. However, if you get three more, to make it five (maximum per new regulations), the cost will still be 150 Euros. So the best is getting three other people who want to share the fee, and each would pay 30 Euros.

You should know the following: First, you can't haggle on the price. Second, they don't take credit cards; third, they are not compelled to find three other people for you. So, best you arrive and meet some "friends" who want to join you. BTW, the maximum now is five people in the gondolier because the gondoliers were complaining that the people were getting too fat (yes, this is not a joke), and for safety concerns, six was too much weight for the gondola. And as stated before, they don't go in the Grand Canal for the standard gondola ride.
>>><<<

After your gondola ride, it should be time for lunch. Lunch in this area is an easy one. As you exit the gondola mooring area, directly next to the Hotel Danieli is an alley (pathway) known as Degli Albanesi. Go down this alley for almost three blocks, and on your left, you will find #4250, The Taverna

Dogi. You can't beat the food, the price, and the service. After lunch, you are ready to visit the other sites in the San Marco area. By the way, avoid the restaurants and bars directly on the Grand Canal (Riva Degli Schiavoni Strada), they define the word "Very Pricey." A glass of wine and bottle of water will be cost $30. The waiter however, will take your picture with a background of the Grand Canal.
>>><<<

>>>TIP<<<
I always recommend a tour of the Doge's Palace and the Basilica in Piazza San Marco. You probably won't be able to get in. So the best is to look online and buy those timed-tickets on Tripadvisor, about a month or two before the date you wish to visit. It will be time spent well. The Doge's Palace is one big museum with painted ceilings and walls; the likes you have never seen. I should note that you can always cancel on Tripadvisor 24 hours prior and receive a full refund. In addition to the Doge's Palace and the Basilica, you need to view the "Bridge of Sighs." This, supposedly, is the most romantic bridge in Venice, connecting the Doge's Palace with the prison next door. The bridge was built in 1600. The best view is from the bridge over the Riva Degli Schiavoni Strada.
>>><<<

If you are still not tired after this point, your next and final stop should be that massive red brick tower known as the Campanile di San Marco. There is usually no waiting at the end of the day or early when it opens up; see below.

173

An Alternative to the Escorted Tour

THE CAMPANILE
Yes, it's a bell tower. However, before becoming a bell tower, the Campanile was a watch tower. The belfry was added in the 20th century. And get this: it collapsed in 1902. What you see is the reconstruction effort of 1912. If you want to bring home an interesting souvenir, see if you can locate the black and white photo of the bell tower as a pile of brick rubble. The original tower was built in 1514. It is one of the symbols of Venice.

The bells were rung to announce the start of the workday, the end of the day, an execution, meeting commencement of the city fathers, and other functions. The tower now stands 323 feet tall. At its base, it is 120 feet wide. On the top of the Campanile is a gold weather vane in the form of Gabriel, the angel. There is a charge of ten Euros to enter the tower, which includes your elevator fee. More at: http://www.basilicasanmarco.it/?lang=en. Tickets run 10-13 Euros, depending on where you purchase them. In the off-season, you should not have any problem purchasing them on-site. The best time is probably first thing in the morning. Check opening times. This is absolutely the best place to take pictures of the entire City.

THE ACQUA ALTA
Mainly in the winter, many of the walkways, alleys, piazzas, etc., become flooded. In addition, most of the canals overflow into the basements of the abutting buildings. There are several reasons for this:
1. The weather, rain, and wind will elevate the water level in the lagoon.
2. A very high tide is predicted on certain days. In addition, cruise ships and oil tankers heading for the industrial port of Marghera will also raise the water level in the lagoon. The railroad and the motorway causeways have also done a number on displacing water in the lagoon.
3. As we all know, the City of Venice is sinking.

174

The sinking is only a few millimeters a year. All of this contributes to the Acqua Alta problem. However, Venice is partially protected for the time being.

When the "Tide Monitoring and Forecast Center" realizes that an Acqua Alta is about to occur, they notify the inhabitants of the City via text message and sirens. At the same time, 79 massive barriers are raised near the three lagoon entrances. It takes about an hour or two to raise them with compressed air. The lagoon is then sealed off, and only a minimal amount of water will raise the level in San Marco Piazza.

When the Acqua Alta occurs, an army of city workers in yellow raincoats and boots erects plywood walkways around certain areas. The areas in and around Piazza San Marco, abutting the Grand Canal, are usually hit hard. It's not uncommon for the water to rise 100 cm (39 inches) or more and come ashore. The Acqua Alta may last anywhere from 12-24 hours or more.
You can check the website: https://www.moseveneqia.eu/

>>>TIP<<<
The best tip I can suggest (even if in doubt) is to pack in your luggage a few of those heavy-duty black contractor bags you can buy at Home Depot or Lowes. Please don't rely on all those boards to be placed exactly where you want to go; they won't be. In addition, you will need a few quarter by 3-inch rubber bands. If an Acqua Alta materializes (the front desk will know), all you need to do is borrow a pair of scissors from the front desk, cut two black bags down to knee height, pull them up over your shoes and legs like boots, and run those rubber bands over them like a garter.

Secondly, the Cannaregio district (the one to the left of the rail station as you come down that ramp) usually does not flood. Best to check the City's

An Alternative to the Escorted Tour

website. And yes, the Vaporetti do run when there is
an Acqua Alta.
>>><<<

EXTRA DAYS IN VENICE
--THE LIDO

If you have extra days to spare and are visiting Venice from April
through October, consider an afternoon on the Lido. I discussed
the Lido in depth at the beginning of this chapter. For Seniors,
there is lots of flat walking, shopping, and of course, a nice lunch
at one of the outdoor cafes. If you are of the Jewish Faith, you
might want to visit an ancient Jewish cemetery that dates from
1386. It is known as the Jewish Cemetery at San Nicolo. You will
find it only one block to the left, as you exit the Vaporetto stop.

--THE ISLAND OF MURANO

There are three islands worth visiting, or at least one. They are
Murano, Burano and Torcello. If you can only spare a half-day,
I would favor Murano. There is also enough time for a whole day
here. It would be best if you figured arriving about 11AM and
departing about 4PM. There are seven small connecting islands.

It won't cost you a penny to go to Murano. You can check with
your hotel concierge, the internet, or with one of the small glass
shops around the Piazza San Marco. It's simple. A boat takes you
over to the island (it's about a mile away), drops you off, and
picks you up later in the day. The boats run approximately every
hour. Hopefully, you will purchase some of the glass as a
souvenir. This is how they make their money. However, it's a free
ride even if you purchase nothing.

If you wish, you can take one of the Vaporetti over and back to
the island. The Vaporetti depart the San Zaccaria stop about
every hour, costing about two Euros. San Zaccaria is one of the
Piazza San Marco stops. Also, that same Vaporetto goes on to

176

Burano. You should check the ATCV schedules as they change throughout the year.

--BURANO AND TORCELLO
I discuss these two islands in the Lagoon because they are very similar. As for Burano, most tourists go here for a few hours to take pictures of those gorgeous houses on the local lagoons. The main product, in addition to tourism, is hand-woven lace.

Romans settled Burano in the 6th century. Because lace-making was labor intensive, it declined until the 19th century, when it was revived. If you visit Burano, the best souvenirs are the lace doilies and those fantastic photos.

Torcello is the third island in the group. The island was first settled in 452AD. They believe Torcello was the parent island from which Venice was populated. The island even had a cathedral and bishops before there was St. Mark's Basilica. In the 10th century, Torcello had a population of almost 20,000. In pre-medieval times Torcello was a more extensive trading hub than Venice. Its primary product was salt. The black plague and other factors lead to a total decline in the population.

As of 2018, the population was reported at 12 (yes twelve). Most of the material used to build the many palazzi, parishes, and cloisters disappeared as they were recycled to create other structures in Venice. That basilica and the campanile were later rebuilt in 1008. There is also a small museum there. The main attraction is the Cathedral of Santa Maria Assunta. It was founded in 639AD and has many Byzantine works, including mosaics from the 11th and 12th centuries.

Torcello is also home to Attila's Throne (nothing to do with Atilla the Hun) and the "Devil's Bridge," a stone bridge. It is believed the original bridge was built during the 13th century and a new bridge replaced it in the 15th century. As recently as 2009, the bridge received an overhaul. If you go to Torcello, the Cathedral and Campanile, along with the Devil's Bridge, are worth a visit.

--GIUDECCA AND SAN GIORGIO

There are two historic islands across the Lagoon that you may want to visit. They are Giudecca and San Giorgio. However, you won't find a lot of souvenir shops here. These two islands are primarily residential. There is not too much activity on San Giorgio as the church occupies most of it, along with the new Vatican Chapels built in 2013. There are, however, some very historic churches. The best known and often photographed is the Basilica of San Giorgio Maggiore. If you are looking at pictures of Venice, you can't miss this one. The basilica sits on a triangle of land jutting into the Lagoon.

Consider having lunch at one of the many cafes on the island of Giudecca, where you will find the five-star Belmond Cipriani Hotel. You should note that the Island of San Giorgio is not connected to Giudecca. There is no connecting bridge. You must take a Vaporetto about three minutes from one island to the other. So plan your day if you visit the Basilica of San Giorgio and the new Vatican Chapels. BTW there were never any Jewish people who lived in Giudecca (pronounced Ju-decca). The source for the name of this island is unknown. Giudecca is worth a visit for a stroll and lunch in any one of the numerous cafes.

PEGGY GUGGENHEIM MUSEUM

Peggy was the daughter of Benjamin Guggenheim. Benjamin was one of seven sons born to Meyer Guggenheim. As we all know the Guggenheims are right up there with the Carnegies, Rockefellers, Rothschilds, and all the other famous people who made their money around the "gilded age of America," 1870-1900. Peggy's father died on the Titanic in 1912. Her mom was Florett Seligman, who came from a wealthy banking family. In summary, she inherited a lot of money. So what did she do with all this money? Simple, she bought works of art.

ITALY Made Easy for Seniors

Peggy moved to Paris in about 1920. In 1938 she opened a modern art gallery in London. Peggy collected contemporary art at the rate of one piece a day. When WWII ended, she moved everything from the south of France to Venice, where she opened a gallery after purchasing a home on the Grand Canal. It was open to tourists every summer. In 1976, she donated the house and her entire collection to the Solomon G. Guggenheim Foundation of New York. The foundation now owns the museum. It is one of the Guggenheims, just like New York and Bilbao.

The Peggy Guggenheim Museum is worth a visit. It contains originals of all the famous modern artists of our time: Jackson Pollack, Dali, Kandinsky, and more. Over 600 pieces of work mostly range in style from Cubism, Surrealism, and the Abstract school. If you are a lover of art, this is the place.

The current entrance fee is 16 Euros, and it's only 14 Euros if you are a Senior. In the off-season, I believe you can purchase tickets at the museum. However, plan your visit and buy your tickets online to play on the safe side. You should figure a minimum of two hours at the Guggenheim. More information can be found: https://www.guggenheim-venice.it/

If you still have extra days in Venice, read on, as you will find more in the next chapter.

CHAPTER 10

VENICE DAY TRIPS

PADUA AND VERONA

If you have selected more than four days in Venice, you might be interested in two excellent day trips. Padua (often spelled Padova) is about 45 minutes away by train, and Verona is a little over an hour. Both cities offer lots of history. What's nice is the trains are very frequent and extremely inexpensive. I won't steal the thunder on Padua, which I describe below. However, few know about Verona.

Where can you view (and stand on) the actual balcony where Juliet said to Romeo: "Romeo, Romeo, where art thou Romeo?" Yes, it was Verona. Verona has more than just that balcony; given the time, you ought to consider a day trip here since there is more to see and do than the balcony.

Another interesting fact, Shakespeare wrote about seven plays set in Italy: *Romeo and Juliet, The Merchant of Venice, The Taming of the Shrew*, and *The Two Gentlemen of Verona, to name a few.* However, Shakespeare never visited Italy! Figure that one out. It has been a topic of discussion of Shakespeare followers for several hundred years.

PADUA DAY TRIP
If you did not know, Padua is best known as the home of St. Anthony (Antonio). Saint Anthony is the patron saint of lost, stolen, and forgotten items. Padua lies about 25 miles due west of Venice on the Bacchiglione River. The Basilica and the complex are the number one draw to Padua. It is also home to

one of the oldest universities in Italy. If you make it a leisurely day trip, you can plan on arriving about 10AM or 11AM and returning about 6PM for a snooze before dinner at 7:30PM.

I won't go into all the details of Saint Anthony's life, but suffice it to be he was a Franciscan monk, born in 1195 in Portugal, and died in Padua in 1231. He is one of the most famous and revered Saints, right up there with Saint Francis of Assisi.

Padua is one of the oldest cities in Northern Italy, dating from 1138BC. It predates ancient Rome by about 500 years. It is interesting to note that this city, for almost 3,000 years, has gone back and forth under the rule of so many conquerors. Far too many conquerors have invaded Padua, even to mention here. It is probably well over a hundred.

What's important, about 50BC, Padua allied and became a part of the Roman Empire. You can still find Roman ruins in Padua. There are ruins of an amphitheater and bridge foundations. In 899, Padua was sacked by the Magyars. The city had to be rebuilt after the fire in 1174. In 1214 Padua went to war with Venice, which Venice won in 1216.

In medieval times Padua, in the year 1405, came under the rule of the Republic of Venice. This domination by Venice lasted about 400 years until 1797. In 1814 with the fall of Napoleon, the city became part of the Austrian Empire. Under Austrian rule, Padua entered the industrial revolution by laying the first railroad from Venice to Padua in 1845. In 1866, Padua was annexed to the Kingdom of Italy by the Battle of Koniggratz. As Italy was an ally of Prussia, Padua and the Veneto regions cities (Venice, Verona, Vicenza) became Italy.

Padua is an enjoyable day trip from Venice, even if you are driving. Almost all trains bound for the west and south of Venice will stop in Padua. It does not pay to board a "Frecci" with a reserved seat for that 30-minute ride. It will cost you about 20

An Alternative to the Escorted Tour

Euros. The best way is to take a local train from Mestre or Venice SL for about 5-10 Euros. Remember to validate your ticket in that small red, yellow or green machine on the platform—also, no need to purchase tickets before you go.

On arrival in Padua, it's a little more than a mile to the Basilica of St. Anthony. I would not suggest the walk even though it is all flat. It is much faster to take a taxi from the rail station. It will cost you about five Euros. You are lucky because in the same area is the old square (Piazza del Santo) and "The Prato della Valle" along with the University. Here you will find lots of shops, eateries and the like.

If you are walking to St. Anthony's, you might want to visit the Scrovegni Chapel and the associated museum. The chapel has exquisitely painted frescoes on the walls and ceilings. These paintings are one of the highlights of the fresco artworks of the 14th century.

The "Chapel" is en route to St. Anthony's. You can view the chapel paintings only on Mondays. However, it is also available with a combination ticket for the museum on all other days. If you need to purchase a timed ticket (not advisable in the off-season), plan to visit 30-45 minutes after your train arrives from Venice. You can also take your luck at grabbing a ticket for time slots later in the day.

On arrival at St. Anthony's, I suggest first viewing this magnificent Basilica and then the tomb of St. Anthony. The Basilica took about 78 years to complete (1232-1310). It's a combination of Romanesque, Byzantine, and Turkish designs. It is unique, and you would never think this beautiful structure is a church.

Then after a light lunch, proceed less than a football field (a two-minute walk) to The Orto Botanico di Padova. This is the oldest botanical garden known. It was founded in 1545 by the then-

182

ITALY Made Easy for Seniors

Venetian Republic to cultivate herbs and unique plants for healing. It is still in its original location and is part of the University of Padua.

Statuary adorns most of the botanical garden. It is just a stone's throw from St. Anthony's. It is definitely worth a minimum of a one-hour visit. Tickets are about 10 Euros. You can find more information at: www.ortobotanicopd.it/it/biglietti.

Also, just a quick note, you will find the facilities to the right of the entrance, about 100 feet near those gardens. And yes, remember to have that Euro handy.

Within a stone's throw of the botanical gardens is the "Prato della Valle ." This is the largest square in Italy and one of the largest in all of Europe. It is unique because it is not a square. It occupies about 900,000 square feet (about 22 acres) and is oval. A trough or canal runs through it. Or shall I say within it?

The "ill Prato," as they call it, is the central gathering point for concerts and other festive events. Here is a quick history.

The Prato was a swampy area used for horse riding events, i.e., jousting in medieval times. The monks of Santa Giustina owned it. The city of Padua purchased it in 1767. There are a total of 78 statues in the inner and outer rings. They are originals carved by artists of the area. All are carved from stone mined in nearby Vicenza. All this work was accomplished between 1775 and 1883. Most statues are of local politicians of Padua, Popes, and famous people of the Venice and Padua area. However, you won't find any Michelangelo or Da Vinci sculptures here. This is an excellent spot for picture-taking.

If you are up to walking and care not to visit the botanical gardens of Padua, you might enjoy a leisurely lunch in the Piazza Dei Signori. There are numerous places around the Piazza and en route from St. Anthony's.

183

An Alternative to the Escorted Tour

As a point in passing, I should note that a canal connects Padua with Venice. In season, there are daily sailings between the two cities. However, with the tours of the abutting mansions, you will have very little time to view the highlights of Padua. If you are staying a week in Venice, this day tour on the Brenta Canal makes another excellent day trip to Padua. My suggestion, of course, is to take the train back to Venice. More can be found on the internet.

VERONA DAY TRIP

While Venice represents medieval times and the Renaissance, Verona is a mix of history. On entry to the city, you are thrown back into Roman times. Verona lies on the banks of the Adige River about 75 miles west of Venice, on the way to Milan, and is surrounded by hills. For Seniors, Verona is a city made for walking; it is all flat.

Ask anyone who has visited Verona, and they will tell you "Romeo and Juliet" and that "big stadium" like the Colosseum in the center of the town. Here is a quick history of Verona:

Little is known about the early history of Verona. We know that the area became Roman in about 300BC and officially became a Roman colony 49BC. The city became important because it was at the intersection of several crossroads to the other cities in the area, i.e., Milan, Venice, Florence, and the towns north of the Italian Alps. The city went back and forth between several powers in the area until King Alboin of the Lombards took it in 569AD. That's about 100 years after Rome fell.

The Holy Roman Empire took over Verona under Austrian control. In 1135 Verona became a free community and integrated into the Lombard League. Many wars continued into the middle ages. And, of course, the black plague of 1346-1353 took a toll on the population.

184

In 1260 the "Della Scalas" rose to power, and the arts and architecture flourished in Verona. Mansions of the wealthy were built. The Della Scalas were also responsible for building the Castelvecchio. If you have extra time you might want to consider visiting the Castle. Castelvecchio is a humongous castle on the banks of the Adige River. It is now a museum. In 1405, Verona became part of the Republic of Venice. It became home to more wealthy merchants as trade flourished. Finally, in 1866, Verona became part of the Kingdom of Italy. The entire city is also a UNESCO World Heritage Site.

WHAT TO SEE AND DO IN VERONA

Verona is the second largest city in the Veneto region, second only to Venice. In 89BC it was a Roman settlement. Most of the history of the City is wrapped up in its medieval past. Parts of the medieval wall and its gates remain.

By now, it should be evident that the home of Juliet "Casa di Giulietta" is a must to see. The actual balcony is located at Via Cappello 23. Note- Parking is difficult in the area, and there are few paid parking lots. If you are coming by train, you need to hop in a taxi for a 2.5-mile ride to Juliet's house. Also, watch out for BnB's name Juliet House or something similar. Using this location may lead you to the wrong place.

William Shakespeare (the Bard) wrote Romeo and Juliet in 1597. To put things in perspective, that's only 23 years before the Mayflower dropped anchor in Plymouth, Massachusetts. As the Bard wrote, the 13th-century house belonged to the Cappelletti family, not the Capulets. The small balcony where supposedly Juliet uttered the words "Romeo, Romeo where art thou" was installed on the house in the 20th century. She spoke those famous words from an open window. Also, there was no Juliet. The Bard made it all up. The house of the Cappelletti (not the Capulets) is now a museum with a small entrance charge. I don't know who invented the "balcony scene."

An Alternative to the Escorted Tour

You must now purchase tickets for the Juliet Museum: https://www.museiverona.com/

There is a bronze statue of Juliet under that balcony. The saying goes, if you rub her right breast, you will be blessed with love and fertility. There is a side of the walkway into the courtyard where you can post a note to Juliet. You might want to consider belonging to the Juliet club. You will find it across the street. One of the staff will write a note to Juliet on a piece of old parchment and post it on that wall for you.

There are many gelato shops in the area, and this is a great place to take some photos, especially with your "significant other," friend, or a family member on that balcony.

In case you missed it. As I said, the Bard never visited Verona. So how did he write this masterpiece? No one knows. Now on to the Arena, the number one ancient attraction in Verona.

The Arena was built outside the walls of the City of Verona. It is now inside the walls of the old city. I don't think they moved the Arena. However, best bet is they built a new wall. A ten-minute walk from Giuletta's house will bring you to the Arena. The Arena was built in 30AD, about fifty years before The Colosseum. Since they did not have the term coliseum yet, they called it the Arena. An alternate name could have been the Amphitheater of Verona. Suffice it to be; it's called just the "Arena."

The Arena is about 1.5 football fields in length and a little more than one across. Gladiators fought here, like the Colosseum, for over 400 years until the Roman Emperor Honorius ended the games in 404AD. For over 400 years, the Arena stood empty. At one time, the structure stood four stories until an earthquake in the 12th century caused so much damage the Arena had to be reduced to three stories in height.

ITALY Made Easy for Seniors

The Arena is almost round and held 30,000 people in ancient times. Today because of the stage, it holds about 20,000 people. The façade of the building was decorated in pink limestone from nearby Valpolicella (the extensive wine-producing area).

The earthquake of 1117 almost destroyed the Arena's outer ring. There are vestiges of the outer ring still standing.

Because of its outstanding acoustics, the Arena has been used to host numerous operas since the Renaissance. It continues to this day with about 4-6 production per year. It's worth a visit. However, you should watch the traffic around the Arena.

There are several sites worth seeing in the old or medieval city:

The Piazza Delle Erbe and the Piazza Bra are excellent places to enjoy lunch and shopping.

If you are into medieval castles, consider an hour of viewing at the Castle Vecchio (Castelvecchio) and its bridge across the Adige River. Just look for a castle with a crenellated roof. The castle dates to 1354. You can't miss it. The Castle is on top of a hill. For Seniors, there is some uphill walking to the castle complex. As usual, it is closed on Mondays. There is an admission fee of six Euros.

You may want to visit two of the many medieval churches of Verona. They are the Basilica of San Zeno Maggiore and the Verona Cathedral. These two churches and many others are beautiful examples of the Italian Renaissance. Not only are the exteriors magnificent, but also the interiors.

The largest church is the Basilica of Sant' Anastasia. It is only a five-minute walk from the Piazza Delle Erbe.

The best approach is to visit Juliet's Balcony first, then have lunch in the Piazza Delle Erbe, then walk about three blocks to

An Alternative to the Escorted Tour

the Basilica. The Corso Sant' Anastasia is lined with shops, so best to visit the area on a weekday since many shops may be closed on Sunday. After you see the Basilica, I recommend visiting the Arena if you have not done so. These visits should round out the day.

** BALANCE OF THIS PAGES FOR NOTES **

CHAPTER 11

MILAN AND THE LAKES COMO, MAGGIORE LUGANO GARDA

INTRODUCTION

The lakes of Northern Italy are a must for second-time visitors. If you are on your first trip and have another week available, I recommend spending it in the lakes region. Since the lakes region is above Milan (except for Lake Garda, which is northeast), I suggest flying out of Milan back to the USA or Canada. Plenty of non-stop flights are available with all the major carriers. Also, pricing is quite reasonable since the Milan route to major North American cities is very competitive.

There is a lot to do and see in Milan. For one thing, it is one of the fashion capitals of Europe, second only to Paris. So don't think you need to spend $150 on a pair of shoes! And, unlike Rome, there is something for everyone when it comes to shopping. All of metro Milan is flat. So walking is easy.

Concerning the lakes, there are two ways to visit them. As we all know, checking in and out of hotels is a pain. It consumes time, and you must check your bags until 4PM when the rooms are available. It's a real drag, literally and figuratively. It is far easier and less stressful to base yourself in Milan for about four days and make day trips to three lakes; Como, Stresa, and Lugano. And for Seniors, this means no "schlepping" your bags around, which we all know can do a number on you. On another point, Lake Garda presents a little problem and is best visited with an overnight stay. I will explain later.

189

An Alternative to the Escorted Tour

MILAN AS A BASE

If you base yourself in a hotel around the Milano Centrale rail station, you will find it easier to visit the lakes since you will not have to take a taxi, a tram, or the Metro (Milan's subway) to the Milano Centrale station.

If you are coming in from Venice on a train, you can easily walk 5-10 minutes to your hotel from the central (Centrale) station. Here are some three- and four-star hotels within 2-4 blocks of Milano Centrale:

Hotel Colombia	Ibis Milano Central	Hotel Terminal	Ibis Styles Milano Central
Spice Hotel Milano	Doria Grand Hotel	Windsor Hotel Milano	Hotel Marconi
Inside By Melia Milano	Best Western Hotel City	Canova Hotel	Hotel Bristol
Club Hotel	Hotel Mythos	Hilton Milan	Crowne Plaza Milan
43 Station Hotel	HD8-Hotel Milano	Best Western Madison	Hotel Sperga

DAY TRIP TO LAKE COMO, VARENNA AND BELLAGIO

This town, along with the Cinque Terre and Positano, has become one of Italy's three most photographed towns. Everyone raves about Lake Como, not to mention George Clooney. There are numerous paintings of the homes abutting Lake Como in Varenna and those small walkways along the Lake. These pictures and photographs are why people love Varenna. Oh, sorry, but you won't find any remnants of Roman civilizations. Here's how we get there:

Walk to Milano Centrale and purchase a ticket to the next local train to Varenna-Esino. You do not want to go to "Como" unless you take a whole day cruise with lunch on the Lake. The tourist spots for Lake Como are in Varenna and Bellagio. This is not on the CITY of Como line. The City of Como is on the rail line to Lake Lugano. Do make sure you don't purchase a ticket to Lake Como. You need to buy a ticket to Varenna-Esino.

190

>>>TIP<<<
Do not purchase your rail tickets from the red machines. Go directly to the ticket agent for "Trenitalia-Trenord" (note there is no service on the competitor "Italo.") BTW, Trenord is part of Trenitalia and operates all the local trains in the Piedmont Region. Ask for two round-trip tickets to Varenna-Esino and then ask for the Senior Discount. Yes, there is one. There is a train every 45 minutes. You might want to walk over to Milano Centrale the day before, note the train times, and purchase your tickets. All seats are unreserved as this is a local train. Even though the ride is only 60 minutes, arrive early to grab some munchies to go. Also, you will be required to clear security to gain access to the rail platforms.
>>><<<

>>>TIP<<<
Make sure you sit on the left side of the train as you face the locomotive. The left-hand side will give you lots of photo-ops as Lake Como comes into view about 30 minutes out of Milano Centrale.
>>><<<

When you arrive in Varenna-Esino, note the return times and follow the crowd down those few steps, or for Seniors, better that ramp. You'll see most people walking down to the Lake on that street to your left. It is known as Via Per Esino. In a few blocks, take that left on the major street known as Via Venini, then take the next right on Via Imbarcadero. You will see the Hotel Olivedo on your left in a few hundred feet. You should note that a taxi stand is just in front of the hotel and outside the restaurant. Seniors, you will need this as there is a long and strenuous "hike" back up to the train station. For Seniors, it would be best to take a taxi for five Euros from the ferry terminal to the rail station.

An Alternative to the Escorted Tour

Directly in front of the Hotel Ristorante Olivedo is the ferry slip to Bellagio and other points in the Lake. Leaving the Olievedo and going to your left will bring you into the village of Varenna.

However, before leaving the Olivedo, you need to make some strategic decisions. Should you explore Varenna and have some lunch, or would it be better to take the 15-minute ferry to Bellagio and have lunch there and return to Varenna for shopping in the late afternoon? My feeling is that there is a lot of walking in Varenna. As they say, it's six of one, half a dozen of the other. So I would favor Varenna till you are shopped out, then spend the afternoon having lunch on the Lake next to the ferry terminal or in the village of Varenna. It would be best if you planned to get to Bellagio at about 2-3PM.

CAUTION- Make sure the ferry is going to Bellagio. They all look the same, and some of them go to other points on the Lake. The ferry fare is relatively cheap.

On arrival in Bellagio, in season, you will find a 30-minute tram tour around the town. I don't know if it operates in the winter months. However, it's only ten Euros and certainly worth it.

The ferry terminal and the area around it in Bellagio are all flat. However, a hill area is behind it with many hotels and BnBs. Seniors who are overnighting in Bellagio should look at some of those hotels before booking them. Many of the accommodations are up several flights of stairs, and you won't have to worry about using the hotel fitness room.

There is not much to do in Bellagio unless you have several days. So it is best to enjoy lunch, the shopping and of course gelato.

When you are done for the day, work your way back to the ferry terminal in Billagio and get the ferry going to Varenna and not to some other point on the lake, e.g., Cadenabbia. On arrival in

Varenna, take a taxi for five Euros back to the stazione and return to Milano Centrale via the Trenord train.

DAY TO STRESA (LAKE MAGGIORE)

You probably never heard of Stresa and Lake Maggiore. It does not get the play that Lake Como does. George Clooney does not live here. Ernest Hemingway made Stresa and Lake Maggiore famous in his novel *"A Farewell to Arms"* (1929 by Scribner). Like the other lakes, it was formed in the last ice age about 22,000 years ago. It is a beautiful lake which is part of Italy and Switzerland. Hotels and parks line the shoreline in the village of Stresa and continue three miles up the Corso Umberto to the town of Baveno. BTW, Maggiore means "major".

The major draw to Lake Maggiore, Stresa, and Baveno is the Borromean Islands. There are five islands less than a half mile offshore. Two are worth visiting as the fifth and smallest, "Malghera," contains lush vegetation and a small beach. Isola Madre and Isolino di San Giovanni are the third and fourth islands, only if you have another day to spare. San Giovanni was the home of Arthuro Toscanini, the famous Italian orchestra conductor during the 1930s and 40's this leaves two remaining islands that are a must to visit: Isola Bella and Isola Pescatore (also called Isola Superiore).

Inexpensive combination ferry tickets are sold for departures from Stresa and Baveno to visit each island separately or two (Isola Bella and Isola Pescatore) together. A government authority operates the ferries. You can see both islands in one day with no problem. There are no roads on the islands, only pedestrian walks. The Islands are small, less than two football fields long and about one wide.

If you are driving out to Stresa, you will find a good amount of parking near the ferry terminal. It is all metered and strictly enforced. You can figure at least 90 minutes to get out to Stresa after you get lost and navigate through the Milan traffic. So, I

An Alternative to the Escorted Tour

always advocate the train for a short one-hour journey of about $15 roundtrip. There are trains every hour from Milano Centrale to Stresa and Baveno. And, you don't have to worry about finding a parking space and worrying about that meter.

Just a point in passing. Avoid going to Stresa and the Borromean Islands on a weekend when it is crowded with locals.

Suppose you are looking for a resort-style hotel and have a family. Your best bet is the Hotel Dino in Baveno, within one block of the Baveno ferry terminal, with frequent departures to Stresa and the Borromean Islands. I have personally stayed at this excellent four-star hotel. More information can be found at: www. grand-dino.hotelslakemaggiore.com

If you take the train to Stresa, it is best to exit the station and follow the signs to your right. Take a left on that main street known as "Via Duchessa di Genova" and follow it till you get to the lake, then go right to the ferry terminal. Seniors should note a slight slope (as opposed to an uphill gradient) as "Via Duchessa" goes down to the lake. Seniors should also note that on returning to the Stresa ferry terminal from the Borromean Islands, it would be wise to take a taxi back to the Stresa rail station for about five Euros. Trust me; you will be bushed from walking all day.

You should anticipate arriving at the rail station in Stresa at about 11AM. From here, best to walk to the ferry terminal and purchase a combination (yes, they will take your plastic) ticket to Isola Bella and Isola Pescatore/Superiore. I always advise Seniors to visit Isola Bella first. You can figure with the grounds and the tour of the Palazzo Borromeo it will take about two hours. So, make sure you bring some snacks to munch on since you won't be in Isola Pescatore until around 2PM for lunch.

I should note that there are about six places to grab a bite on Isola Bella. However, you will find many more restaurants and lots of shopping on Isola Pescatori, including even a hotel. You will have a greater selection of eateries if you can hold off the hunger.

Seniors should take note if you want to stay on Isola Pescatore for the night at the Albergo Ristorante Belvedere: I believe the island is shut off late in the evening till sunrise, so if you have any medical conditions which may require emergency attention, best to stay on the mainland.

Here is a quick history of Isola Bella:
The main attraction is the gardens and the palace. There is an entry fee, and well worth it. I cannot tell you how incredible the gardens and the palace are. There is no comparison if you have been to places like the DuPont estate in Wilmington, DE, the Biltmore Estate in Asheville, NC, or any other famous gardens. Both Isola Bella and the smaller Isola Madre (where there is also a small palace) are mentioned in *"1,000 Places To See Before You Die"* by Patricia Schultz. And by the way, there is more to these gardens besides the fauna and flora! It is a MUST-see!

In 1632 Carlo III of the House of Borromeo started construction on a barren island, about four football fields off the shores of Stresa, a palace dedicated to his wife "Isabella" (hence the name of the island is Bella, for the beautiful one.) Construction stopped about 1650. Milan was struct by a plague. Further work started after the plague by Carlo III's sons, Giberto III and Vitaliano VI. However, the gardens were not completed until 1671. Construction continued for almost 400 years.

In the 1800s, the palace hosted Napoleon and Josephine, the Prince of Wales, and others.

In 1935, the palace hosted representatives of Italy, France, and the United Kingdom, resulting in the "Stresa Front."
You should depart the ferry terminal and make your first stop the Isola Bella. If the first stop is Isola Pescatore (Superiore), stay on

An Alternative to the Escorted Tour

the ferry till the next stop. They are less than 10 minutes apart. For Seniors, visiting Isola Bella first is the easiest way to see both islands. It would be best if you went to the ticket booth, bought your tickets, and took a tour of the palace and gardens.

>>>TIP<<<
On exiting the ferry at Isola Bella, ask the attendant (with the white hat) when the next ferries are to Isola Pescatore. He usually carries a card with him and will tell you when ferries are usually in about two hours. Knowing the departure time for Isola Pescatore will give you time to plan your stay on Isola Bella, and, further, you won't wait at the ferry terminal for a long time for the next ferry to Isola Pescatore.
>>><<<

The Isola Pescatore (or Superiore) is just what it is. It is an island of the fisherman and working people. You will find many restaurants, souvenir shops, and other shops selling fine goods here. And, yes, gelato. After lunch, do your shopping and walk around the whole island. Once again, when arriving on the island best to see when the return ferries are to Stresa about 4-5PM.

Some quick facts about Isola Pescatore:
It is just a charming place. As a New Englander, it's very much like Nantucket. Cobblestone streets, shops, and houses line the streets. The island was first occupied in the 10th Century. The chief "industry" was, fishing. There still are fishermen here. However, in the past 70 years, tourism has taken over. If you have a few minutes, visit the church, which dates to the 11th Century.

On arrival back in Stresa around 4-5PM, time permitting, consider taking a walk over to the Grand Hotel Des iles Borromees. Have a drink at the lobby bar and think about how it was for young Hemingway (Frederic Henry) and Catherine

Barkley as they contemplated rowing across Lake Maggiore the following evening to Switzerland. And yes, they did it in the dark of night, it was cold and raining, and would you believe she was pregnant? You will have to read the book (*A Farewell to Arms*) to see how it ended. It was one of Hemingway's best sellers.

>>>TIP<<<
Best to take a taxi back to the rail station. It will cost you about five Euros. You can usually get a taxi at the ferry terminal or better at the Grand Hotel Des iles Borromees. Seniors should remember that the walk back to the station is up a slight grade for about six blocks.
>>><<<

If you are staying overnight in Stresa or Baveno, several other attractions are worth visiting. First, if any of your friends advise you to take that cable car up the mountain in Stresa, it is still closed due to that horrific accident in May 2021 which killed 14. However, it is still possible to hike the mountain the cable car served. It is known as Monttarone. Here you will find breathtaking views of Lake Maggiore.

Fabulous views of the Isola Bella palace and gardens are all lit up at night. Check with the tourist information booth about hiking the mountain. Also, check with the ferry people or the information booth about illumination tours of Lake Maggiore. You will find more information at www.isoleborromee.it

DAY TRIP TO LUGANO
Lugano is in Switzerland, the province or canton known as Ticino. By the way, the abbreviation for Switzerland is "CH ." It does not mean CHeese or CHocolate. It is an abbreviation for Confederation Helvetic, which goes back to 400 BC. Over the years, the confederation of "Cantons" (provinces) decided to keep the abbreviation. While places in Lugano will accept your Euros, the official currency is called the Swiss Franc, abbreviated

An Alternative to the Escorted Tour

CHF. As of this writing in late 2022, the CHF is almost equal to the US dollar. Locals don't use the words Swiss Francs. They just refer to them as Francs.

About one-third of Lake Lugano lies in Italy. There are tiny villages on the Italian side of the Lake. I should note Lake Lugano is the most polluted Lake in Europe. Over the last hundred years, pollution has been caused by dumping untreated septic water into the Lake. Efforts are underway to build pollution control facilities. As of now, no swimming is allowed.

The draw to Lugano is the village and the beautiful Lake. I would only suggest a day trip if you have an extra day to spare and wish to see a small part of Switzerland. There is a train about every hour. However, the cost is high compared with points in Italy. It will cost you about 48 Euros round trip per person. So expect to pay over $100 for two people for the day. The high price is because even though the Italian rail system goes to Switzerland, it is considered an international destination. Therefore, for a one-hour trip, you would be paying almost three times what you would expect to pay for a one-hour journey in Italy.

Lugano can also be reached by car, and it is pretty straightforward. As expected, you can figure more than an hour after you clear out of the Milan traffic. And remember, you may need your passports, so best to take them anyway.

I have been to Lugano twice and can tell you the best time is to get there by 11AM. Going by rail, you will find the stazione on a hill overlooking the town. From here, you take the escalator down to the village. At the base of the escalator on Tuesday and Friday mornings (till 2:30PM), you will find a moderate size outdoor food market consisting of stalls selling everything from cheeses and meats to you name it. My favorites are the baked crusty loaves of bread and, of course, the pastries. There are also nearby cafes so you can fuel up on Cappuccino or, should I say, hot chocolate since we are in Switzerland.

ITALY Made Easy for Seniors

On weekends, there are other flea markets (swap-meets for our California readers), and all are walkable from the train station or the Lake. On a point in passing, you should know that Switzerland is different from most of Europe. A plain croissant may cost you five dollars, and everything else may seem like a lot of money. And it is. However, the labor cost is almost double ours in the USA. So the person serving you that $6 cup of coffee is getting $50,000 a year. In the USA, it would be $3 for the coffee, and the server gets $25,000 a year. It defines the phrase "it's all relative." However, since you are coming from Italy, where things are "normal," expect to pay a lot more in Switzerland.

If you are visiting Lugano outside of the winter months, consider making some sandwiches (or buying them in Italy) and head down to one of the parks on the Lake. Some of the stalls in that Tuesday and Friday market may be able to make a sandwich. Or better, I am sure that they have one of those ham and cheese croissants to go. Do make sure they warm them up.

>>>TIP<<<
If you are having trouble finding a parking space, finding your way to the rail station is best. You will find lots of parking here, and you can take that escalator down to the town.
>>><<<

Before or after you are shopped out, consider going over to the Monte Bre incline. This funicular goes up to the top of Monte Bre for a spectacular view of the Lake. The only problem is that it is located about six miles from town. No problem if you are driving. However, you should check what a taxi driver would take a party of four over to the base station from the rail station, where there are always taxis waiting. More information can be found at: www. Montebre.ch.

An Alternative to the Escorted Tour

A DAY TRIP TO LAKE GARDA

Lake Garda is the largest lake in Italy. It lies between Milan and Venice and north of Verona. The lake covers three provinces of Italy even though it is only 34 miles long and 11 miles wide at its widest point. Parts of the lake and its towns lie in Brescia, Verona, and Trento. While it is also a product of the last ice age of about 25,000 years ago, it is not in the same region as Lake Como, Maggiore, and Lugano. Garda is a region prone to earthquakes, being a seismic "3." The last quake occurred in 2014. I would not worry, as these tremors occur every 100 years.

There are a few towns worth visiting. Several can be seen in one day. If driving or taking the train, get to Desenzano del Garda or Peschiera del Garda. These are only about 90 minutes from Milan. These two towns can also be reached by bus from Milan.

One of the best-known resort towns is Sirmione. It is on the lake's southern bank in the province of Brescia. Like Montecatini Terme, it is home to natural baths. A peninsular of about two miles juts into the lake. This peninsular is cut in half by a small canal. The historical center lies in and around the Scaligero Medieval Castle, which dates to the 13th Century. It is stunning and well-preserved. Supposedly the castle was built by Mastino I della Scala, the same Scalas of Verona.

Control of Sirmione and its castle passed back and forth between Venice, Verona, and finally, the Hapsburgs under the Austro-Hungarian empire. It eventually became part of the Kingdom of Italy in 1860. The Grotte di Catullo ruins are at the peninsular's far end. These ruins were the home of the Roman poet Catullus which he built in the 1st century BC. However, the timeline of Sirmione dates from about 6000 BC.

There are very few main roads in Sirmione, as most of them have been converted into narrow winding paths for tourists. Cars and taxis are, however, allowed to drop you off at hotels. Like many other towns in the Lakes district, the city is excellent for picture taking. Sirmione is best enjoyed from May through September.

You can only experience all the small towns around Lake Garda if you drive. There is a road that circumvents the entire lake. However, you will need to arrive in the closest town you wish to start in no later than 10 AM to circumnavigate (about 100 miles).

If you want to visit Lake Garda and its towns, the best approach is to rent a car in Milan and spend a day or two in Sirmione. On one of those days, you can circumvent the Lake.

If you are visiting Lake Garda, you might consider flying in and out of Bergamo, which is due east of Milan. From here, you can fly to most European hubs.

WHAT TO DO AND SEE IN MILAN

Milan is great for shopping. On Saturday there is massive outdoor market selling everything. Two blocks away is the major shopping street known as Corso Buenos Aires. If you care to do some upscale shopping with lots of designer shops, check out the Galleria Vittorio Emanuele II.

No trip to Milan is complete without a visit to its Gothic Catheral of Milan. This magnificent church is the largest in Italy and took 600 years to build. If you take a walk over to the Santa Maria delle Grazie church, you will find one of Da Vinci's most famous paintings *The Last Supper.* For an opera, do consider a visit to the La Scala Opera house (purchase tickets online).

The Sforza Castle is another big draw in Milan. It is a converted castle that now contains ten separate museums. Not too many Roman ruins here; Milan is an affordable shopping town!

If you are flying out of Milan (MXP) there is direct train service from Milano Centrale, else, taxi service is available.

CHAPTER 12
UMBRIA
ASSISI, PERUGIA, GUBBIO

WHERE TO STAY IN UMBRIA

I have always felt that Umbria is the sister province (or land) of Tuscany. Settled by the Etruscans thousands of years ago, it is much like Tuscany. It is loaded with medieval hilltop towns with ancient walls, Assisi, Gubbio, Spoletto, and Todi, to name a few, and vineyards still farmed by generations of families. If it's not grapes, it's olives or both. If you look west from Assisi, right across that last valley is Tuscany. Like Florence is the capital or the hub of Tuscany, Perugia is the hub of Umbria. However, Perugia is one up on Florence; it's the chocolate capital of Italy. Yes, chocolate! You can even stay in the Chocohotel! However, you should be aware that this hotel sells out early. If you intend to stay at the Chocohotel, I suggest you make your reservation immediately. You can always cancel.

Also, here are two items you should note: I have addressed the hilltop town of Orvieto under day trips from Rome. While Perugia is over two hours away, Orvieto, on the border with "Lazio" (the province of Rome), is only one hour by train or car. It also is part of Umbria.

The other item; is in October of each year, Perugia hosts the Euro Chocolate Festival. You can expect many hotels within a 50-mile radius to be sold out for this European event. Not only is Perugia chocolate celebrated, but most chocolates from all over Europe will be present. You should make your reservations a year in advance if you plan to attend. You should be aware that most hotel prices will be sky-high because of the annual event. If you were not attending, the best would be to avoid the area during the chocolate festival. Best to check the internet for the ten-day festival in October. If you are attending, it would be best to overnight in hotels and BnBs within 40 miles of Perugia.

I have always regarded Perugia as a real city like Florence. It's big, but not as big as Florence. However, the smaller towns, especially Assisi and Gubbio, are really not "cities"; they're towns or villages. The only one that is a 100% historic district is Assisi. If you have been to San Gimignano, this is the best comparison. And once again, if you want "quaint," Assisi is it.

If you are driving, I suggest you base yourself in Assisi or Perugia to visit these three unique places (Assisi, Perugia, and Gubbio). If you are relying on public transportation (buses are good in the area), my suggestion for Seniors would be to base yourself around one of the bus terminals in Perugia. If you will be taking the bus to Assisi or Gubbio, it's best to locate the current CENTRAL bus terminal, where all the buses depart for points in Umbria. You will find the three-star hotel Alla Rocca about three blocks away. Or, if you prefer, the four-star Sangallo Plaza Hotel directly across from the central bus station on Piazza Partigiani. If you want something more romantic, "historic," and Italian, stay in or around Assisi. Here is an overview.

I have been to Assisi so many times you could put a blindfold on me, and I could walk from one end to the other without bumping into anything. If you want to visit all three of these towns, I suggest staying in one of them and making day trips to the two.

Both Perugia and Assisi are made for Seniors. I will explain why later. Gubbio, on the other hand, is not; however, it deserves a visit, and there is a way of getting around that big hill.

Assisi, Perugia, and Gubbio are key historic cities in Umbria, which abuts Tuscany to the west. All three are medieval hilltop towns built to defend against invaders (organized armies) and marauding tribes. If you want to stay in a historic city, my

An Alternative to the Escorted Tour

choices would be Assisi or Perugia. You are in luck if you are driving, as Perugia has what I would call a non-historic area with several American style hotels, including a modern four-star Best Western hotel called the Quottrotorri (means four towers). The Best Western is located in an industrial park far away from the historic center of Perugia. However, it's a good deal and away from the buzz of being in the city. If you are driving, you will also find, right down the road, the famous Perugia Chocolate company, which offers free tours and plenty of samples.

STAYING IN ASSISI

If you stay in Assisi, you can stay in the old city. However, parking becomes a problem or the non-existence of close-in parking. You really can't park at your hotel in the ancient town. You must park in the muni-lots or the underground garage and walk back to your hotel. In addition, you really can't drive in the old city. Please see, later on, my write-up on parking in Assisi. There is another area of Assisi that does offer modern hotels with easy parking. This area is not in the old city but on the switchbacks leading up to it and about four miles away in the village of Santa Maria degli Angelli. There is also a rail station here and a bus every 30 minutes to Assisi. I might note the rail station is called "Assisi – Santa Maria degli Angelli." staying in Maria degli Angelli is ideal for Seniors who do not wish to overnight in the old village of Assisi. It's less expensive, and there are plenty of restaurants.

If you decide to overnight in Assisi and you want to stay at an interesting place, do check out the Domus Laetitiae. It's a convent. My favorite hotel in the old city is the three-star Hotel Umbra. Note the way I spelled it. There is no "I." It is not Umbria! However, you cannot beat the location. Conrad Hilton said, "location, location, and location." Hotel Umbra is it! Here is how you find the Hotel Umbra:

Suppose you are in the central square of Assisi, Piazza del Comune, and you are looking at those ancient columns of the

Tempio di Minerva. In that case, you will find the Hotel Umbra directly behind your left-hand shoulder down that covered alley. It is less than half a block away. Outside, you will find a lovely café for a light lunch. What I like best about the Hotel Umbra is that it is about a ten-minute walk to the Porta Nuova, and if you go the other way, it is a fifteen-minute walk to the Basilica of St. Francis with plenty of shopping along the way. There are loads of restaurants and shops off the main streets. In addition, Hotel Umbra offers excellent views of the rolling Umbria countryside. I have visited this hotel but have never stayed or dined there. If you want something like the Hotel Cisterna in San Gimignano with those incredible views, then the Hotel Umbra is the place. And, do request a room with a view— "visualizza."

STAYING IN PERUGIA
If you did not know by now, Perugia is a medieval hilltop town, better, I should say a city. It is also the capital of the province of Umbria. It is now very commercialized. You should not expect anything like San Gimignano or Assisi. However, the town management has done an excellent job preserving the town and the historic district over the years. There is virtually no parking for any cars in the historic district or the hotels located there. All parking is paid for, and most are underground. However, for Seniors, no worries. There are numerous escalators in every underground parking garage. In addition, there is the "mini-metro ." You will see this sometimes spelled as "mini metro."
It's part cable car and part subway transportation system. You can ride it for 1.5 Euros for 70 minutes. Once exited in the historic district, an escalator will whisk you to the surface. However, if you stay close to the historic district, you won't need to use the mini metro.

QUICK HISTORY OF PERUGIA
Perugia is one of the original Etruscan cities. It was an Umbrian settlement around the year 310BC. In 212BC, it assisted Rome in the Second Punic War. There were no writings on Perugia until 40BC, when Luciu Antonius took refuge in the City. The town

was burned in 40BC, leaving only the temples of Vulcan, Juno, and the Etruscan terrace walls. Whoever wanted to occupy the destroyed City did so. Resettlement of the City occurred in 251AD. The City is surrounded by a mile-long monster double wall. It is said the Romans could not conquer this City because of the size of its wall.

In 547AD, the conqueror, "Totila," captured and destroyed the City. The City's bishop, "Herculanus" became the representative of the town's people. Totila did not like him, so he had him executed. Herculanus subsequently became the patron saint of the City. In the 9th century, control of Perugia was passed onto the popes and Charlemagne. By the 11th century, the small commune found itself warring against the neighboring hilltop towns, i.e., Assisi, Spoleto, Todi, Arezzo, etc.

WHAT TO SEE AND DO IN PERUGIA

First, like Bologna and Padua, Perugia is home to the university. So expect to see loads and loads of students. Perugia is full of history. It has the remnants of the Romans and what's left of the medieval and renaissance periods. There is very little to see of the Roman remains since most are located below the underground City. Fortunately, we are lucky as most remains of the medieval and renaissance period are in the underground City, not below it. I'll describe more below.

The main square in the historic district is the Piazza IV Novembre. Here you will find the city hall, covered market, cafes, restaurants, and numerous chocolate shops. It's also the central hangout place.

If you do one thing in Perugia, you must visit the underground City known as the "Rocca Paolina. In medieval times, the rulers of Perugia were the lords. The popes took over control in about 1540 and built the Paolina as a fortress. In 1848, the underground City was systematically destroyed. It was not until 1860 that control passed as Perugia became part of the new Kingdom of

Italy. It was in 1965 that the underground City was "unearthed" into what we know today. For Seniors, there are four entrances, all with escalators. Tunnels connect the underground rooms. For Seniors, it's all flat walking. If you are driving, it is easily reached from the Piazzale Partigiani car park or station Via Baglioni on the minimetro. You will need at least two hours, and it's free!

>>>TIP<<<
If you want to explore the underground City, I suggest speaking to your concierge and setting up a 90-minute walking tour. The best would be to form a group of 4-6 people.
>>><<<

The other places worth a visit in Perugia are:
The Etruscan Arch (Arch of Augustus or Augustus Gate) is one of eight gates that were part of the Old City. There are only two surviving gates. The Arch of Augustus was constructed in the second half of the 3rd century BC. The arch is part of a massive set of walls that are 30 ft (9.1 m) tall and 9,500 ft (2,900 m) long, made of travertine and set without mortar. It covers approximately a quarter of a square mile over three hills.

The other surviving gate is the Arco d'Augusto (Arch of Agusto). It was built in the second half of the third century BC by the Etruscans but took its name from the Roman emperor Augustuo who restored it in 40BC.

The Palazzo dei Priori or Comunale is one of the best examples in Italy of a public palace from the 11th century. It takes its name from the Priori, the highest political authority governing the City in the medieval eras. You will find it in the central Piazza IV Novembre, the town's main square. It still houses part of the municipal offices and, on the third floor, the National Gallery of Umbria, where you can view the period's paintings from the 13th to the 19th century. The collection is presented in 40 exhibition rooms in the Palazzo. On the second floor of the Gallery, there is

An Alternative to the Escorted Tour

an exhibition space for temporary collections, which change several times a year. If you enjoy art, this is the place for an hour. This piazza has been the social and political center of Perugia. There is a 13th-century fountain there (Fontana Maggiore). Nicola and Giovanni Pisano carved it. Note the trio of bronze nymphs and the urn spilling water.

If you want to check out an interesting Gothic church, head to Porta San Pietro, where you will find the church of San Pietro. It was built in the 12th century and incorporates 18 ancient columns. It was completed between 1535 and 1591. Gothic wooden choir stalls adorn the inside of the church, as well as a painted and gilded wooden ceiling from 1556. On the southwest section of the church, you will find the gardens with great views.

I would strongly suggest that if you stay in Perugia, you visit all the unique churches. Here are two of the most notable:

The church of Sant' Arcangelo is a round church built between the 5th and 6th centuries. It uses sixteen Corinthian columns salvaged from an older pagan temple.

Another interesting church is that of San Domenico. It is unusual because it's made of bricks. It was built in 1305. Soon after the church was completed, the topmost section was found to be unstable and had to be demolished. In 1614 as predicted, the roof caved in. So much for bricks! Reconstruction took place from 1621-1634. Most Baroque decorative additions were removed and replaced with a Gothic appearance which can be seen in the exterior. So much for Perugia. Now on to Assisi.

SOME FACTS ABOUT ST. FRANCIS OF ASSISI
Saint Francis of Assisi was known as Giovanni di Pietro di Bernardone of Assisi before he was made a saint in 1228. He was born in 1181 in the village of Assisi and died in October of 1226 at 44 in Assisi. He was the founder of the Franciscan order. St. Francis is one of the most famous saints, if not the most famous.

He was inspired to lead a life of poverty. He is usually depicted in a robe with a rope as a belt. Francis is associated with patronage of animals, and the environment became customary for churches to hold ceremonies blessing animals on his feast day of the Fourth of October. He is known for his devotion to the Eucharist. Along with Catherine of Siena, he was designated patron saint of Italy.

THE DETAILS OF ASSISI

If you did not know by now, the main draw of Assisi is the Basilica of St. Francis. Saint Francis is the saint of patronage of animals and the environment. Not only can you visit the Basilica, but if you go to your right on entry, you can go down a flight of stairs (sorry, no elevator or lift) and visit the actual tomb of St. Francis. There is no talking or taking pictures allowed. However, if you would like to light a candle, you may.

Three parcheggi (municipal parking lots) are at the base of the hill or mesa if you are driving. They are pretty large, and one is strictly for buses. It is known as the "Giovanni Paolo III" parking lot. The other, located about 1.5 miles away, is on the other side of Assisi and is known as the "Porta Nuova" parking lot. There is another parking lot known as the "Porta Mojano." However, this brings you to the center of the town near the Piazza del Comune. You need to pay at all three municipal parking lots. Most of the hotels in the old town do not have parking lots.

If you are taking the train, you need to take a train to the village of Santa Maria degli Angelli (note- the station is still called Assisi), then take a bus ride of about 15 minutes to Assisi. No connection trains make the journey from Florence to Assisi in 2.5 hours at about 16 Euros. The bus runs from the rail station to the parking area in Assisi every thirty minutes. If you are staying in Perugia, there is a direct bus to Assisi for about five dollars.

Assisi was made for visiting Seniors, as all three parking lots have escalators in addition to the garage. There is also an escalator at

An Alternative to the Escorted Tour

the Basilica of Saint Francis. Make sure you don't have any items you wish to part with clearly visible in your vehicle. It would be best if you packed them in the trunk before you departed for Assisi. As mentioned, there is also a parking garage with security. The way you visit Assisi is a walk through the town. You start at one end and finish at the other. That garage and one of the parking areas are not in the center of the town. So beginning at Porta Nuova or Giovanni Paolo III parking areas is best.

>>>TIP<<<
If you are arriving late in the day, start at the Giovanni Paolo III parking area and visit the St. Francis Basilica and tomb first (since it may close late in the day), then walk the town till you exit at Porta Nuova.
>>><<<

The walk from the Porta Nuova lot to the Giovanni Paolo III parking lot is about one mile long. If you have taken a day trip from Perugia, you should arrive 10-11AM. Start at the Porta Nuova lot. It's a flat walk once you take the escalator to the top. This escalator will minimize walking uphill, as it is difficult not to do in Assisi. When you finish your walk, you will take the escalator down to the parking lot on the Giovanni side near the Basilica of St. Francis. Then it would be best if you took the bus or a taxi back to the Porta Nuova lot where you started.

YOUR VISIT TO ASSISI

Starting at the Porta Nuova parking lot, take the escalator and follow the crowd onto the Borgo Aretino, along the souvenir shops, and under that big stone gate and tower. Take a look to your left, and you will see the Basilica of Saint Clare. Construction of the church started after the death of St. Clare 1257-1265 around the ancient church of San Giorgio, which until 1230 had kept the remains of St. Francis. Clare's remains were subsequently buried at the church of San Giorgio. The remains

210

of St. Clare were buried under the altar of the new church in 1265. The crypt which houses the saint was built in 1850. In 1852 they found the original bones of St. Clare and buried her in a new tomb. Saint Agness is also buried at this Gothic church.

Note the flying buttresses which support the walls from outside the structure. The flying buttresses were used for many Gothic churches during the Renaissance period. This is much like the upper Basilica of San Francesco d'Assisi, which you will see at the end of your walking tour. The church is all late 14th-century design with a façade fabricated with rows of white and pink local stone. The square-based bell tower stands on the side, with mullioned windows and a large single window. In addition to the exterior design, the inside is also worth visiting.

This region of Umbria is a high-risk area for earthquakes. Several have occurred in 2022. However, substantial damage occurred in 1997 to the Basilica di Santa Chiara and the Basilica of St. Francis when the roof caved in. Four people were killed at St. Francis.

After you view the Basilica of Saint Clare, continue walking to the left (on the Corso Giuseppi Mazzi) until you come upon a building on your right that looks like an old Roman temple. It is. That's the Temple of Minerva, which sits in the Piazza del Comune. The Piazza is the main square of Assisi. You can't miss it. There are six well-preserved Corinthian columns supporting the main cross beam. The temple with those columns dates to the 1st century BC. It was converted to a church in 1539 and later renovated in the 17th century to the Baroque style. The temple housed a court with an annexed jail in the Middle Ages. The Italian painter "Giotto" depicted the Corinthian columns of the converted temple in a fresco which is in the Basilica of St. Francis up the street. When visiting St. Francis, you will see it, as the portrait of the church has windows and bars.

The central square is home to the Palazzo del Capitano del Popolo, a mid-13th-century design with merlons added in 1927.

An Alternative to the Escorted Tour

That tower you see is the Peoples Tower, built in 1305. The fountains with the three lions on the southern side date from the 16th century. About a block to your left en route to the Basilica of St. Francis is the Forum and Archaeological Museum. If you have an extra hour, or if you are staying in the old city, it is worth a visit. There is a charge of nine Euros.

Like many of the other cities in Italy, Assisi, because of its strategic importance as a defensive hilltop town, was conquered and reconquered by practically every waring people.

When you are finished with your visit to the Piazza del Comune, continue your walk up toward the tower next to the Temple of Minerva toward the Basilica of Saint Francis. It's a good 15-minute walk to Saint Francis. The street will come to a junction in about 100 feet. On the right is the Via San Paolo. Take this street. You will know you are on the correct path when you pass the Carabinieri (police department). There is shopping on this street as well as BnBs. Continue walking in the direction of the auto traffic until it ends at Porto Giacomo. Take a left here and continue with the traffic for about two blocks until you come upon the Basilica of San Francesco. If you want to grab a light bite or a café, there is a "Ristorante Bar San Francesco," just off that grassy area in front of the upper Basilica. Best to use the facilities at this bar since the main pubic facilities are located on the square below the upper Basilica, known as the lower square "Piazza Inferiore San Francisco."

>>>TIP<<<
When leaving the Piazza del Comune en route to Piazza San Francisco and you accidently go to the left of that small museum on the Piazza Commune, don't worry, it will still get you to the Basilica of St. Francis. No worries.
>>><<<

212

ITALY Made Easy for Seniors

For Seniors, I should note any there are slight gradients on any walkway from the Commune to St. Francis.

The Basilica has a lower and upper part. The upper is a beautiful church with paintings on all the walls. The lower contains the crypt of St. Francis. If you enter the lower Basilica to visit the crypt area and view the tomb of St. Francis, you will have to navigate a small stairway of about twenty steps. No big deal, hold onto those wrought iron railings. You will return to the lower Basilica through another staircase on the other side of the crypt area. You should feel free to light a candle. However, there are no flash pictures or talking allowed. So turn your flash off.

After leaving the Basilica, you must work your way down to the Giovanni Paolo III parking lot. I should note for Seniors that once you leave the Basilica area, there is a long slope down to the parking lot. Once you take that hard right under the old city walls (you won't miss this place), you will spot the massive parking lot and check-in point for all the tour buses. For Seniors, hold on to that railing as you walk down that path.

If you have parked your car in the Nuova Porta parking lot, you must take a taxi or that local bus. There should be ample time to return to your hotel in Perugia for a nap and dinner later. If you are staying in Assisi, all you need do is walk back to your hotel and shopping, of course.

An Alternative to the Escorted Tour

A QUICK HISTORY OF GUBBIO

The Romans conquered the Town about the 2nd century BC. However, the occupation of the hills around the Town of Gubbio dates to about the Bronze Age, 3300BC. In pre-Roman times the Umbri people occupied the land and the other Umbrian hilltop defensive towns like Assisi, Todi, Spoletto, and Orvieto. Gubbio contains the second-largest surviving Roman theatre in the world. Gubbio was mighty during the middle ages and peaked in the first half of the 16th century. It is rumored that Gubbio sent 1,000 knights to fight in the first crusade.

DAY TRIP TO GUBBIO

If you do not have a car, there is a bus (Busitalia.it) which runs every few hours between Perugia and Gubbio. It takes one hour and costs about five dollars. The only problem is that Gubbio is built into a hill or, better, the slope of Mount Ingino. Sorry to say there are no escalators, not even stairs. So walking up that hill presents a problem, especially for Seniors. No worries. First, historical items like the Roman Theatre are in the flat area at the base of Mount Ingino. By the way, the Romans called this place Ikuvium. I can't even pronounce it!

All you need do is pay six Euros for a round-trip ticket to the top of Mount Ingino. If you are a Senior, on arrival, the best way to visit Gubbio is to take a taxi from the main square (or drive over) to the end of via San Girolamo where you will find the Colle Eletto Funivia www.funiviagubbio.it. There is plenty of parking at the Funivia. From the top of the Funivia, there are breathtaking views of Gubbio. Once at the top of the Funivia, don't count on a town to visit. There is none.

You should note that this funivia is more like a ski lift. The attendants will put two people in a bucket, and you stand for six minutes as it lifts you to the top of the hill. There is a basilica on top of the hill. In the Basilica lie the remains of San't Ubaldo. To reach the Basilica of San't Ubaldo you would need to walk the equivalent of several blocks on a winding path behind the

214

funivia. Seniors may find this a real challenge. When they remove you from that basket at the top of the mount, look at the Basilica and see if you are up to this moderately strenuous walk.

After you visit the top of the funivia, you need to take it back down and work your way over to the Piazza del Quaranta Martini, the main square. The square is a semi-circle. Here you can grab a bite before exploring the other highlights of Gubbio. There are at least six outdoor cafes in addition to food trucks. However, before heading down the hill, If you walk across the slope, in other words, not down the hill, you will come across the Palazzo dei Consoli in the Piazza Grande. It's an old palace but looks like a castle with a crenelated top. You will know when you see it. This place contains the seven Iguvine Tablets with ancient inscriptions from the bronze age. About a block further up the hill is the Duomo of Gubbio. You should be ready now for lunch.

After lunch, you are ready to view the Roman Amphitheatre. The actual name is the "Teatro Romano d Gubbio". It's a short flat walk of no more than 10 minutes. However, it isn't easy to describe just how to get there. So, I will do my best. All you need to do is go over to that small rotary. Then walk to your right along Route 298 until you see the signs to the Teatro Romano d Gubbio. You can also walk to the right of the Chiesa di San Francesco (the church in the square), down Via Ortracci, and then take a right on Route 298. You can't miss it. Just look for a smaller Colosseum on your left. Before returning to Perugia or Assisi, enjoy a café, pastry, or gelato. You arrive at your hotel at about 5PM, enough time for a snooze and a drink in the lobby bar before dinner at 8PM.

On a note for Seniors, if you follow my instructions, you will take a taxi to the Funivia. Once you get back down from the Funivia, all you need do is head for the Piazza Grande and walk down the hill. It is an easy walk.

CHAPTER 13

NAPLES AREA
SORRENTO, POSITANO
RAVELLO, AMALFI,
PAESTUM, HERCULANEUM
CAPRI & AMALFI DRIVE

OVERVIEW

If you are going to extend your itinerary to include a minimum of three full days in the Amalfi area, you need to review this chapter in detail.

You should note that I have included many details on the Sorrentine Peninsular under "Day Trips from Rome, Chapter 6. However, suppose you are basing yourself in Sorrento (highly recommended for Seniors) and plan on just taking it easy or visiting the ruins of Herculaneum and Paestum. In that case, you will need an additional two or three days in or around the Sorrentine Peninsular, and the Amalfi Coast.

First, if this is your final destination on your visit to Italy, consider flying back to the USA or Canada from Naples. As of now, there are no non-stops back to North America. So, you will have to fly to a European hub, e.g., Paris, Rome, Munich, Lisbon, and then fly home non-stop. If you are starting your Italy visit in the Naples area, the same holds, i.e., you would probably fly to one of the hubs mentioned.

ITALY Made Easy for Seniors

As discussed in Chapter 6, staying in Sorrento is best if you are a Senior. Amalfi would be my second choice. Why? First, unlike Positano, it's flat and easy to walk for Seniors. Second, it's clean, with many pedestrian-only walkways selling everything, including wine and cheese of the region, to all those Italian souvenirs. It's also excellent for finding an apartment for 4-6 nights. And finally, it's centrally located for all your day trips. You can't ask for anything better.

For Seniors, if you elect to stay in Positano, remember that it's all walking up and down that beautiful hill dotted with buildings of different colors. Very much like the Cinque Terre towns. Most bed and breakfasts will offer to port your bags from a convenient drop-off point. However, they won't carry you.

Hotels on the "water," or the lower side (below the SS163 road), will take your bags and may port you via a golf cart. If you base yourself in Sorrento, my feeling always was to go for the day trip to Positano. See Chapter 6, "Day Trips from Rome."

Several hotels do have access to the narrow streets and allow taxi access. If you are a Senior and want to stay at a hotel in Positano, I suggest using Google Earth to locate it before you book it. Booking.com also provides a map of the area with the hotels indicated on the roads and the paths. Those small dotted lines are paths. Also, for Seniors, be aware that in most cases, you will do a considerable amount of "inclined" walking to access restaurants and shops.

Also, if you insist on staying in Positano, consider instead of the Circumvesuviana railway to Sorrento and then a mini-bus or a taxi, the ferry service directly from the port in Naples. You can get more detailed information at www.naplesbayferry.com. If you want to get excellent photos of the town of Positano, make sure you take the ferry after 1PM. Positano faces west and looks great when the sun sets, and there is no cloud cover. So if you can time your ferry departure from Naples, you may be able to get incredible photos. The fast ferry is only $20 and makes the journey in about one hour and 20 minutes. In summary, if you are a Senior in excellent shape, I say, "go for it." And stay in Positano!

>>>TIP<<<
If you are driving a rental car and wish to stay in Positano, be aware that you will have to negotiate the Amalfi Drive. You also need to contact the hotel for parking accommodations, if any. In this case, you may want to reconsider and stay in Sorrento.
>>><<<

CONSIDER STAYING IN AMALFI OR SORRENTO

If you want to take it easy and live with the locals, consider staying in Amalfi. There are many hotels in what I call the "Flat Area" abutting the main road known as SS163. There is not much walking unless you stay at one of those touristy hotels in the hills. Further, the town is not that touristy, and you can find excellent restaurants, dine with the locals and spend a lot less.

Like Positano, you should also note that there is a ferry service from Naples to Amalfi. During the off-season, the ferry schedule is minimal. So this is one boat you won't want to miss, or you will spend the night sleeping in Naples. Also, remember that you will probably do your sightseeing in reverse, i.e., Amalfi to Positano, then Sorrento in those Blue SITA vans. Not much to do in Amalfi but enjoy the locals.

There are two areas of Sorrento with hotels. If I had to design the town again, I would have placed the central railway station closer to the center of the city, known as Piazza Tasso.

Later, when you walk through the town, you will see that statue of Tasso. Torquato Tasso was a late comer to Italian history.

ITALY Made Easy for Seniors

The current rail station of the Circumvesuviana, the only rail station in town, is located about five football fields from the Piazza Tasso. It's not a big deal and an easy short walk of about 10 minutes from Piazza Giovanni Batista de Curtis station to Piazza Tasso. The best way is to walk down the Corso Italia. Hopefully, the hotel you have selected will be closer to the Piazza Tasso, where all the action is.

You should note the last stop on the train (Circumvesuviana) is called "Sorrento." If you don't know where your hotel is and prefer not to walk, there are plenty of taxis at the station. And, as I have stated before, it's best to hire a car and driver for Naples Centrale or the airport. See my notes on Sorrentocars.com.

THREE & FOUR-STAR HOTELS NEAR THE STATION:

Hotel Nice	Hotel Michelangelo	Hotel Capri	Hotel Sorrento Sorrento City

THREE & FOUR-STAR HOTELS NEAR PIAZZA TASSO:

Hotel del Corso	Hotel Tasso Suites	Hotel Rivoli Sorrento	Imperial Hotel Tramontano
Antiche Mura **	Grand Hotel Cesare Augusto	Hotel Eden	Europa Palace
Hotel La Meridiana	Hotel Regina Sorrrento	Hotel Palazzo Tritone and Avagnale	Hotel Plazza
Hotel del Mar	Grand Hotel de La Ville		

If you are wondering who this guy "Tasso" was, I can tell you the following: His full name was Torquato Tasso, and he lived from March 1544–April 1595. Supposedly, he was one of the famous Italian poets of all times. And why is his statue in the central square? Simple, he was born in Sorrento!

** - Antiche Mura - This is Bob's favorite hotel in Sorrento

.

An Alternative to the Escorted Tour

DAY TRIP TO THE TEMPLES AT PAESTUM

First, I have stated: "The Temples at Paestum." However, the entire complex is an architectural park sprawled over about 300 acres. It is massive and not only contains three of the best-preserved temples in the world but also the ruins of the ancient city of Paestum. Most of the city walls are still intact. At least, their foundations are. In addition, there is also a museum worth a visit. Admission is about ten Euros and includes the museum. You should note that the park closes at 1:30PM on the first and third Monday of the month. So, best to plan accordingly.

None of the temples in the ancient world, including the Parthenon in Athens, and the Valley of the Temples in Agrigento, compares to these temples. Why? They are mostly still intact, and secondly, they are a marvel of construction. Unlike Stonehenge and the Acropolis, you can enter all the temples, sit on those ruins and take as many photos as you wish with no security people chasing you.

Some quick historical facts. Way before the Romans arrived, Paestum was part of ancient Greece. The territory was Magna Graecia and dates to about the 8th Century BC. The region of Salento in Southern Italy still speaks a Greek dialect known as Griko, a blend of Italian and Greek. On my most recent trip to the heel of Italy (Salento), I was amazed that there are over 30,000 Italians who speak Griko in this region.

Yes, after the Greek god of the sea, Poseidon. The actual complex, now known as Paestum, was originally a Greek colony known as Poseidonia. While the entire complex is also Greek and Roman ruins, most people visit it because of the three well-preserved temples.

Here is a basic recap of the three temples: Hera One was built about 550BC, Hera Two about 450BC, and the Temple of Athena about 600-500BC. These temples were built by the ancient Greeks and later taken over by the Romans. They were

220

constructed as all temples were built to honor the gods, i.e., the god of the ocean, Neptune, Polaris, etc.

A quick overview. First, the two temples are about half a football field apart. They are Hera One and Hera Two. By the way, Hera was a Greek Goddess. She is best known as the goddess of marriage, women, and family and the protector of women. As you enter the complex, you need to take a quick left-hand turn, and you will see the two temples. If you take a right-hand turn about five blocks up, you will find the Amphitheater of Paestum. After exiting the amphitheater, go right for another five blocks, and you will come upon the Temple of Athena, which also dates to about 500BC. The Romans took over the entire area at about 237BC and renamed it Paestum.

About these three ancient temples, there are two interesting facts to note. First, observe the columns. They are all tapered as they rise to the top, where there was probably a roof. Secondly, the one on your left (the most southern temple) is called Hera I (Hera One). Inside there are seven columns down the center. The one on your right is Hera Two, initially thought to be the Temple of Poseidon.

As for the Temple of Athena, it was also built in about 500BC. The architecture is known as transitional. Some of the columns are Doric in nature, and some are Ionic.

Of an interesting note, the amphitheater you see is only half of the remains. In 1930, a local builder built a road right through the center, burying the eastern half. The locals stated that the responsible civil engineer went to trial, was convicted, and received a prison sentence that was described as wanton destruction of a historic site.

You will need 2-3 hours to take in the entire complex, including an hour in the museum. There is lots of walking here for seniors, but it is all flat. In addition, you will not be able to exit the

An Alternative to the Escorted Tour

complex via that restaurant abutting (The Netunno). You will need to leave where you came in and walk around the entire temple ruins complex.

To get to Paestum, you have two alternatives. I assume you are staying at a hotel or an apartment in Sorrento.

The first budget approach is to take the train. As a rail buff, I can tell you this is a drag. You must spend 90 minutes on the Circumvesuviana railway from Sorrento to Naples. Then you would need to walk that underground passageway to Napoli Central. Then you need to catch a train to Paestum. It is the same line as Regio Di Calabria. That's another 90 minutes. On arrival at the rail station, you need to walk about one-third mile to the entrance booth at Paestum. All told you would spend about four hours each way, not a good idea. I'm getting tired just thinking about this! For Seniors and anybody else, there is a better way!

Just like you would spend some good money for a nice day trip down the Amalfi drive, you ought to consider the same for a trip to Paestum. It will be a few dollars less on what you leave your kids. The best approach is to contact www.sorrentocars (www.leonardotravels.com). His name is Ugo, and trust me, he is very reliable, having worked for National Travel Vacations. As in your Amalfi day, he can pick you up at about 10AM, take you to Paestum, take you to Agropoli for lunch, and return you to your Sorrento hotel at about 4-5PM. If you would like to stop and take a one-hour tour of a mozzarella factory in Paestum (Annulli Farms) before your visit, I suggest you leave at about 9:30AM. It would be best if you invited another couple(s) to join you, thereby splitting the cost.

Annulli Farms is only open in the mornings for tours. If you don't like cheese, there is ample time to have lunch in Agropoli and then do about one hour of shopping before starting your drive back to Sorrento. The best is to contact Ugo on the website.

ITALY Made Easy for Seniors

DAY TRIP TO HERCULANEUM AND SHOPPING

Herculaneum is also a nice day trip from Sorrento, and it costs very little, no more than eight dollars per person. There is a major street market daily on the streets abutting Herculaneum, and you can shop here for anything and then have lunch in several local restaurants.

For some reason, Herculaneum, also known as Ercolano, does not get the play that Pompeii receives. Perhaps because it's part of Naples? I don't know. I don't know anyone that jumps up and down and says, "I want to go to Italy and see the ruins at Ercolano," but they do with Pompeii.

Don't count on Herculaneum being on the same magnitude as Pompeii. The current excavated size is about a tenth of Pompeii. Herculaneum is on the south side of Naples. It is easily reached from Sorrento in about 50 minutes and from Naples Centrale (Garibaldi Square) by taking the Circumvesuviana railway for about 20 minutes. Trains run every 20 minutes. If you leave your hotel in Sorrento at about 11AM you should be at Herculaneum at about 12:30. If you are coming from Sorrento, it is the first stop marked "Ercolano Scavi ." If you are coming from Naples, make sure you get off at the Scavi stop. You only need 30-60 minutes to take photos of the ruins and head for that massive street market. After you are shopped out, consider lunch with a return back to Sorrento at about 5PM with just enough time for a nap before dinner at 8PM of course.

Here are some quick facts on Herculaneum:
It was buried in the same Mount Vesuvius eruption of 79AD, which also buried Pompeii. There are few ancient cities preserved intact. Ercolano was discovered by accident while drilling a water well in 1709, compared to Pompeii in 1748. Unlike Pompeii, Ercolano was covered by pyroclastic material, not lava and ash. This material preserved more "organic material," i.e., wood, papyrus, etc. It had a population of only 5,000.

An Alternative to the Escorted Tour

Because it was located close to the sea as opposed to Pompeii, Ercolano was a vacation spot for the Roman elite. The eruption covered the city to about 60 feet. Only a fraction of the city has been unearthed.

The heat (480 degrees F) of the eruption, which occurred on October 17, 79AD, had a radius of seven miles and killed everyone in sight, even those sheltered.

The entrance fee is 13 Euros per person. You do not need to book tickets online. You should figure one hour here at most.

>>>TIP<<<
If you plan your day accordingly, you can visit Herculaneum and Pompeii on the same day since they are on the same Circumvesuviana rail line, only 20 minutes apart. I would visit Pompeii first, then go to Herculaneum for lunch and shopping.
>>><<<

THE AMALFI DRIVE
 I have covered this topic in detail in Chapter 6; Day Trips from Rome. There are only three practical ways to "do" the Amalfi Drive: 1) If you have a rental, drive it yourself, 2) take the blue SITA bus from the Sorrento Circumvesuviana rail station and 3) Hire a private driver for the day e.g., "sorrentocars.com." If you are a Senior, the best way, without question, is to hire a private car and driver for the day. Once again, don't worry about the grandchildren's inheritance. Enjoy this once in a lifetime experience now!

SORRENTO AND POSITANO
Sorrento is on the Sorrentine Peninsular, and Positano is a few miles from the end of the Sorrentine Peninsular. You will find all the details about these two towns in Chapter 6 as they can be visited from Rome as a day trip.

224

Here is a quick recap:

The two popular towns of the area, Sorrento and Positano, have been discussed in my overview above. People love to stay in Positano because of its beauty. You can't beat that picture of all those colorful homes glued to that hillside. It is very similar to some of the towns in the Cinque Terre. However, as discussed, Seniors need to consider where their hotel is located; else, they will be walking up and down those hills. On the other hand, Sorrento is flat, and as Seniors, you won't have any problem.

Neither Sorrento nor Positano has much history compared to other towns mentioned in this book. However, there are some Roman ruins in Sorrento. You can view these ancient ruins from the lobby of Hotel Antiche Mura.

RAVELLO AND RUFALO

I have discussed both the town of Ravello and the villa at Rufalo in Chapter 6, under the topic of The Amalfi Drive. You will find all the details there.

THE ISLAND OF CAPRI

You will find all the details of a day trip to Capri in Chapter 6.

CHAPTER 14

BARI

MATERA, ALBEROBELLO

INTRODUCTION

This chapter is unique. If you have been to Italy a few times or have a third or fourth week to explore this beautiful country and its people, I would strongly suggest you explore the highlights of Matera, Alberobello, and Bari. I really can't group them into one province since they lie in Basilicata (Matera), Alberobello (Puglia), and Bari (Puglia). Forming a triangle, they are about one hour or less apart. If you want to visit all three towns, your best approach is to take the high-speed train to Bari from Roma, visit Bari, then go to the Bari airport and rent a car for a few days. Here is your itinerary, which will minimize check-ins and maximize your site-seeing time:

Day 1 – Morning high-speed train or fly into Bari directly from one of the European hubs.
Note: I suggest you do not fly from the Rome airports.
Between check-in, etc., it takes too long. The trains run every two hours and cover the distance in four hours.
Check into a hotel in Bari o/n Bari

Day 2 - Visit the old City of Bari o/n Bari.
Day 3- Drive to Alberobello o/n Alberobello.
Day 4- Day trip to Matera o/n Alberobello.
Day 5- Drive to Bari airport, turn in a car train back to Rome,
        or fly home via a European Hub.

ITALY Made Easy for Seniors

OVERVIEW OF THE THREE TOWNS

Bari is the hub of the northern part of Apulia (sometimes called Puglia). Bari is quite cosmopolitan, with excellent shopping, good restaurants, and history. Secondly, it's a rail hub featuring trains to Rome, Milan, and Italy via the Trenitalia and the new Italo systems. There are frequent daily flights to Rome, Milan, and other European hubs.

Alberobello is the home of those cone-shaped houses. In and around the area, there are over 1,500 of them. Unlike Bari, Alberobello and Matera are unique historical cities on their own.

Matera is also a unique city. You will not believe this place when you visit it. It is nearly impossible to describe. This place is massive, and the recent James Bond movie only shows a small part of Matera. Matera has been featured in numerous motion pictures, the most recent being *"No Time To Die"* (2021, by producers Barbara Broccoli and Michael G. Wilson.) The first well-known film was "Ben-Hur" (1959, Charlton Heston). To date, there have been over 137 movies filmed in some parts of Matera. If you want to visit Matera, I would strongly suggest you see the film "*No Time to Die*" first.

If you want to visit these three towns, I have constructed your visit so that you do not have to overnight in Matera. It's a hassle. For Seniors, there is a lot of walking and numerous ramps and flights of stairs in and around the City. It's like negotiating a three-dimensional maze. In addition, most of the streets and walkways are cobblestone. The historic area where the caves are is called the "Sassi."

Using the rail system is not an option for visiting Matera. It takes too long to get there from Bari and other key points. In addition, the entire historic area (The Sassi) is a ZTL (Zone Traffic Limited) controlled area, and you cannot drive around or even park in the historic area. Do not even attempt to enter the Sassi area. If you care not to drive, I suggest hiring a car and driver.

An Alternative to the Escorted Tour

Another idea, instead of a private car and driver, is to go back to the Bari Airport and rent a car for two full days. It's easy and inexpensive. I should note that there are only rental locations at the Bari Airport. There are no in-city rental locations.

>>>TIP<<<
If you rent a car at Bari Airport, a taxi from the City will cost you $35. However, there is a train every 30 minutes to the airport at the Bari train station, and it will cost you only $5 per person. Also, remember that when you drop off the car and return to your hotel in Bari, you can take the train back. If you stayed at the Hotel Excelsior, it's just across the street.
>>><<<

>>>TIP<<<
There is a bus from Bari airport to Matera several times a day. There is also a bus from Bari airport to Alberobello. You can research these buses on the internet as the times change with the airline times. They are not a lot of money, and they make the journey in about an hour.
>>><<<

You can extend the above five-day itinerary by adding two or three days in Lecce, another historic town, and making day trips to Otranto and other places in the Salento region of Apulia. I will not cover these two cities. However, using Lecce as a base in what is known as the Salento region of Apulia (or Puglia) would be a plus.

BARI - POLIGNANO A MARE AND MONOPOLI
If you arrive in Bari by rail, you can walk to the four-star Hotel Excelsior. It is only one block from the station. The only negative about this hotel is that it is in an intense graffiti area. This area will be a real plus if you are into modern art.

To reach the Excelsior, take the elevator down to the under-tracks tunnel and exit to Via Giuseppe Capruzzi; follow signs.

There are other fine hotels within walking distance of the rail station. The rail station's other (eastern) side defines the words "the other side of the tracks" with parks, fountains, shops, restaurants, etc. Other hotels within walking distance are the Hotel Cristal and the Hotel Colibri. I might note, for Seniors, that all of Bari is flat, so walking is easy. After you drop your bags at one of the downtown hotels, you are ready to explore the City. Otherwise, you may take a taxi to your hotel for 5-8 Euros.

If you walk across from the rail station, you will come to the main walking street (pedestrians only) known as Via Sparano da Bari. It's lined with parks on both sides. Follow this until it crosses the Vittorio Emanuele II, a major boulevard. Here you will find at least eight outdoor cafes to enjoy lunch or dinner. The old City and its medieval walls lie just behind all those outdoor cafes.

Once in the Old City, bear to your left. Follow the signs to the Castello Svevo di Bari in a few blocks. This castle (the moat has been filled in) was built in 1132 by the Norman King Roger II. It is also known as the Swabian Castle. At one time, the castle extended to the port but was filled in to make way for the Corso Antonio de Tulio boulevard. The castle was destroyed in 1156 and rebuilt in 1233 by Fredrick II of the Holy Roman Empire and was later acquired by Duke Ferdinand of Aragon and later donated to the Sforza family, who returned to the King of Naples. The Aragon walls remain along with the Hohenstaufen tower. The castle is now used for exhibitions.

If you have another full day in Bari, I suggest driving down to Polignano a Mare. You probably don't know much about Polignano, but you have seen many pictures of that famous restaurant under that massive rock or cave. It's also a hotel. The official name of this five-star hotel and restaurant is "Hotel Ristorante Grotta Palazzese ." And if you want to spend those

An Alternative to the Escorted Tour

big bucks to have dinner there or stay overnight, you need to make a reservation 3-6 months in advance. I might note there is a "guard" or, better, a "bouncer" who will not let you into the restaurant or hotel, even to take a few pictures. You would probably have to be a member of the "A-List" club and arrive in a Rolls-Royce with a private driver. In addition, you would need to have a write-up in Wikipedia. However, I'm not sure if that bouncer would know what Wikipedia is. That bouncer denied us entry. Would you believe Bob Kaufman, author of books on Italy, was denied entrance?

I usually suggest taking the train down to Polignano. It's only $8 round trip and takes about 30 minutes. On arrival, you can either walk down to the old town or take one of those Tuk-Tuk three-wheeled taxis for 10 Euros from the station to the old town.

The old City is perched on a limestone "mesa." There is excellent shopping and great spots for lunch. Two other things worth doing are the beach and the cave boat tours. The beach is small but very nice, sandy with that turquoise green water. So, do pack a bathing suit. You can also sit on the beach and enjoy the view. If you want to spend about $30 per person, there are one-hour tours of the caves by speed boat.

If you make an early start, say 10AM, out of Bari to Polignano, another 15 minutes down the Adriatic, you will find the town of Monopoli. After having lunch in Polignano, take the train to the next major stop or drive down 15 minutes to another fascinating town Monopoli. It will cost you about two Euros. If driving, consider the coast road for great views of the Adriatic and an excellent view of the City coming up in front of you. Once again, Monopoli also sits on a mesa or "bluff" of stone. It's flat walking, and there is municipal parking. If arriving by train, consider a Tuk-Tuk tour or a transfer to the old City located half a mile from the train station. A taxi will cost you about 6 Euros to the old City. Before leaving Bari or arriving at Monopoli, check the return times for the Trenitalia trains or the new sleek-looking regional trains. The trains stop in Bari. Trains operate about every half-hour.

Okay, now we are in Monopoli, so what will we do? First, like many of these coastal cities on the Adriatic, they went back and forth between all the conquering entities over 2000 years. Just too many to name. The town dates to 500BC. The new Italian Kingdom chased the Spaniards out in 1860.

Monopoli is a walking city. Lots of small quaint streets, the real Italy I love. Monopoli has many squares abutting whitewashed buildings, well over 100 years old. Two places worth visiting are the Castello di Carlo and the Palmieri Palace. Like so many places, the Castello was also a prison and barracks. The Spaniards built it for coastal defense in 1552. In later years it was abandoned until the 1990s, when it was reconstructed and turned into an exhibit hall.

With no heirs to the Palmieri family's succession, the Palmieri Palace was turned over to the government in 1921 to be used as a museum and school of art. You can't miss it. When in the Centro Storico, you will find it on Palmieri Piazza. The Palace is modeled after the palaces you see in historic Lecce. The old town consists of many Baroque fountains, plazas, and other ornamental designs of the mid-1700s. Most of the design comes from the mid-1800s, known as the late Baroque. The Palace is worth a visit unless you are heading to one of the beaches. Most of the excellent beaches lie south of the town; however, unless you are here during the summer or shoulder months best to skip them. So best to enjoy that gelato while you stroll the Old City.

I would suggest the Basilica of the Madonna della Madia as another place to visit. Construction started in the 12th Century; however, as it goes, construction stopped when they ran out of wood beans for the roof supports.

An Alternative to the Escorted Tour

It would be best to have a pastry (Il Pasticcino) and café before heading back to Bari at about 6PM.

ALBEROBELLO

If you have not done so, you will need to check out of your hotel in Bari and go to the airport to rent a car. I should note that there are no rental car pickup points in Bari. You need to back to the Bari airport via the fast shuttle train (from Bari Centrale) or take a taxi which will cost you about 30 Euros. Taking your luggage with you would be best so you don't have to return to the City and can get on the main road to Alberobello. Just a word about Bari airport and the train from Bari Centrale. The airport has elevators and a new escalator system outside the south door. It's not like Rome. You don't have to walk a lot. If you are taking a taxi, you still need to be deposited at the terminal building to sign up for your car at the rental counter. If you have luggage, spend the extra $25 and go by taxi from your Bari hotel to the airport.

It is a four-block walk from the rental counters to where the cars are located. If you care not to drag your bags, have your partner watch them outside arrivals as you bring up the rental car.

It's less than an hour to Alberobello, and your rental car will also be used the next day to visit Matera (from Alberobello). Alberobello, like Matera, is one of my favorite towns in Italy and, in fact, in the world. It is so unique. You may have seen pictures of Alberobello (pronounced AL-BER-OH-BELLOW) with the town and the countryside filled with all those cone-shaped houses. Those cone-shaped houses are called "Trulli." the City and the outlying villages are UNESCO World Heritage Sites. The singular is a Trullo.

On arrival, I suggest you check into your hotel for the two nights. If the room is not ready, check your bags with the bellman. Do not leave it in your car since you will park and walk 3-4 blocks

232

into town. Since there is plenty of municipal parking, you can also drive into town. My favorite hotel in the area is the four-star Grand Hotel Olimpo. It is exceptionally reasonable and includes breakfast as usual. You may want to drive into town as the main road has a slight incline. Before booking at the Hotel Olimpo, check if you can stay at one of the Trulli hotels in town. However, they are usually booked up several months in advance.

So, what's with these funny-looking Trulli houses?
First, they are only found in the southern region of Puglia (also known as Apuglia). They are examples of mortar-less (no cement) drywall construction. They are a pre-historic building technique that has stood the test of time in this area. The Trulli are made of chiseled blocks of limestone boulders that came from the neighboring fields. There are several types that, when placed together, form domed buildings. They were built for "Thermal Balance." They keep the inside cool in the summer heat and warm when it gets cold.

There are two sections of Alberobello:
The section Rione Monti has 1,030 Trulli, and the Rione Aia has 590 Trulli. There are four specific locations (Casa d'Amore; Piazza del Mercato; Museo Storico; Trullo Sovrano).

The houses with the "corbelled roofs" are still being constructed today. They serve as temporary field shelters, storehouses, or permanent dwellings for small-scale landowners or agricultural laborers. The domed (corbelled) roof rests directly on the structure's walls. The walls are double-skinned with a rubble core (probably for insulation against the hot sun). It is also double-skinned. The buildings are whitewashed. Water is collected from the roof's runoff to a cistern beneath the house. How restoration and maintenance of the Trulli are undertaken is prescribed in local legislation, and it is illegal to demolish, reconstruct, add floors, or construct fake Trulli.

Now that you know about the Trulli houses, what do you do?

An Alternative to the Escorted Tour

Alberobello is a shopping town. The central shopping district is on Via Indipendenza (yes, that's the spelling) and extends for about ten blocks. Here you will find everything, including all types of food and a supermarket. It is all flat walking. However, Seniors should note that to your right, paralleling Indipendenza is Via Colombo which is a traditional shopping area (non-Trulli). There are stairs of about 10-12 feet every so often leading up to Via Colombo. Between the two streets, there are also shops.

I might note that since you will be overnighting here for two nights, you might want to scope out a place for dinner before you go back to your Alberobello hotel and snooze. Our favorite was the Ristorante Terminal Pizzeria next to the large municipal parking lot on Indipendenza on your right as you enter the commercial section of Alberobello. Don't let the name scare you. This place is a lot more than a pizza place! Also, it is owned by the same folks who own the Grand Hotel Olimpo.

Remember, tomorrow is a day trip to the ancient (and I mean ancient) the City of Matera. So, if you missed a good dinner, you will have a second shot at it.

MATERA
You may have noticed that I have saved the best or most interesting for last. So here we go:

The original settlement of Matera lies between two canyons carved by the Gravina River. The "Sassi" is a complex of cave dwellings dug into the canyon walls. Matera was occupied by the Romans, Longobards, Byzantines, Saracens, Swabians, Angevins, Aragonese, and Bourbons. All these people made their homes in those caves. There are several hundred of them.

By the way, "Sassi" is Italian for "stones." Here is a quick history of the Sassi: Archeologists believe the caves were dug out of the soft stone walls about 10,000 years ago during the Paleolithic era. These caves are almost "pre-historic" history. To put this

234

timeline into perspective: The digging of these cave homes was accomplished during the time of primitive man when he was the hunter and the gatherer. It would be almost 10,000 years before Ancient Rome would come along. This is also several million years after the dinosaurs became extinct.

In the 1800s, the cave dwellings became houses of poverty with poor sanitation and meager working conditions coupled with rampant disease. The Italian government evacuated these "modern" cave dwellers in 1952. The Sassi area of Matera lay abandoned until about 1980, when the government and private sectors started converting many caves into hotels, restaurants, museums, shops, and an art community. In 1993, Matera was declared a UNESCO World Heritage Site.

The actual town of Matera (not the Sassi) was founded in 251BC by the Roman Lucius Caecillius, who named it Matheola. As stated above, the control of Materia over the centuries passed between various warring peoples. In the 15th century, Matera was controlled by Aragon (Spain). In 1806, Bonaparte assigned Matera to be held by Potenza, also in the province of Basilicata.

In 1927, Matera became the capital of the new province of Matera. On arrival in Matera, don't get surprised. Matera is a modern city with shops, restaurants, hotels, and the like. The new and modern section of Matera is not the Sassi. You need to follow the signs to the Sassi, then park in one of the municipal areas.

>>>TIP<<<
Here is another way to see Matera. If you can fly into Bari by 11AM, there is a one-hour bus to Matera. You can visit Matera and then, at about 5PM or 6PM, take the bus back to the Bari airport. No car is needed. However, timing is critical here, and it may be a stressful day.
>>><<<

An Alternative to the Escorted Tour

>>>TIP<<<
The best way to see Matera is via a 40-minute "Tuk-Tuk" tour. Tuk-Tuks are small three-wheeled mini-taxis that accommodate two people behind the driver. Some of them are like golf carts and can accept four people. The government sets the rates. You will see them all over Matera. However, the best way to get one is to go into any bar or hotel and ask one of the staff to call one for you. The cost is 50 Euros (total for two people) if you want an English-speaking guide. An Italian-speaking guide with no English will cost you only 40 Euros. And if you are going into a bar, thank the barista and order a café. If at a hotel, please tip the one who called the Tuk-Tuk. There are not that many Tuk-Tuks, and the best is not to wait. So, you might want to email "Cosimo" at menavento@virgilio.it. His phone is 39-329-619-3820. Best to give him a time frame for your arrival. In this way, he will provide you with a priority once you arrive.

All Tuk-Tuks are privately owned by the drivers, most of whom have been driving in Matera for over 30 years. Also, **CASH ONLY**.

Usually, the Tuk-Tuk guide will stop at one of the famous churches in a plaza and allow you, if you would like, to visit it. One such church is the Cattedrale di Maria Santissima della Bruna e Sant'Eustachio on the Piazza Duomo. I might note that the driver will stop a few times for picture-taking of the entire Sassi area. After you complete your tour, ask the guide to bring you back to where you parked your car. You can grab a bite before returning to Alberobello or Bari.
>>><<<

CHAPTER 15

SICILY WEST
PALERMO, TRAPANI
ERICI
SEGESTA, SELINUNTE
AGRIGENTO
THE VALLEY OF THE TEMPLES

INTRODUCTION

For some reason, Sicily doesn't get the play or promotion it ought to get. I spent almost a month in Sicily, circumventing the entire island. You can't beat the history of this island. The people are warm, and the food has a little different flare. And, if you like seafood and fish, Sicily is the place.

What I like best about Sicily is that it can be visited in winter and will feel like a mild spring day. Would you believe in December and January, they are growing tomatoes? If this is a subsequent visit to Italy, you can't beat the weather in the winter months. January and February temperatures can reach 70 degrees during the day. If you are planning on visiting Italy during the winter months, plan on 7-10 days in Sicily.

The island is varied with its terrain and ancient sites. Not to mention Mount Aetna (a not-so-dormant volcano) in the Catania area, which seems to blow up every few years and spill lava all over its slopes.

An Alternative to the Escorted Tour

Because of the size of the island, I have divided Sicily into West and East Sicily. This way, you can spend anywhere from 6-14 days in each region. If you want to visit Palermo, the best is to add extra days onto the six day minimum. After visiting the West side you can fly home or go over to the east side i.e., Syracuse and Taormina. I don't detail the days since you may add on a few in these two towns. Sicily is best visited with a rental car. However, the train is an excellent second choice. Minor problems are taking the train, which I will get into later. If you want to make a comparison, you should compare Milan in the northern part of Italy with Palermo. I mean that you can easily make Palermo a base for day trips to the Western side of Sicily. However, my suggestion is to rent a car at Palermo airport. It is inexpensive, and you don't have to worry about those crazy Italian or Sicilian drivers, for there are no major Autostradas (at least the ones with those maniacs) in Sicily. Once you rent that car, hopefully in your planning state, you can follow the itinerary below. You can skip certain towns, making your visit to Sicily "compact."

If you are on Italy's mainland, I suggest flying down to Palermo or Catania. It's less than an hour and not a lot of money. There are frequent flights from Rome and Milan. Also, consider flying into Palermo or Catania as your first stop on your visit to Italy. All the major European airlines have excellent connections. For example, you can fly JFK, ORD to Zurich or Amsterdam, then connect to Palermo (PMO) or Catania (CTA). This way you don't have to go down from Rome, Milan or Venice. This way, you can start your visit to Italy by going directly to Sicily.

Another alternative is to take the train down. However, I have to tell you; there are only two trains a day from Rome's Termini station. And, further, it's a long "schlep"; about 10-11 hours. It would be better to get that train in Naples going to Palermo and save 90 minutes (instead of from Rome). A quick summary: avoid taking the train down if possible, as it will also waste an entire day. If you take the train down, make sure you are in the correct coach, as the train breaks apart once it crosses the Straits of Messina on the ferry. One half goes down the east coast toward Syracusa, and the other goes west toward Palermo.

On another subject, if you are flying in and can schedule your arrival into Palermo before 2PM, you won't have to overnight in the Palermo area, as Trapani and Erice are only an hour away.

So, in summary, it's best to rent a car at Palermo, Airport (PMO). This way, you can add Palermo on as a day or two before or after your visit to the west side of Sicily. At the end of this chapter, I will give you all the information on Palermo, i.e., history, where to stay, and all that good stuff.

So, here is a suggested itinerary for Western Sicily:

SICILY WEST DAY 1 FLY INTO SICILY

If it's dark or late consider staying overnight in a suburb of Palermo called "Mondello." It's only a few miles from the airport. Here you will find several three and four-star hotels in a quaint Italian (or should I say Sicilian) village. My favorite is Conghiglia D'Oro.

As mentioned, if you have at least two hours of daylight remaining, consider the 1.5-hour drive to the hilltop town of Erice; else, it's only one hour to Trapani.

Both towns are "linked" together by a cable car system (Funivia). Hence, you can visit Erici and Trapani the same day.

>>>TIP<<<
If you are not renting a car at the PMO airport and instead taking the airport bus or a taxi into Palermo, you can visit Trapani and Erice the next day. Forget the train as it takes 3.5 hours. However, a bus line (Segesta Bus lines) operates hourly buses to Trapani

239

An Alternative to the Escorted Tour

from Palermo. It is reasonable, costing only 11 Euros and taking 1.0 to 1.5 hours. This way, you can enjoy Trapani and then take a day trip via the Funivia or a taxi to Erice. Just an idea if you are not renting a car. >>><<<

SHORT HISTORY OF ERICE

The Phoenicians founded the ancient hilltop town of Erice (2500ft above sea level). It was destroyed in the First Punic War by the Carthaginians. In 831, it was ruled by the Arabs and renamed the Mountain of Hamed. In 1167, the Normans invaded and renamed it Monte San Giuliano. In the mid-20th Century, the town took on its present name of Erice from the ancient Greek name of Eryx.

Two well-preserved castles remain and can be visited. The Pepoli Castle dates from Saracen times, and the Castello di Venere (Venus Castle) from the Norman period. This temple was built on the ancient Temple of Venus. The city walls still remain.

SHORT HISTORY OF TRAPANI

The Elymians founded Trapani, originally called Drepana, and still serves as the port of Erice. The City sits on a promontory, surrounded by water on all three sides jutting into the Mediterranean Sea.

Like many medieval towns, control of Trapani went back and forth between at least a dozen warring tribes. Carthage seized control in 260BC until the Romans took it in 241BC. It was taken by the Vandals, Ostrogoths, and Byzantines until 827 when the Arabs took over. Roger I of the Normans took control in 1077AD.

In the 17th Century, the City decayed rapidly from plagues, famines, and revolts. However, the population grew from 16,000 to 30,000. Because of its strategic natural harbor, Trapani became a jumping-off spot for the Crusades to reach the Holy

240

Land. Trapani continues to be a large fishing and processing port. Later the City became part of the Kingdom of Naples.

SICILY WEST DAY 1 OR DAY 2 – CHECKING INTO YOUR HOTEL IN TRAPANI OR ERICE

First, there are about the same number of hotels in Trapani as Erice. Parking is relatively easy in Trapani. It's all flat walking with lots of shopping and restaurants. For Seniors, Trapani is ideal. On the other hand, if you want to stay in an Italian village with lots of history, then Erice is the place.

However, on the other side, Erice (pronounced Err-Ree-Chee) has limited parking, stone streets (sampietrini), a half-dozen hotels, and what's most important for Seniors, is that the streets all have slight inclines. However, that being said, if you have no major mobility impediments, best to stay in Erice. It's a medieval town perched on top of a hill. Also, if this is your first stop from an overseas flight, staying two nights is a must since you will need a full day for recovery to just sleep and work that jet lag off.

One hotel I recommend is the Hotel Moderno. I have stayed here, and for the price and location, you can't beat it. However, you must park temporarily in the main square, about two blocks away, and summon the hotel bellman, who will lug your bags up the slight hill to the hotel. The problem is that he won't carry you up the hill in a rickshaw. Also, be advised that to go to any restaurant you will have to navigate the slight inclines or eat in the hotel, which I might add is excellent and very reasonable.

You can find parking after you check in by moving your car about 5-7 blocks up the incline. It's not a big deal. Also, it's free parking on the street. For Seniors, if you have a walking or a cardio problem, I suggest you stay in Trapani and make a day trip to Erice. If you are staying at the Hotel Moderno, request a room with a balcony overlooking the Via Vittorio Emanuele. It's like a Romeo and Juliet balcony. And, yes, the Moderno Hotel has an elevator.

An Alternative to the Escorted Tour

>>>TIP<<<
If you cannot make calls in Italy on your smartphone and if you are overnighting in Erice you need to advise the hotel to help you with your bags. From the square, suggest you ask any of the taxi drivers or one of the locals to do you a favor and call the Moderno. Make sure you have a piece of paper with the phone number and the name Hotel Moderno on it. It would be best to offer that person a Euro for a café and a "Grazie".
>>><<<

Here are some of the hotels you will find in Erice. If you are booking late and need to "get a room" somewhere in Erice, make sure you ask about a private or en-suite bathroom.

Here are some three star hotels in Erice. However, many hotels, Albergos (just a term for a small hotel) and B&B's may not be rated. Readers are encouraged to check the reviews. Also, many may not offer breakfast. There are however, places to purchase pastry goods and cafes.

HOTELS IN ERICE

Hotel Moderno	Hotel Elimo	il Carmine Dimora Storica	Residence San Martino Rooms and Suites
Albergo Hotel Edelweiss	Bella Vista B&B	Hotel Al Postal 17	Antico Borgo

>>>TIP<<<
If you are overnighting in Erice, best to use Google Maps as TOMTOM and GARMIN tends to route you another way with numerous switchbacks. If you are following a taxi or a bus coming up from Trapani, you are on the correct road, and yes there are switchbacks here that the buses can negotiate.
>>><<<

ITALY Made Easy for Seniors

One more item. If you have any intention on staying at the Moderno or the Elimo. You should book directly and book early. These two places fill up very fast. Remember, you can always cancel your booking several weeks in advance. You should check with the hotel about their policies.

A word about Trapani. This is not a touristy town. Expect to find inexpensive restaurants and 99% locals. If you want to live with the locals, this is the place. If you want to visit the medieval hilltop town of Erice, you can go for a few hours via the inexpensive Funivia.

If you are wishing to stay in Trapani. Here is list of hotels. Unlike Erice, Trapani is 100% cosmopolitan. Shops of all types. A bustling main boulevard (Corso Piersanti Mattarella/Via Giovanni Battista Fardella) is loaded with shops, hotels and restaurants.

HOTELS IN TRAPANI

Best Western Palazzo Art Hotel	Hotel San Michele	Palazzo Barlotta	Dimora Botteghelle
Casa Trapani	Grand Hotel Palace Divino	Residence Porta delle Botteghelle	Historico Loft and Rooms

There is lots of shopping in Trapani. The town is split into two sections: the new section and old section. However, you will come upon the old section when you get down to the park at the end of "Fardella." After you work around the post office, you will find bakeries, pastry shops, restaurants, and churches as you stroll the streets toward the end of the peninsular. If you make it to the end of the peninsular in the old city, you can take a photo of the Torre di Ligney. It houses an architectural museum that dates to about 1670.

It's a long day of walking. If you are bushed, you can always take a taxi or one of the buses back to your hotel from the old section or the railroad/bus station opposite the park. Also, suppose you stay in Erice and come to Trapani for the day on the Funivia. In that case, you can ask any taxi to take you to the Funivia (about 8-10 Euros as it's only about 2.5 miles) or ask any bus if they go up to the Funivia. If they do, jump on and buy a ticket. The driver will advise you when you get up to the Funivia entrance. If you care not to take the Funivia back up the hill to Erice, I am sure the taxi driver will take you back to your hotel in Erice. I should note that the bus takes about 30 minutes. So you might consider spending the extra five Euros and just taking that taxi. You can usually pick up a taxi at a hotel or ask a bar to call one. If all else fails, you probably can "hail" a cab on the main boulevard. You should be able to return to your hotel at about 5PM for a snooze and shower before going to dinner at about 7:30 or 8PM.

SICILY WEST DAY 3- DAY TRIP TO THE TEMPLE OF SEGESTA

You probably never heard of Segesta. No one knows anything about it. It is only speculation. The Temple predates Greece and Rome! You probably never learned about it when you studied the Punic Wars in high school history class!

Segesta is only 25 miles from Erice or Trapani and will take about 45 minutes. It's a short day trip without beating your gums out. It's best to leave Erice or Trapani by 10AM, and visit the Temple and the abutting Greek amphitheater. After the visit, you can have lunch in one of the towns, then head back about 3-4PM.

The Temple at Segesta is so eerie and steeped in history that I don't know where to start. The Temple of Segesta is a well-preserved Doric Temple. Some quick facts. It dates from 420BC and is of Greek design, but the ancient City of Segesta had no Greek population. Figure that one out. The view amongst historians is it was built by the indigenous people known as the Elymians. The Temple sits on a slight mound in a valley of tall grass backed by hills with moderate size outcroppings of rock.

244

The Temple has six columns in the front and fourteen on the side. It measures about 65 feet on the short side and 175 feet in depth and is on a platform of about three steps in height.

The Temple was never completed. Indications are that the bosses in the blocks were never removed after the columns were assembled. Strangely, the Temple lacks a roof. Also, there is no altar site. It is believed that the construction of the Temple halted when Segesta went to war against Selinunte. The Carthaginians in the 5th Century AD spared the Temple's destruction.

In addition to the Temple of Segesta, there is a Greek Amphitheater (Teatro di Segesta) located about a quarter mile away in the same complex. The amphitheater is built into the side of Mount Barbaro, which lies about 300 feet higher than the Temple of Segesta. It is still well preserved, being constructed (the latest renovation) in the 2nd century BC. It appears that the theater held about 4,000 people.

To visit this Greek theatre, you must walk about a third of a mile up Mount Barbaro over a few switchbacks. However, no need to worry. The park authorities provide a mini-bus that will take you up and down Mount Barbaro.

>>>TIP<<<
If you take the mini-bus (there is a charge of 1.5 Euros), it is best to sit on the right-hand side as you go up the mountain. This way, you can take excellent photos of the Temple of Segesta off in the distance.
>>><<<

On arrival at the complex, tickets are offered for a combination of a visit to the Temple and the Greek Amphitheater. The price is only six Euros. The Temple lies about a football field behind the ticket booth and the facilities. It is easily walkable; however, for Seniors, you should note that there is a very slight grade.

An Alternative to the Escorted Tour

If you have extra time, you can visit some of the ruins of the ancient Segesta dating to about the 2nd century BC. Another village was recently discovered from Muslim times in addition to a Norman settlement with a castle on top Mount Barbaro. After the expulsion of the Arabs, the Normans built a castle on Mount Barbaro. The entire site of the ancient city of Segesta was found in 1574 by the Dominican historian Tommaso Falzello. Ruins unearthed to date are available for viewing.

For lunch, 2-3PM, you will find two excellent restaurants on the OLD main road SP68, less than a mile from the Segesta Architectural Park entrance. Follow the SP68 going west toward the ocean. The SP68 is the road that leads you into Architectural Park from the main highway. Just before the E933, you will find the Ristorante at the Tenute Pispisa Segesta, and after you pass under the bridge of the highway, the Ristorante Mediterraneo Segesta. Best to make your lunch (pranzo) the day's main meal. At about 5PM you should arrive back in Erice or Trapani for a snooze before dinner at 8PM. If you are staying in Erice, an excellent restaurant is "Osteria di Venere" located on Via Abatti just up the street to the right of the Hotel Moderno.

SICILY DAY 4- TEMPLES AT SELINUNTE AND ON TO AGRIGENTO VALLEY OF THE TEMPLES

If you are staying at the Hotel Moderno, see if they will let you drive your car up to the side street entrance or help you down to the taxi plaza. You will have to bring your car down from your overnight parking spot.

Here is a quick re-cap of the day. We visit the temples at Selinunte in the late morning. Then head to Agrigento in the afternoon. We overnight in a suburb and then see the Valley of the Temples the next day before heading to Syracuse. You should check out of your hotel by 10AM and head for Selinunte. You will be in Selinunte for a few hours.

246

ITALY Made Easy for Seniors

What I like best about Selinunte is that it sits on the Mediterranean. The ocean makes a great backdrop against the ruins of the still-standing temples. And you can take selfies with yourself perched on top of those ruins.

The temples at Selinunte are a 90-minute run, about 60 miles due southeast of Trapani (or Erice) on the Mediterranean. Covering almost 700 acres, Selinunte is the largest archeological park in Europe. It was founded as a Greek colony in 628BC, perhaps as early as 700BC. It was an extensive Greek city founded by a Greek colony (about 20 miles from Athens) known as Megara. At its peak, it had a population of over 30,000. It was destroyed and abandoned in 250BC and never reoccupied. There are many temples on the site, with the earliest dating to 550BC.

The name Selinunte is a Greek word for celery. Wild celery grew in the area; hence the Greeks named their city after it.

Now that your know the background of Segesta, you should know the following facts: First, Segesta (you probably visited it yesterday) and Selinunte always fought each other. Then the Carthaginians aided Selinunte only to come back later and conquer Selinunte. This went on for several hundred years. Wars went on and on. It is believed that as early as 580 BC the Selinuntines were engaged in hostilities with the non-Greek Elymian people of Segesta, whose territory bordered their own. So much for a short history.

If you are taking the train, you must go to Castelvetrano and take a quick shuttle bus to the park. Getting to this place is not easy. It is operated about four times a day by the Salemi bus company. You need to get the exact times; else, you may be forced to take an expensive taxi ride back to Erice or Trapani. There is a six Euro admission fee, and parking is free.

247

An Alternative to the Escorted Tour

The best way to get down to Selinunte is to go by car (private car and driver for the day. You would then return to Erice or Trapani. If you are fortunate your driver will accompany you to Agrigento or perhaps your entire visit to Sicily.

It's a fast drive down on the A29, then take the Castelvetrano exit and follow SS115 to Marinella di Selinunte. You will be there in a few minutes.

At the entrance, there is a moderate size museum and very modern facilities. You can tour the complex on a tram for an additional fee. Please see below.

There are paths connecting all the ruins. Seniors should have no problem unless you are visiting in the hot summer and shoulder months, to be avoided. In any way, best to bring your water and snacks. You may even want to get your hotel or an "Alimentaria" (convenience store selling cold cuts and crusty bread) to make you a sandwich or two. You can also buy sandwiches and drinks before you enter the park. It makes a great photo op, downing a sandwich on one of those ancient Greek columns in the grass.

You should note that the park closes at 6PM. So don't arrive about 5PM and expect to spend several hours here since there are two clusters of ruins and temples about a kilometer apart (a little more than a half mile). You may want to take the mini-tram around the park for 12Euros or better 3Euros between stops.

Now here is what you need to see:

Most of the ruins were discovered and excavated in the 19th Century. In the 20th Century, the temples on the eastern hill were excavated. In as little as 1950 Temple E was reconstructed. At the same time the excavations of the Acropolis began.

First, the ruins and the temples all are addressed with an alphabetic charter: A-B-C-D and O are right up against the

248

water. The other cluster E-F-G is near the entrance and the museum. Once again, all these temples were built to honor the gods, Zeus, Dionysus, Apollo, Hera (Goddess), and more.

>>>TIP<<<
The best approach is to take the tram from the entrance, where they always hang out to the temples on the water A-B-C-D and O, and then either take the tram back or walk back to the entrance. Also, you may want to visit one of the necropoli and view the foundations, which date back several thousand years.
>>><<<

A rather large necropolis of part of the old city is also located about a kilometer from the entrance. It lies at about two o'clock as you enter the complex. All temples and ruins are located in this massive park. You cannot compare Selinunte with Pompeii or any of the other ruins in Italy or even Greece. This archeological park is spread out and huge.

On my entrance to Selinunte, my jaw dropped as I viewed temples E, F, and G for the first time.
It was an "OMG."

After completing your visit to Selinunte, you are ready to make your way over to Porto Empedocle, a suburb of Agrigento and on the Mediterranean. There are lots of hotels in Agrigento. However, my favorite area is Porto Empedocle. Lots of good restaurants abutting the beach and a fabulous four-star hotel at the end of the beach road. Villa Romana is on the beach and also has an excellent restaurant. If you want to stay here the night before your visit to the Valley of the Temples, do request a room with an ocean view if you are arriving during daylight hours to see that gorgeous sunset.

An Alternative to the Escorted Tour

SICILY WEST DAY 5 AGRIGENTO- THE VALLEY OF THE TEMPLES

The Valley of the Temples is a must-see if you visit Sicily. Like many of the archeological sites in Italy, it is also one of the 58 UNESCO World Heritage Sites.

After checking out of your hotel at about 10AM, it's only a 15-minute drive on the SS640 road to the Agrigento. Once in Agrigento, follow those signs to the Valley of the Temples.

On arrival, there is a free parking lot before you gain admission. You should note that there are two entrances. A shuttle bus goes between them for three Euros. So, if you walk to the other side (about 2.5 miles), you can take that shuttle back to where you came in.

If you decide to base yourself in Palermo, there are trains every few hours to Agrigento, and the journey only takes two hours. If you are in Catania, the journey will take around five hours with at least two or three changes of trains; not advisable.

First, if you are attempting to visit in June-October, be advised that you need to purchase a timed ticket, or else you won't be able to gain admission to the park. Secondly, if going during this time frame, I can tell you from experience that this place is beastly hot.   Once again, for Seniors the best time to visit Sicily is in the shoulder and winter seasons.

You can purchase tickets directly from the Italian Government-authorized website: www.ecm.coopculture.it/index.   The entrance fee is 12 Euros. However, if you want to go to the museum it will cost you an additional 3.5 Euros. Also, at the entrance, a map of the complex is advisable for one Euro.

Now on to the history of the Valley of the Temples:
First, this place was originally called Akragas. Like many communities in Sicily, it was founded about the 6th Century BC

250

as a Greek colony, actually an outpost. The complex does not lie in a valley but on a bluff. All the temples, or what I would say, the remains of the temples, are on like a boulevard. For Seniors with severe mobility issues, you can arrange a no-charge power chair. However, you need to make a reservation. It is strongly recommended that you pick up an audio tour and headset.

Better if you are with another couple or can arrange with another couple you can take a guided tour for two hours. This place also is mind-boggling. An ancient wall surrounds the entire complex of about 2300 acres. Here is a quick overview of the temples:

The most famous and best preserved is the Temple of Concordia. When you see pictures of the Valley of the Temples, this is the photo they often show you, indeed not a pile of rubble with a few standing columns as many of the other temples are. Here is a quick overview from Wikipedia:

The "Valley" contains the remains of seven temples. They are all of the Doric Greek style. The actual names you see here are from the Renaissance period, as they had Greek names when they were built.

The Temple of Concordia was built in the 5th Century BC. The name Concordia comes from a Latin inscription found nearby. It probably had a different name when it was built. The Temple of Concordia was converted into a church in the 6th Century AD.

The Temple of Juno was also built in the 5th Century BC. It was burnt down by the Carthaginians in 406BC.

The Temple of Heracles was one of the most revered deities of the ancient city of Akragas. An earthquake destroyed it. Today, only eight columns remain standing.

The Temple of Olympian Zeus was built in 480BC to celebrate the victory over Carthage.

An Alternative to the Escorted Tour

Temple of Castor and Pollux.
Only four columns remain. It is now the symbol of modern Agrigento.

The Temple of Hephaestus (Vulcan) also dates from the 5th Century BC. It is now one of the most eroded.

Temple of Ascipepius (I can't pronounce it either, but I know it's Greek) is located far from the town's walls. It was the goal of pilgrims seeking cures for illnesses.

Also in the Valley is the Tomb of Theron. It was built to commemorate the Romans killed in the Second Punic War.

You will need 2-3 hours to digest the temples fully, take pictures, etc. After you visit the Valley, you have several options. On exiting the Valley, best to grab a bite.

For Seniors, if you are bushed best is to overnight in Agrigento or Porto Empedocle and head back in the morning to Palermo for two nights and three days of sightseeing. Or, if you will be visiting Syracusa and Taormina on the east side, the best would be to overnight in Agrigento.

The road to Syracuse on the side of the island, via Catania takes about 2.5 hours without stops. It's not the best road in the world, either. However, you can drive about one hour late in the day to arrive at a hotel in Caltanissetta. Or see if you can make it to Syracusa. However, my feeling is that you are gaining little. So if you are going to Syracusa and Taormina, the best would be to drive one hour to arrive at your hotel at about 5PM.

You should be aware of the sunset in the late afternoon if, for some reason, you have decided to go back to Palermo instead of Syracuse. While going north to Palermo the road also goes west and you may have the sun in your eyes. The roads in Sicily are simple local roads. For Seniors, exercise caution when passing.

252

As a final point, you may want to adjust your time to visit the Valley of the Temples and depart no later than 1PM. This, will allow ample time to drive to Syracusa or Palermo with no problem. Remember, you need time to re-fuel your rental at the PMO airport before dropping it. Either you will be flying home or taking a taxi to your hotel in Palermo. If not then you are en route to Syracuse and Taormina on the east side of Sicily.

 The east side of Sicily: Catania, Syracusa and Taormina, are discussed in the next chapter.

SICILY WEST DAY 6 SEVERAL DAYS IN PALERMO

PALERMO

Palermo Is famous for its history, culture, architecture, churches, and gastronomy. With three major outdoor markets in the city, you might want to rent an apartment and consider self-catering. You can broil a piece of fresh fish every day and still not sample all that fish from the Mediterrean. You can always have dinner out and breakfast in your apartment with goods purchased from the four outdoor markets. Shopping at these markets is part of the Palermo experience.

What comes to mind when people say, "our cruise will be stopping in Palermo for the day"? Is it the Sicilian Pizza that is so different than the pizza we enjoy so much? Perhaps it's because Palermo is synonymous with the Sicilian Mafia? Or is it because of how quaint and Italian (or should I say Sicilian) the Old Town is? Most of us know that Palermo is the capital of Sicily. However, like Sicily, Palermo doesn't get the tourist traffic it deserves. There are lots of reasons. A week here would be best, but three days will do the highlights.

If you are considering a few days in the capital of Sicily, you might want to consider going first to the PMO airport and dropping off that car. You won't need a car in Palermo.

An Alternative to the Escorted Tour

>>>TIP<<<
If you want to try your hand at driving in Palermo, drop your luggage off at your hotel. Then proceed to the PMO airport. Once at the airport follow the signs to the new (Metro) subway and take it back to the final station which Palermo Central rail station. It takes almost one hour with about 16 stops. If you are flying into PMO, it is best to take a taxi to your hotel instead of lugging those bags.
>>><<<

Palermo is made for walking. Using a car becomes a pain between the traffic, small streets, and the parking. If you are bushed after a day of walking, the best is to take a taxi back to your hotel. I also suggest that you stay at a hotel near the central rail station if you make any day trips to Agrigento, Trapani, the cathedral, or the waterfront. Buses depart near the main rail station for many points in Palermo and the abutting towns.

PALERMO HOTELS IN THE CENTRAL CITY

Ballaro Hotel	55 Aira	Hotel Palazzo Bruaccini	Hotel NH Palermo
Hotel Porto Felice	Palazzo Santamarina	Hotel Concordia	Hospitality Hotel
Hotel Politeama	Hotel Mediterraneo	Hotel Joli	The Grand Hotel Wagner
Astoria Palace Hotel	Albergo Athenaeum	Casena dei Colli	Best Western Ai Cavalieri Hotel
Grand Hotel Et Des Palmes	Hotel Tonic	Quintocanto Hotel	Ibis Styles Palermo President

MORE HOTELS IN PALERMO

Ibis Styles Palermo Cristal	Hotel Plaza Opera	Hotel Vecchio Borgo	Artemisia Palace Hotel
Hotel Posta	Grand Hotel Piazza Borsa	Hotel Principe Di Villafranca	

A SHORT HISTORY OF PALERMO

Here is a quick history of the City:

It was founded by the Phoenicians in 734BC almost 2700 years ago. Palermo then became a possession of Carthage. Subsequently, the Greeks established two colonies here. They were called Panormos after the 5th Century BC. Panormus became part of he Roman Republic and Roman Empire for over one thousand years. From 831AD to 1072AD, control of what we know as modern day Palermo passed on to Arab rule becoming the Emirate of Sicily. The City was known as Balarm. The Normans took over in 1130AD until 1816AD when it became the Kingdom of Sicily. In 1860 it became part of the Kingdom of Italy. The influence of the Roman, Arab, Gothic and Baroque cultures made their mark on the churches, palaces and other buildings throughout the City.

The inhabitances of the City speak Italian and the Palermitano dialect of the Sicilian language.

WHAT TO SEE AND DO IN PALERMO
I strongly suggest that you spend the first full day exploring Palermo. In other words, an orientation. See your front desk clerk and obtain a map (plan) of the city. Have him/her circle the three markets. Then set out by visiting them. You can have a late lunch in Old Town. I would suggest you also visit some of

An Alternative to the Escorted Tour

the famous churches en route to the markets. Here is a recap of the major markets:

The most famous is the Ballaro Market. It is located on Via Ballaro. It is the largest of the three major markets.

The del Capo Market is located on Via Cappuccinelle in the Capo neighborhood. It is known for fresh fish. There is also a fish market near the marina.

The Vucciria Market can be found in the Piazza Caracciolo. This place is ancient! It is located in the very old quarter known as Castellammare. Small alleys with buildings falling apart and graffiti all over make this place a real "gotta see" for the tourists. There are hawkers all over, shouting is an added attraction.

In addition to the above food markets you will find other smaller markets throughout the City selling everything from antiques to shampoo and housewares.

>>>TIP<<<
Visiting street markets in any city (even Paris or London) is a hangout for pickpockets. They sometimes work in teams. Ladies, don't put your handbag down on those lovely peaches! See my write-up under security in the back of this book. You should be extra vigilant in all open markets.
>>><<<

All the street markets which usually sell food are closed on Sunday. There are some markets which sell antiques and sundries which open on Sundays for a few hours.

THE CHURCHES AND ARCHITECURE OF PALERMO
Most of the churches and historical building of Palermo were built during the Baroque Period (1600-1750). You would need at least three full days to visit them all. Keep in mind that many of

256

them do charge minimal entrance fees. Check to see if they are open on Mondays. So here is an overview:

The Cattedrale di Palermo was built in 1185. It is definitely not Baroque. The Catherdral is a complex of several buildings buildt over 500 years. It appears to be a castle as it has the crenilized roof. The Church was buildt over the remains of a Muslim Mosque. The front entrance appears definitely to be Moorish. You need at least two hours to take in the entire complex.

The Cathedral at Monreale can be visited in a half day. But you should plan on a whole day. It's located about an hour away. It is also a complex mostly of Moorish and Norman design. The valuted painted ceilings are incredible. If you have a rental car no problem, else it is best to take the #389 bus. If you take other buses with connections you will be forced to walk about a half mile. Allow extra time to have lunch about 2PM in the village of Monreale. It is best to see your concierge. Seniors note, this place closes about 3PM, so don't plan on getting there late.

Santa Maria dell'Ammiraglio is best known as "La Martorana". It is part of the Byzantine Eastern Orthodox Diocese, as opposed to the Western Roman Catholic Church based in the Vatican. Since WWII it is home to the 15,000 Albanians who lost their church during the bombing of Sicily in World War II. La Martoran is a must see because of its painted and frescoed ceilings and walls. You will need about 1-2 hours here. There are many more churches. However, here are two interesting places which are must to see.

The Piazza Pretoria (also known as the Grand Square) contains a large fountain erected during the Inquistion. It contains statues of nymphs, nudes and more.

Other places worth a visit are the Palermo Opera House and the Museum of Tiles.

CHAPTER 16

SICILY EAST
TAORMINA
SYRACUSE
CATANIA & MOUNT AETNA
CEFALU

INTRODUCTION

You have reached this chapter either because you are driving in from the western portion of Sicily i.e. Agrigento and the Valley of the Temples or you have driven down directly from Palermo or you have flown into the Catania airport (CTA) and perhaps just wanted to visit the eastern side of the island.

Two things that are a must to see: Syracuse and Taormina. Both deserve a minimum of two full days. So if you arrive in the evening you can count the next day as the first full day.

SYRACUSE (SYRACUSA)

First you should know that there are two parts of Syracuse. There is an island called "Ortigia", separated by a canal which connects it from the mainland portion of Syracuse. The canal is spanned by two small bridges no more than 200 feet each. Ortigia as well as the mainland contain Greek and Roman ruins. Please see my history below.

There are hotels on both Ortigia and the mainland side. Syracuse is a small place compared to a Palermo or a Catania. You can walk the entire place in less than an hour.

ITALY Made Easy for Seniors

My favorite place to stay is on the island of Ortigia. First its rather quaint. Secondly, there is a major food and street market everyday (except Sunday). There are lots of restaurants and gelato shops. And finally, it's a small place to walk around as compared to the mainland portion of the town. No question, Ortigia is the best place to stay.

My favorite hotel is the three star La Posta. It is quite reasonable and you can request a balcony overlooking the canal (channel). If you want to spend the big bucks, best is to stay at the five star Grand Hotel Ortigia; do request a water view.

If you can't find a place in Ortigia to sleep, one of the best places is the Grand Albergo Alfeo. It's easy walking to Ortigia and central to all.

If you are arriving by train, there are lots of hotels within a few blocks of the rail station. The entire mainland of Syracuse and Ortigia island are flat. So, no worries if you enjoy a long walk.

Ortigia is a walking island. So best to park your car here and if necessary move it each day. The mainland is auto friendly. However, you can walk it with no problem on the main boulevards of Corso Umberto I and Via Malta. If you are bushed, you can taxi back to Ortigia or take one of the buses.

>>>TIP<<<
The Corso Umberto is a one way boulevard going away from Ortigia and the Via Malta goes the other way. Best to walk one way on one of the boulevards and return on the other. Note direction of the sun since they both run east and west.
>>><<<

A QUICK HISTORY OF SYRACUSE
The city of Syracusa dates back to about 2,700 year ago. It was found by the ancient Greek Corinthians and Teneans and

became a powerful city-state. Later it became allied with Sparta in addition to Corinth. It was part of what was known as Magna Graecia. By the 5th Century BC it equaled Athens in size.

It wasn't 663AD that it became part of the Roman Republic and the Byzantine Empire under Emperor Constans II. In fact, it was the capital of the Byzantine Empire from 663-669AD. Palermo took over later as the capital of the Kingdom of Sicily.

The Kingdom of Sicily was united with the Kingdom of Naples to form the Two Siciles unit the Italian unification of 1860.

Syracuse is one of the UNESCO World Heritage sites along with the Necropolis of Pantalica.

Syracuse is mentioned in the New Testament in the Acts of the Apostles book 28:12 as Paul stayed there. The patron saint of the city is Saint Lucy. She was born in Syracuse on December 13 So if you visit Syracuse over this time frame you should be aware that hotel rooms may be in short supply. I include more history in what to do and see in Syracuse.

WHAT TO SEE AND DO IN SYRACUSE
With the exception of that great street market in Ortigia, you will find most of Syracuse wrapped up in either Greek or Roman history. Oh, I forgot to mention, Syracuse is the home of Archimedes (287BC-212BC). He lived here all his life until being killed accidently by a Roman soldier during the siege of Syracuse by the Romans in 212BC. He is best known for his laws of buoyancy, mathematics and of course the Archimedes Screw.

Syracuse was founded in 734BC by Greek settlers from Corinth. There are several origins of the name. Some say it came from the Phoenicians from the words Sour-ha-Koussim, which meant "Stone of the seagulls". The Phoenicians were a people who lived in what is now the seacoast region of modern Lebanon. In ancient time various village in and around, what is now Syracuse were also occupied by other peoples from the Mediterranean. The center of the city was on the island of Ortigia. Native tribes farmed the land outside of the island.

Under Greek rule the city grew and prospered until it was the most powerful Greek city on the Mediterranean. There is so much history here that I would need a book of at least 600 pages to describe it.

THE OUTDOOR MARKET
This is a place you want to visit in the morning. Grab some olives (or bruschetta), a loaf of bread, a wedge of cheese, some slices of proscitu and head on down to the harbor where you can sit and have lunch. If you are too early for lunch, grab your goodies and stash them in your Ortigia island hotel. Oh, and don't forget that bottle of wine you need to stash in the frigo-bar. Oh, if you forgot to bring one of those swiss army knives, now is the time to purchase on at the outdoor market and make sure it has a cork screw.

TEMPIO OF APOLLO (TEMPLE OF APOLLO)
As you cross that small canal on Via Malta take note of the flower cart and café, you will see the Temple of Apollo straight in front of you. I should I really say "the remains of the Temple of Apollo." It, like most other Greek temples is of Doric design and was built in the 6th Century BC to honor Apollo. The Greek and Roman deity "Apollo" is probably the most revered and best known of all the Greek and Roman Gods. He was the god of archer, music, dance, truth, prophecy, healing and diseases, the Sun and light and more. There are remnants of temples built to honor Apollo all over what was the ancient world.

Since hopefully, you have been to the temples of Segesta, Selinunte and Concordia in the Valley of the Temples, you will find this temple to Apollo a letdown. It's mainly ruble with about six column stubs remaining. Would you believe this was a smaller temple compared to the others of the ancient world. The temple was only xix columns in the front by seventeen in length.

The temple had several transformations. It became a Byzantine church in the late Roman Empire. You may be able to make out the old iron gate in the front. Later it became an Islamic Mosque when the entire island of Sicily was ruled by the Muslims 831-1091AD. When the Normans defeated the Saracens, it was turned back into the Church of the Saviour in the 16th Century.

The building was built with 42 monolithic columns which were probably delivered via the sea and erected on site. The temple had a wood roof. Monolithic columns are made of one piece of material, chiseled from one solid piece of marble or stone, then fluted. A hole was bored in the center to aid in its lifting and manufacture. Other temples are made of disks which are then piled on top of each other to reach the desired height and then the Doric supporting block is placed on top. The temple and its remains are free to view. The balance of the remains of the ancient world are on the mainland. Please see my discussion later in this chapter.

THE MANIACE CASTLE

The Maniace Castle sometimes called the citadel. is located at the far point of Ortigia island after you cross through the Piazza del Duomo and head due south past the small university. You can't miss it, there are plenty of signs. It sits on a promontory with water to each side except for the connection to the island. At one time there was a moat, but it has been all filled in. It was constructed 1232-1240AD by Emperor Frederick II.

The first fort was built on this site by an Armenian general by the name of George Maniakes. He captured Syracusa from the Arabs on behalf of the king of Sicily.

The Castle was used by the queens of Sicily until the 15th Century. It later became a prison. In the 16th Century it became a harbor defense for the city. In 1704 a huge explosion damaged the fort and it was then renovated to incorporate guns.

It houses now a museum. However, you should take note that it is only open in the mornings. The entrance fee is small two Euros. You need no more than one hour here.

PIAZZA DEL DUOMO

As you work your way to the Piazza del Duomo you will pass a small rotary. That's the Palazzo of Archimedes. It also contains the status of Diana in a fountain. In a few blocks you will come to the Piazza del Duomo. This is the central square (it's not really a square) of Ortigia. It contains the Cathedral of Syracuse (the Duomo), the Town Hall and the Archbishop's Palace. Here you will also find the Chiesa di Santa Lucia all Badia church.

In addition to the historic buildings there are cafes, shopping and gelato shops.

What I find most interesting about the cathedral is the fact that it is a mix of Gothic with Greek columns. I find this kind of odd. However, if you look at the history of this UNESCO World Heritage Site (within the Syracuse UNESCO site) you will understand.

About the 5th Century BC the great Temple of Athena was built of the same site as the Cathedral of Syracusa. Like many other Greek temples it had six columns on the short side and 14 on the long side. Excavations around the Duomo 1907-1910 showed that the ancient Greek Temple was built on even older foundations.

The present cathedral you now see now was constructed in the 7th Century. The Doric columns of the original temple were incorporated in the walls of the church. And in 878 the church was again converted into a mosque. And further in 1085 the mosque went back to being a church. After the 1693 earthquake,

263

An Alternative to the Escorted Tour

the cathedral was rebuilt 1725-1753. The style is called High Sicilian Baroque.

If you see that small rotary, that's the Palazzo of Archimedes. It also contains the status of Diana in a fountain.

There are so many sites in Ortigia, again, I could write a book about them. However, if you visited the places I have described you will have visited the major ones. Oh, I forgot to mention that this little island with only a length of 2.5 miles also had an old Jewish Quarter. It no longer exists, but in 1998 while excavating for a house a Jewish Bath (Mikvah) site was unearthed. It now is below In the basement of the "Residence Alla Giudecca" which is a 3 star hotel. Supposedly this is the biggest and oldest Jewish ritual bath in Europe. If you care not to stay at the hotel you can take a tour of the baths for only five Euros.

Now on to the mainland section of Syracusa. The number one must see site is the massive Archaeological Park.

ARCHAEOLOGICAL PARK
The archaeological park in Syracuse, is one of the most important archaeological sites in all of Sicily and one of the largest in the Mediterranean. It spans several eras of the history of Syracuse. The park is located in the Neapolis (the new city as opposed to Necropolis) section of Syracuse, which is entirely situated on the mainland sections (not on Ortigia island). What is interesting to note is that the park is relatively new. However, the "finds" date back several thousand years. To see this entire complex and the "Pantalica," you probably need two full days. However, you should spend 2-4 hours just seeing the highlights.

You should be advised that the Necropolis of Pantalica is located about 25 miles from Syracuse. Best to drive or taxi over.
By the mid-1800s, most of the monuments at the park had been unearthed. It was only around 1950 that a master plan was

264

developed to protect the park. Outside the park's core, homes were being built over ancient temples, baths, and streets. This rampant building over precious antiquities had to be protected, and by the 1980s, the park was fully established.

Here is what is in the park:
The park is located on a hill known as the Temenite Hill. Seniors, take note it's not very high, just a hill. The hill divides the park in two. The quarries are to the North, and the South contains most monuments. The park is located near the Anapo river (or what used to be a river).

For the details and locations of all the monuments, it would be best to pick up a map/plan at the ticket booth. Note the ticket booth is located in the park on Via Francesco Saverio Cavallari.

There is plenty of parking on the Corso Celoni and in all abutting streets in addition to a public parking lot on Corso Celoni. For Seniors, there is an awful lot of walking at the park. So, you may want to take a minibus tour; check with the ticket booth. On a positive note, the Greek Theatre is located just across the street from the ticket booth (Biglietteria). There is not a lot of walking to visit the Greek Theatre.

Here are the must-sees:
The Greek Theatre was built in the 15th Century BC on the southern slope of the Temenite hill. It was subsequently rebuilt in the 3rd Century BC. It was renovated once again, now by the Romans. Later, in about 1500, when the Spaniards controlled the area, they spent no time taking the Theatre apart and shipping those blocks of stone back to Spain. What you see now is pretty much a rebuilt Greek theatre. Do not confuse this theater with the Roman amphitheater across the way.

If you see an odd-shaped structure off the side of the road with people walking around it, that's the "Ear of Dionysos," known in Italian as "Orecchio di Dionisio." If you are curious about the

An Alternative to the Escorted Tour

"Ear", I suggest you visit it. The ancient Greeks carved this limestone cave into the Temenite hill. It was given the name in 1608 by Michelangelo. It supposedly looks like the shape of a human ear. It is said that people's voices can echo up to 16 times. I suggest you visit the Ear because of the unique acoustics. The actual purpose of the cave was to be a water storage tank. It was dug in Greek / Roman times. An earthquake struck the area and caused severe damage, so the water tunnel is not useable now. In the medieval period it became a prison.

This "Ear" is massive. It is about 70 feet in height and extends about 195 from front to back. It is tapered from top to bottom like a teardrop. The Ear is definitely worth a visit.

The Church of San Nicolo ai Cordari dates from 1093 and was constructed during the Norman period. It can be seen on entering the Neapolis. The church is a building made of stone blocks. However, I never understood why a Catholic church would be built in a Greek amphitheater area. The church is closed right now. When it is open, it is used for receptions.

With respect to the Roman Amphitheater: Is a short walk from the Greek theater. However, unlike the Greek theatre, which is well preserved, the Roman theater is all ruble in a grassy field. At its prime, the theater measured about 150 yards in depth and about 120 yards across. That rectangular pit was an entranceway that led to tunnels under the Theatre to allow gladiators and animals, etc., to enter the "stage." Roman remnants of an old water tank still exist. These tanks held water for the Roman nautical games and water fights. They were fed by the Galermi aqueduct, parts of which are still standing.

Parts of the Triumphal arch of Augustus remain.
It is located in the southern part of the Roman amphitheater. It was a large arch of about 35 feet wide, about 19 feet deep, and about 40 feet in height. This arch was the entrance to the area during the Augustan period. In and around the area, there are

remains from the Hellenistic period. Again, only bases remained while most of the blocks were removed (yes, again) by the Spanish to build a fort in the 16th Century.

The Mills of Galerme was a complex of water mills. These were located above the caves of the Greek Theatre. However, they only date from the late medieval period. Today only the millers' house remains visible. These mills ground grains, i.e., Amaranth, Kamut, Spelt, etc., so they could be baked into bread.

As for Pantalica (also a UNESCO World Heritage Site), if you are into history or archeology, this is the place for exploring. It's free. But don't expect lots of ancient ruins here. What is left is an ancient cemetery. There are 4000-5000 tunnels built into rocky outcrops. This place dates from the 13th Century BC to the 7th Century BC. That's pretty old, about 3500 years. This place is a catacomb built into the rocky walls as opposed to underground tunnels. The actual town ceased to exist sometime around the 12th Century AD. Archeologists believe the town had a population of about 1,000.

After you have spent a minimum of two full days (suggested) in Syracuse, it's time to move on to Taormina.

TAORMINA
If you are visiting the eastern side of Sicily, this is one of the highlights. You can also come down from Rome for the day via an early flight to Catania (CTA) and then fly home in the evening. Please pack an overnight bag, fly down, and return to Rome the next day.

If you are driving from Syracuse, it will take you about 90 minutes (70 miles). The taxi ride from the CTA airport is about one hour. It will cost you about 80 Euros to go directly to your hotel. The drive from Palermo is a hike. The 175 miles run will take you 3.5 hours. I wish I could have stayed several days on my last trip to

An Alternative to the Escorted Tour

Taormina. A drink and some olives at the five-star Grand Hotel Timeo Belmond didn't do it.

Taormina dates before Ancient Greece established its first colony on Sicily in 734BC. Taormina is also as old as some of the other ancient sites you probably have been visiting in Sicily. Taormina ranked as one of the essential towns in Sicily and followed its history of being ruled by successive foreign monarchs.

After the Italian unification in the mid 1800s, it began to attract tourists from northern Europe. It received lots of notoriety when the 43rd G7 summit was held here in May 2017. Like Capri keep your eyes peeled for the "A-List" people and the Paparazzi.

The town of Taormina lies on a massive outcrop at the end of a large hill that extends along the coast from Cape Pelorus. The old town lies about 820 feet above sea level. About 500 feet higher than the actual town, you will find a Norman castle. There are still ancient walls around the town. Numerous pieces of old buildings are scattered about.

If you are driving, those switchbacks which take you to the top of Taormina are extremely challenging. Seniors should take a taxi to the top or, better, take the Funivia. If you are driving, you will find paid parking in a massive concrete structure where there is a capacity for almost 1,000 cars. There are other paid parking areas. They are all government-run and charge the same price. Depending on the parking area, shuttle buses are available.

>>>TIP<<<
Seniors should note that the best way to visit Taormina for the day is to park at the base of the Funivia, then take the Funivia to the top of the hill. The Funivia is on the main seaside road. If you are staying at a hotel or a BnB, you must take a taxi to the top as it is pretty challenging to take 40-pound

luggage bags on the cable car; see the above paragraph about parking garages.
>>><<<

QUICK HISTORY AND WHAT TO SEE AND DO:

The only remnant of the Greek/Roman era, remaining and still used, is the Ancient theatre of Taormina. Originally it was a Greek theatre. The Romans later rebuilt it. It was rebuilt in the 2nd Century. It is pretty impressive, with a span of 358 feet. You will find the walkway down to the theatre on the left side of the Grand Timeo hotel. Best to have a drink, and some olives there.

Other sites to be visited are the 14th Century Palazzo Corvaj, a 1635 Baroque fountain, the Church of San Domenico, and the municipal gardens. Below Taormina lies the seaside resort of Giardini Naxos. You will see the Isola Bella nature reserve and beach in the bay.

The church above the town is the Santuraio Madonna della Rocca. If you have the energy, you can climb steps on the path leading to the church. Seniors should be aware that there are a lot of steps. If you are inclined to visit the church, there are superb views of Mount Aetna in the distance.

There are several other churches perched high on the slope overlooking the town, in addition to some castles. Seniors should be aware that there is lots of uphill hiking.

So what's the draw with Taormina? Simple, it is highly romantic. Many Europeans consider this an excellent place for a honeymoon. In addition, there are incredible views of the sea. There are numerous shops and cafes on the main boulevard, the "Corso Umberto ." About halfway down this boulevard, which spans about 15 blocks, is the Piazza IX Aprile. Late in the day, a pianist is playing the classics on a baby grand piano.

An Alternative to the Escorted Tour

I cannot tell you how much I enjoyed the shopping, or should I say the looking. There are great places for a honeymoon. There is a superabundance of hotels and BnBs. You can figure the count is at least a hundred. However, you will have to find a beach. The best is to stay perhaps in Taormina Mare for part of your stay. You might also consider Giardini Naxos or the Letojanni beach area.   As for dinner or Pranza (lunch), you will find an abundance of restaurants. However, best to ask the locals where they go.

>>>TIP<<<
If you are going to stay at a BnB, Seniors should be aware that off the Corso Umberto there is a slight slope as you walk with the sea on your left. The best would be to check it out on Google Earth before you make your booking. You won't have a problem with many of the three, four, or five-star hotels as they are in flat areas.
>>><<<

After you have enjoyed your visit to Taormina, it's time to depart to Catania or Palermo for a fly-out. If you are going back to Palermo, I suggest one or two nights in Cefalu (pronounced Chef-a-loo.) It's only a four-hour run from Taormina instead of nine hours to the PMO airport. So you can easily leave Taormina at about 3PM and head for dinner in Cefalu. Please see my next section on Cefalu's beautiful village and seaside town.

CATANIA AND MOUNT AETNA
No question, the draw to this area is the drive around Mount Aetna. Also, remember that Aetna is still an active volcano.

If you are overnighting in Catania before a flyout to one of the European Hubs or have an additional night in Taormina, I strongly recommend a day trip circumventing Mount Aetna. If you don't have a rental car, you can take the train down to Catania, then catch the special train which goes completely

270

around the volcano. However, you must remember that it is an actual "U" and not a true cirecle. It returns to a different location in Catania where you can also get the train back to Taormina. It's definitely a nice day trip.

If you are not in love with volcanos, there are several sites worth visiting in the old section of Catania. They are the ruins of the Greek and Roman theatre, the Castello Ursino which dates to the 13th Century (it's a castle) and the Cathedral di Sant' Agata. The Cathedral was built 1078-1093 but needed to rebuilt several times because of eruptions from Mount Etna and earthquakes. The lastest rebuilding was in the Baroque style.

CEFALU

Cefalu (pronounced CHEF-A-LOO) is just the town you want to stay in before you leave Italy. It's not touristy! So don't expect to buy coffee mugs, snow globes, and refrigerator magnets (made in China, of course) in this quaint seaside town.

The best place to stay is at the Hotel La Calette and Bay, about four miles due east of the town. It is a five-star hotel on the ocean, modern and very reasonable. And, do request a room with a view of the pool and ocean, if you are visiting in the shoulder season.

>>>TIP<<<
If you are overnighting in Cefalu and visiting the town, do not, repeat, do not attempt to drive in the city. Some of the streets are too narrow, and you risk getting stuck in one of them. Please take it from my experience. If you are staying at the Hotel La Calette or any hotel outside of the village itself, my advice is to take a taxi for no more than six Euros to the center of the town, walk around, shop and then come back to your hotel after lunch.
>>><<<

An Alternative to the Escorted Tour

Cefalu is a resort town. However, sitting on the small beach won't be in vogue if you are there in the off-season. The village itself is great for local shopping. And, further, I love mixing in with the locals. The main drag is called Vittorio Emanuele (named after the first king of unified Italy). It's all cobblestone. After you go through the portal at the end street, you will emerge at the sea. Just turn around and take those pictures

La Rocca, called the castle, is a fortified cliff about 820 feet above the sea. Rocca has ridges facing east, west, and south. Scaling the cliffs is impossible since the lower half is fortified. The path fortified in the middle ages allowed climbing to the top, where a castle was built.

Note, climbing "Rocca" is NOT advisable. Whether you are a Senior or not, you need to be skilled at hiking on steep paths. It is best viewed at sunset with the Rocca di Cefalu in the background behind all those houses.

There are numerous churches in the village. My suggestion is not to stay in the village but to stay in one of the lovely beach resorts. It is best to visit the town from 11AM- 3PM. You should note that many shops will be closed 1PM-4PM for siesta.

The following day it is a fast run of about 60 miles (a little over an hour) to PMO airport to drop that rental car and fly home to Rome or drop into one of the hotels in Palermo itself. And remember you won't need a car in Palermo.

See my write-up on things to do and see in Palermo in the prior chapter, "SICILY WEST."

CHAPTER 17

CORTONA (TUSCANY)
A BONUS CHAPTER

INTRODUCTION

If you enjoyed San Gimignano, you will really enjoy Cortona. It also is a medieval hilltop town without the towers of San Gimignano. The town and the abutting rolling hills are so inviting that Frances Mayes chose Cortona as her town in *"Under the Tuscan Sun."* If you decide to visit Cortona and perhaps spend a few days in this romantic town, and beautiful town, you can visit the Villa Bramasole, the home where the movie was made. The name Bramsole means in Italian "something that yearns for the sun." The Villa is now a private residence, however, you can take pictures from the outside. I might note that Francis Mayes enjoyed this town so much, she now spends a good part of the year living here.

So you may ask yourself "what is so unique about this medieval town besides the fact that *Under the Tuscan Sun* was filmed here?" Good question. I just can't describe it. You must see it for yourself. And if you do stay at a hotel in the old City e.g., Hotel Villa St. Lucia or the Hotel Villa Marsili, insist that you have a room with a view of those rolling hills. That valley is called "Valdichiana.". And yes, you can use the term in your emails to the hotels.

Cortona is best visited with an automobile. You are lucky if you are going by train since Cortona is on the Rome-Florence mainline. However, most of the high-speed trains don't stop here. So you need to take a local. The rail station for Cortona is

An Alternative to the Escorted Tour

called Terontola-Cortona. It is a two hour run from Rome at a cost of $15-35 and from Florence about one hour at a cost of $12. You will need to take a taxi 12-15 Euros to the center of Cortona.

Most of the hotels in the old City are accessible by auto and taxi. Many of the hotels on the hilltop towns like Cortona, Assisi and San Gimignano will not have hotel parking. So do enquire via email if and where you can park your car. And for Seniors, do ask how far is the walk to the hotel from the parking area. I should note, there is metered parking along the ring road along with parking lots abutting the back streets of the medieval City.

For Seniors, there are steps and ramps leading from parking lots up to the main streets and the **Piazza della Repubblica and** Piazza Garibaldi.

With respect to hotels in the old City. For Seniors, make sure they have an elevator or else ask for a quiet room on the ground floor not facing the street as these rooms tend to be noisy. If they cannot give you a room with view, take a room facing the courtyard or a side street.

There are about two dozen hotels in the old city and about 100 others (including BnBs) within five miles. There are also several five-star resorts at the base of the hill.

As for restaurants Cortona is loaded with them and they are all excellent. Many of them are located in old stone buildings with rustic beamed ceilings.

HISTORY OF CORTONA

Cortona for several centuries was believed to be Etruscan. In the 8th Century BC it is believed they were part of the Etruscan League. Cortona became a powerful city because of its strategic position in controlling the valley.

274

ITALY Made Easy for Seniors

The walls you see surround the town were date from about the 4th Century BC. In 310BC Rome made an alliance with Cortona which was shortly lived. Rome took over Cortona and made it a colony. The Romans built the Via Cassia road between Chiusi and Arezzo bypassing Cortona. During the Second Punic War, Hannibal attacked Cortona.

During the Gothic war (535-554AD) Cortona was sacked and destroyed. Cortona was subsequently attached by other warring tribes and further controlled by wealthly families, including the Medicis. In 1861, Cortona became a part of the new Kingdom of Italy along with the other towns of Tuscany.

The restored city is mostly medieval in character. Seniors should watch out for steep narrow streets abutting the main streets.

WHAT TO SEE AND DO IN CORTONA

In the past I have found it is best to use Cortona as a base for several day trips. If you decide to make it a base the following towns are less than one hour away by car: Florence, Assisi, Perugia, Gubbio (1.25 hrs), and Montepulciano. If you are into shopping for the locals, the major town of Arezzo is about four miles up the road. The best is to shop the Saturday market for fruits, vegetable and everything else.

If you are into architecture and beautiful church, you will find The Duomo of Cortona a must to visit. The second one I would recommend is the **Basilica di Santa Margherita**. However, Santa Margherita is someone of a challenge for Seniors who want to hike up that hill. If you wish to visit the Basilica, my suggestion is to take a taxi to the top.

The Piazza della Repubblica is one of my favorite places to just hang-out, and "do nada". Imagine just people watching in the square for an hour while enjoying your Americano Café and a pastry. The Piazza della Repubblica is the main gathering point

An Alternative to the Escorted Tour

for the town. That building you see with all those steps and the campanile is the city hall.

Off the piazza are the main streets lined with places for lunch or dinner or just to enjoy a glass of local wine. This brings me to the next "thing" you do in Cortona. You walk those narrow streets; and there are plenty of them. Seniors should note that the only truly flat street for easy walking is the Via Nazionale which starts at the Piazza della Repubblica. Most of the other streets off the Via Nazionale are either steps or moderate gradients. For Seniors with mobility problems, some of these streets may be a challenge.

There is an Etruscan museum in Cortona which may be worth an hour of your time. Other than that, most visitors come here just for enjoying the beauty of this hilltop immersed in those those rolling hills. So just enjoy Cortona!

CHAPTER 18

HOTEL SELECTION
ALL YOU NEED TO KNOW

HOTEL SELECTION PROCESS

Did you know that even five star famous hotels e.g. The Waldorf Astoria in New York, The Savoy in London, etc. all have some negative reviews? So how do you choose a hotel? It's quite simple. First, convince yourself that you will do the best you can. Once you arrive if there are any issues, resolve them at once. And as a seasoned traveler remember, nothing is perfect. So here is what I do:

First, find the hotel on Booking.com or Hotels.com. Spot them on the map and see if they are close enough to where you want to stay. Pay attention to hotels which are on a main boulevard or a busy drag. Then go to Tripadvisor.com. and read some of the reviews. Pay attention to the bottom two ratings i.e. Poor and Terrible. Tick them off and read some of them. Discount comments like "the martini at the lobby bar was warm" or the desk clerk defined the word "grumpy." Pay close attention to the real bad ones, "throughout the hotel there was a musty odor." Now, add up the Poor and Terrible comments. Then add up all the categories.   Here is an example:

Excellent   980
Very Good 1287
Average   390
Poor   330
Terrible   400

So the ratio would be: $(330+400)/(980+1287+390+330+400)=.21$

An Alternative to the Escorted Tour

In summary 21% of the total reviews were made up of either poor or terrible. You can rationalize that one out of five (20%) will have a bad experience. If you can tolerate this choose this hotel. It is best to compare three hotels. And, also remember, if you are using "points" it probably doesn't matter, since who wants to pay cash with all those. If the ratio is far above the 20%, make sure you explain this well to your travelling partner.

Secondly, do consider other critical items. Will you have to pay for parking? Is breakfast included? Many five star hotels do not offer breakfast. I was in a five star hotel in Madrid and the breakfast was $36 per person. Great buffet, but I could have done with a slice of frittata and a coffee for $5 at a café down the street. You need not worry about any resort fees of $25 per person unless you are staying in resort areas e.g. Portofino in July.

Once you choose your hotel, you are ready to make the reservation. What you don't want to do is make it through the OTA i.e. the Online Travel Agents. Lot's of reasons. You need to make it directly through the hotel's official website. It may appear on page 2 or even page 4 of your Google search. The Rialto Hotel in Venice official website is Rialtohotel.com. It is not "thehotelrialto.reservations.com/." Make sure you go to the official website to make your booking. Also note that many hotels pull their listing from OTA's once they are up to perhaps 60% occupancy. So even though it says "no rooms left on our website" doesn't mean the hotel is sold out. Also, don't be afraid to ask for multi-night discounts or senior rates. They usually will want a credit card guaranty for the first night.

On your email make sure they state "Breakfast included with private bath," and 20 Euros (or whatever) per night for parking, if not included. And, do request a room NOT on the ground floor (zero floor). They tend to be noisy. For Seniors, make sure they have an elevator. And, finally make sure they state their cancellation policy on the email.

CHECKING INTO YOUR HOTEL

On check in, always ask to see the room first. Leave your bags in front of the reception desk. If the room is too small or facing the main street, do ask the clerk if they have a nicer room facing the courtyard and perhaps larger. Turn on the heat or air-conditioner and make sure the fan does not rattle. If you have a noisy mini-bar, you can always unplug it.

>>>TIP<<<
If the garage is too small to navigate in (which they usually are), do ask the front desk to have the bellman park your rental car for you. This way you will avoid damaging your rental as you squeeze it between two other cars.
>>><<<

And one final point, once the lights go out there is very little difference between paying $150 per night or $400 per night. You will still get a good night's sleep! All I ask is that it is clean and comfortable with no plaster falling off the ceiling. It is best to read those "current" comments.

On check-out make sure you pay the bill on your credit card in EUROS. In this way you will get the bank exchange rate.

CHAPTER 19

MONEY, CREDIT CARDS, ELECTRICITY, FACILITIES DRESS AND INTERNET/TELEPHONE

MONEY

The best suggestion is "don't run down to your bank to order Euros." They will "soak" you. They usually give you the worst exchange rate. Then they tack on all types of fees. There is a far easier way to do it.

On arrival in Rome, there is usually an ATM just outside those sliding doors from customs where you meet all those your private drivers. If you have a private driver (good idea), tell them you would like to get some Euros before leaving the airport. Your driver will accompany you to the ATM. It is advisable to get the maximum amount which is 250 Euros. The total fee assessed by your bank will be about $7.50 whether you get 100 or 250 Euros, plus the rock bottom exchange rate. So it is best to get the maximum allowable, which presently is 250 Euros. An alternative is to forget the ATM and postpone it for later in the day or, better, tomorrow. Your driver and hotel bellman will accept your dollars. Just explain that you do not have any Euros. A good idea is to take a fist full of one dollar bills (Canadian five dollar notes) with you. Most of your small tips will be $3-5. And by the way, in Italy we don't tip taxi drivers. However, it's a practice to let them keep the change i.e. THE COINS.

ITALY Made Easy for Seniors

>>>TIP<<<
Contact your bankcard (not your credit card company) directly or online and ensure you can use an ATM in Italy. Many major US banks, e.g., Bank America, have Partner Fee agreements with Italian banks. If you use the Partner bank ATM, Bank America will waive their foreign ATM fee. In Italy, Bank America is partnered with BNL d'Italia. There will be no foreign transaction ATM fee which is usually $5 or $7.50. If using the Bancomat ATM of BNL d'Italia, there will be no fees. If the ATM is not a BNL, you can figure a $5-7.50 total fee, which Bank America levies. You only pay the actual bank exchange rate.
>>><<<

>>>SENIOR NOTE<<<
As a Senior, we all grew up using "Traveler's Checks." Before that road trip to Florida, my Dad would visit the AAA office or our local bank and purchase American Express traveler checks. Fast forward 60 years. They are now useless and have been replaced by those ATMs. Secondly, if you ask your hotel to cash a $100 traveler's check, they will charge you 5% and offer you the worst exchange rate. They don't want to deal with those obsolete traveler's checks. In summary, you don't need them, even if your brother-in-law Harry said you do!
>>><<<

Make sure you use your Euros. Some restaurants may not take credit cards, and others usually take your dollars at a steep exchange rate. However, be advised that it is illegal for them to give you change in dollars. So, If you want to buy those silk ties for 15 Euros, that vendor at Nuovo Mercato in Florence will charge you $16 US dollars and return four Euros, not four dollars. To add insult to injury, they have the Financial Police

An Alternative to the Escorted Tour

(Guardia di Finanza) running around and checking on the vendors to make sure they also give you a receipt with their tax numbers on it and did not give you dollars as change.

It is best also to read my security notes later on in this chapter on when to use the ATM, money belts, etc.

CREDIT CARDS

First, you need to inform your credit card company the dates you will be in Italy, else you run the risk of a charge being declined. Secondly, make a copy of your card(s) and stash it in your suite case. It is best to take a VISA and a Mastercard. Most hotels will take AMEX cards, however, smaller establishments may not.

There are two types of cards. Some banks will add 3% to each foreign transaction. It's just a money maker. So, if you charge over a ten day period $1,000 you will pay an extra $30. Best is to make sure your credit cards do no incur any foreign transaction fees. If you are more than 30 days in advance of your trip, my suggestion would be to get a new credit card which has no foreign fees. Best to consult "thepointguy.com" and also pick-up some frequent flyer or hotel points at the same time.

If you use a credit card in Italy, you will find that they are a little more advanced than Americans. They don't take your credit card away from you. It is always in your possession. If you are at a restaurant or any other place where you need to use your credit card, they will bring a little machine to you to complete the transaction.

>>>TIP<<<
If offered to pay in DOLLARS, don't. Always pay in Euros. If you pay in dollars they will give you their exchange rate, which is usually not competitive with the bank rate.
>>><<<

ITALY Made Easy for Seniors

Also, remember, that restaurants include the TIP (they call it the service charge) and the TAX in their prices. Many times the restaurant will state at the bottom of the menu "All prices service and VAT inclusive." You will find no place on the credit card machine to input the tip. However, it is a custom to drop a few coins on the table when you leave. I usually drop 2-4 Euros on the table

>>>TIP<<<
If anyone tells you that the tip is not included in the price and that you need to tip 15%-20% in cash, don't believe them. Service is always included. Please see more of my dining comments.
>>><<<

ELECTRICITY
Italy, like most of Europe (not the UK) is on the 220 Volt A/C small prong system. If you are using mobile phones, laptops and tablets, you will need a USB charger with those two prongs on it. This is not the same ones we use in the USA or Canada. Many USB charges will accept the 220Volt Euro voltage, however, you need a physical adapter which takes your 110Volt A/C "blade" adapter and converts it into a two prong adapter. Here is what you need to purchase at Amazon before you leave for Italy:

AMAZON SKU- B09CT1TMRD – USB EURO CONVERT
        COMES AS A 3 PACK. THEY BURN OUT!

If you have a 110Volt plug in USB cube, check to see if it will Accept 220Volts. If it does all you need is a physical blade to prong unit, also known as a Type C adapter. Note do not get any wider units. This is the skinny unit and will go into all the European female sockets.

AMAZON SKU- TYPE C ADAPTER – EURO TO USA
        COMES IN A 6 PACK $5.99 (TiKeTaoKe)

An Alternative to the Escorted Tour

As for appliances, you may want to forget about taking that blow-dryer, as most hotels will have to borrow or in the room. If you have your own, make sure it has the knob or screw your turn for 220 volts. You will still need a Type C adapter. Please see above. This also applies to any curling iron or those heated rollers. I can tell you that you will not find any of these in the hotels. Another idea I tell folks, is to go into a CVS/Walgreens type store and purchase a travel size unit with plug and voltage for 220V operation.

FACILITIES

You will find at most hotels that odd shaped toilet next to the regular toilet. It's known as a "bidet," pronounced, "Bid Day." I won't go into the details since most Americans and Canadians don't use it. I think it is hold over from the Roman period. The next thing I suggest is that you bring a roll of your own soft toilet paper. The toilet paper tends to be like "crepe paper." Yes, in some hotels you will find it soft, however, if it's not you can pull out your roll or Charmin or whatever.

In terms of public toilets, everyone asks me "What's with those missing toilet seats"? At one time I thought it was because of the shortage of Home Depots or Lowes stores. Then I found the truth. There are over 350 models of toilet seats. Those two mounting holes are all different. In the USA and Canada we have a standard for round and elongated toilet seats such that Kohler, Delta etc. all fit the same holes. In summary, once a toilet seat breaks in a café, restaurant or whatever, they just leave it alone. If you need to use public facilities, I always suggest a large hotel. Trust me, they will have a nice toilet and it will definitely have a nice toilet seat. Oh, one more item, there are still some ancient toilets left from the Roman Empire, however they are very rare. For us guys, they are fine, for ladies you need to do a balancing act to use them. If you can't to the balancing, best to seek another bathroom that is more modern. And remember to have that one Euro coin in your pocket, just in case there is a matron there to keep the place tidy.

ITALY Made Easy for Seniors

INTERNET/TELEPHONE

I usually group these two subject together since they are related. It is my believe that Verizon and ATT charge their customer's just too much for the travel plans. If you use their travel plans it will be pricey. Just call them. The better approach is to make all your calls and access the internet when you are in your room for the evening. I used to use the Verizon travel plan, but they don't give you a lot in terms of talk time, text and data.

First, most carriers allow you to receive texts at no charge. However, if you don't have a plan, you can't text out. No big deal. The six hour difference from Eastern Time works to your advantage. If you are back in your room by 10PM, it's only 4PM in New York, 3PM in Chicago, and 2PM in Denver. So just hop on WIFI from your hotel room and use Messenger, and all those other apps to make your calls. Also, take a look at those texts and return the calls via WIFI or email.

>>>TIP<<<

Under settings turn Mobile Data off. Turn Roaming off. Don't answer any calls. If you do it will cost you. Just let them go to voice mail if you must. Also, don't access voice mail with your carrier, it will cost you. You can also put a message on your voice mail that you won't be able to return calls till (date). Advise them to email you instead. If you do have a Google Voice number tell them to call it. You can research more on Google Voice numbers on the internet. Make sure you charge your Google Voice account with perhaps $20 on a credit card so you can make WIFI calls for as little as ten cents a minute, instead of $1.75 a minute. I used to advise travelers to get an Italian cell phone for $40 and charge it with 10 Euros. I found it did not pay off. If I have to make an urgent call, I swing into a stand-up bar or café and ask the barista if he would be so kind to make a quick call for me. As long as its local, no big deal.

285

An Alternative to the Escorted Tour

Also, if you are making local calls, you might consider picking up a telephone card at any tobacco shop. All you need to is swipe it on the Italian pay phone (must be Telecom Italia) and make your call. >>><<<

In summary, don't use your US Carrier cell phone to make or receive calls or access the internet, use WIFI. You might want to check with you carrier, most allow you to receive texts, however, if you respond and send an outbound text, your "travel pass" will start, which can be as much as $20 per day.

DRESS

Dress in Italy is laid back. There are only two exceptions: in the Vatican, men cannot wear tank tops (muscle shirts), and women must cover their knees and no short-shorts or halter tops with plunging necklines. If you are not appropriately dressed (modestly), you will not be allowed to enter St. Peters. It is best to check with the Vatican website.

If you are checking into any five-star hotel, I find it best to pack a dark blue blazer, as you may be denied entry to the main dining room. Make sure you bring comfortable walking shoes, preferably sneakers, for both men and women. Do not try to break in any sneakers or shoes on your trip. Best to bring what I call "peel-off clothes." Consider the new "puff coats" and a heavy sweater in winter. Walking around Rome in a snow parker may be too hot, likewise for winter corduroy pants. Blue jeans are acceptable all over. Ladies should consider leaving high-heels and "uggs" at home.

I suggest bringing a sweater to dinner as the air-conditioning may be blowing your way. Also, after you pack, un-pack everything and ask yourself, "Do I need ten shirts"? You can always buy a shirt at the street fairs. Every time I go on a trip, I find I only wear half of what I bring. And, don't forget EXTRA meds, incase you need to spend an extra night in Venice.

286

CHAPTER 20

DINING & CUSTOMS

EURAIL & SECURITY

DINING

Dining, whether dinner or lunch is a ritual with most Italians. Most of you will probably have a lite lunch because of all your touring. So I will skip the lunch and proceed to dinner. First, most places will open at 8PM. You may be able to find a few places that open at 7:30PM, however, don't expect it. You can figure you won't eat anything until a half hour after you are seated. It this presents a problem best is to have a snack after you wake up from that snooze. By the time you leave the restaurant at 9:30PM the place will usually be packed. Second, there is a cover charge for all dining. This is usually about 2-4 Euros per person. It includes the table cloth, the utensils, bread and olive oil and may include olives. You can always ask.

>>>TIP<<<
Before you go out to dinner ask the desk clerk, where he goes to dinner. You can bet the prices will be better and they will not have a menu but a chalk board. They may only take cash. So before you sit down, check out the menu. If you care not to dine there go to your selected restaurant. I should note most restaurants post their menus outside so you can make a decision. Do walk in and ask the owner if there are any specials tonight. If you are near the coast, expect the specials to be fish.
>>><<<

An Alternative to the Escorted Tour

Wine by the glass, usually of the region is pretty inexpensive. So expect to pay about $3 a glass for Chianti when you are in Florence or $3 a glass for cold Frascati in Rome. Don't ask for exotic mixed drinks like a Pina Colada. Unless, you are at a resort or a high end hotel, they will not know how to make it. So best just to stick with wine and straight mixed drinks e.g. a Martini, a Gin and Tonic (the Brits enjoy the this) or an Italian aperitif (Aperitivo) like Compari and Soda. Also, you will find Coke, Sprite and all that other stuff expensive at about $4 a can.

When you walk into the restaurant, greet the matre 'd (usually the owner) with a "Buona Serra" and smile. If there is a non-smoking area do ask for it. Remember, all of Europe smokes and Italy does not have a Surgeon General.

After you are seated the waitperson will present you with a menu. It's usually in Italian and English. The wait person will ask you if you want bottled water. As far as I know all of the tap water in Italy is fine. However, I usually order a liter of bottled water. They will ask you if you want natural, without gas (sin gas) or with gas. It's usually ice cold and great with a piece of lemon. All water is relatively inexpensive and cost about $2-$4 per liter.

Most restaurants will offer you a Tourist Menu or you can dine ala carte. Best deal is always the Tourist Menu. It includes, an appetizer (the starter), a pasta dish, a main course and dessert. If they offer a salad it will be served before dessert. Many Tourist Menus also include a glass of house wine. Take it from me..It's always a good deal. If you don't want that full course dinner, it's okay to order some appetizers and a main dish. Don't feel embarrassed to ask the waiter that you will share all with your partner. It is perfectly acceptable.

Two things you should realize. Dinner is slooooo. Expect to wait between courses. Better, as soon as you order dessert, ask for the bill. In the USA I always figure 90 minutes for a dinner. In Italy, best to figure two hours. And don't think the service is slow. It is no reflection on the establishment. They are all slow. It is their way of life. Take it easy and enjoy it. Order some garlic bread and have another glass of wine. And one final point. You won't find spaghetti and meat balls on the menu. It's not Italian! So do have the antipasto and the Osco Bucco with the sautéed broccolini (it's a contorni, a side dish) or the spinache and enjoy. One more item, you must always ask for the bill (il conto per favore), means the count please.

CUSTOMS

Italy has some strange customs. Here are just a few. There is no such thing as salad dressing. So don't request creamy Italian, Ranch, or Blue Cheese. They only use oil and vinegar.

Pizza is only eaten with a knife and fork. You don't pick the slice up and try to bite off a piece. Also, it is ordered only for dinner unless you find a slice on a street shop for lunch.

Cappuccino is usually consumed up to 12Noon. However, after dinner an expresso is served. Most tourists will of course have a Cappuccino. You will find that most Italians will finish their dinner off with a pony of lemoncello or grappa. Lemoncello is that lemon liquor from the Naples area and grappa is made from the leftovers from the wine fermentation.

When you leave the restaurant you are required to carry the receipt with you for 100 meters. This keeps the Financial Police on their feet, making sure that you paid all those VAT taxes. In the USA many restaurant take the cash and destroy the handwritten bill, no can do in Italy!

EURAIL

Most of your friends who probably have never been to Italy will suggest that you get Eurail passes for unlimited travel through Italy. WRONG! The *Italian* Eurail pass only allows travel on a few days during the time period. In other words, you can take the train say five days in a 14 day period. It only pays off if you are

An Alternative to the Escorted Tour

doing some "long haul" routes e.g. Venice to Palermo in a day, Genoa to Brendisi, etc.

If most of your travel will be rail, it is best to get my companion book *ITALY The Best Places to See by Rail,* which explains the rail system in detail. A simple suggestion at this point is just purchase point to point tickets.

SECURITY

Comparing Italy to the USA, crime in Italy is non-existent. There are no mass shootings every day. Very few, walk around with or even have guns. Police are well respected. It definitely has to do with their culture. To prove the point, turn on the TV in your hotel room. You will only see programs which fall into four categories: Soccer (or some other sport), Game shows e.g. Wheel of Fortune, Entertainment e.g. "America's Got Talent" or better "Dancing with the Stars", and finally news. The only violence you will see is a re-run of a John Wayne wild west movie (probably in black and white from 1955) or some news involving the Ukraine war.

The crime in Italy and most of the European countries involves what is called "Petty Crime." It takes the form of everything from scams to hand-bag snatching. Now before you come to any conclusions, I can tell you that petty crime is rare. So there is no need to be concerned, especially if you follow my rules.

1. Don't bring anything you can afford to part with. Ladies leave the diamond cocktail ring home. Men don't wear your Rolex. You don't need to impress anyone.
2. Men should purchase a money belt. Best is Amazon B015HXS2KY or equivalent. They are only $20 or less. I suggest this and not the pouches. However both work.
3. Ladies and also men, should purchase a handbag with a zipper and a wide strap which fits over the shoulder. Where it across your chest and always walk with away from the curb. In other words, NOT toward the gutter

290

where it can be easily snatched by someone on a motor-scooter. Always zip it up after you take something out.

4. Always take your wallet and smartphone to breakfast with you. While the staff at all the hotels is honest, you never know who will slip in the room when the maid is cleaning.

5. When leaving for the day, take that Ipad or tablet, bury it with your soiled underwear and zip up your luggage. Also take the charging unit and bury them also.

6. Italy law requires that you have your passports in your possession at all times.

7. Purchase a cheap "sacrificial" wallet. Place a five Euro note in it with an expired AARP or library card and keep it in your back pocket. Take your real wallet and put it in that large front pocket where you can easily put your hand on it as you walk around that large outdoor market.

8. Beware of setups. If someone sits next to you on a park bench, consider getting up and moving. Watch out for people wanting to take your picture on the Rialto Bridge. While distracting you, the "partner" may bump into you and remove that wallet in your back pocket. Ha, all they got is five Euros and an expired library card.

9. Beware of people willing to help you with directions or show you to your hotel.

10. If you need to look at a map or your smartphone, back yourself up against a building where no one can come from behind and pick that sacrificial wallet; better to slip into a stand-up bar or a café.

11. Don't use the ATM when it is dark. Have someone accompany you to the ATM. Or better, use the ATM inside the bank and not the one out on the street.

CLOSING REMARKS

I thank you for reading this book and hopefully your travels through Italy will be as enjoyable as mine have been!
Bob Kaufman, thegelatopress@gmail.com

An Alternative to the Escorted Tour

UNESCO SITE	CHAPTERS	1,000
Historic Center of Rome	2,3	Yes
Last Supper Milan	11	Yes
Historic Center of Florence	7	Yes
Venice and The Lagoon	9	Yes
Piazza del Duomo of Pisa	8	Yes
Historic Center of San Gimignano	8	Yes
Matera Sassi	14	Yes
Historic Center of Siena	8	Yes
Trulli of Alberobello	14	Yes
Cinque Terre	8	Yes
Pompeii	6,13	Yes
Herculaneum	12	Yes
Amalfi Coast	6,13	Yes
Agrigento- Valley of the Temples	15	Yes
City of Verona	10	Yes
Assisi	12	Yes
Basilica of St. Francis	12	Yes
Syracuse-Pantalica	16	Yes
Mount Aetna	16	Yes
Montecatini Terme	7	
Padua- St. Anthony	10	Yes
Orvieto *	6	Yes
Trapani / Erice *	15	
Perugia *	12	Yes
Bari *	14	
• =Proposed		

The Italy has 58 UNESCO World Heritage Sites, more than any other country. In addition, Montecatine Termi is one of the eleven UNESCO World Heritage Spa towns of Western Europe. An asterisk means that the town/site is a candidate for inclusion. "1,000" column denotes a mention in *"1,000 Places To See Before You Die."* By Patricia Schultz, Second Edition, 2015.

Made in the USA
Monee, IL
01 August 2023

40269023R10166